Series Editors

W. Hansmann
W. T. Hewitt
W. Purgathofer

D. Thalmann and
M. van de Panne (eds.)

Computer Animation
and Simulation '97

Proceedings of the Eurographics Workshop
in Budapest, Hungary,
September 2–3, 1997

Eurographics

SpringerWienNewYork

Prof. Dr. Daniel Thalmann
Computer Graphics Laboratory, Swiss Federal Institute of Technology,
Lausanne, Switzerland

Ass. Prof. Dr. Michiel van de Panne
Department of Computer Science, University of Toronto,
Toronto, Ontario, Canada

© 1997 Springer-Verlag/Wien

Typesetting: Camera ready by authors

Graphic design: Ecke Bonk

Printed on acid-free and chlorine-free bleached paper

SPIN: 10635823

With 121 partly coloured Figures

ISSN 0946-2767
ISBN-13:978-3-211-83048-2   e-ISBN-13:978-3-7091-6874-5
DOI: 10.1007/978-3-7091-6874-5

Preface

This volume contains the research papers presented at the *Eighth Eurographics Workshop on Computer Animation and Simulation* which took place in Budapest, Hungary, September 2–3, 1997. The workshop is an international forum for research in human animation, physically-based modeling, motion control, animation systems, and other key aspects of animation and simulation.

The problem of realistically and efficiently modeling the motion of people, objects, fluids, etc. remains a significant challenge in computer graphics. This workshop is representative of the continuing interest in this field of study.

This year, animation and simulation of human shape and motion is of particular interest. In fact, nine of the papers in this volume deal with techniques which are applicable to human animation. Others are concerned with equally interesting dynamic natural phenomena, such as clouds, plant development, and coastal scenes.

The call for papers required submission of the full papers for review, and each paper was reviewed by at least 3 members on the international program committee, consisting of:

Bruno Arnaldi (IRISA/INRIA Rennes, France)
Norman Badler (University of Pennsylvania, U.S.A.)
Ronan Boulic (Swiss Federal Institute of Technology, Switzerland)
Michael Cohen (Microsoft, U.S.A.)
Sabine Coquillart (INRIA, France)
David Forsey (University of British Columbia, Canada)
Marie-Paule Gascuel (iMAGIS-IMAG, France)
Gerard Hegron (Ecoles des Mines de Nantes, France)
Jessica Hodgins (Georgia Institute of Technology, U.S.A.)
Annie Luciani (ACROE-IMAG, France)
Nadia Magnenat-Thalmann (University of Geneva, Switzerland)
Kees van Overveld (Eindhoven University of Technology, The Netherlands)
Demetri Terzopoulos (University of Toronto, Canada)
David Zeltzer (Massachusetts Institute of Technology, U.S.A.)

Several others also contributed their expertise in providing reviews:

Jean-Dominique Gascuel (iMAGIS-IMAG, France)
Rama Bindiganavale (University of Pennsylvania, U.S.A.)
Pei-Hwa Ho (University of Pennsylvania, U.S.A.)
Pascal Volino (University of Geneva, Switzerland)

Based on the reviews, 12 papers were accepted and the authors were invited to submit a final version for the workshop. We wish to especially thank all reviewers for their time and effort in working within the constraints of the tight schedule, thereby making it possible to publish this volume in time for the workshop. We also thank the authors for their contributions to the workshop, without whom this unique forum for animation and simulation work would not exist.

We would like to thank the Eurographics Association and Werner Purgathofer from the Technical University of Vienna, for his support in publishing the workshop as a volume of the Springer-Verlag Eurographics Series. We are also grateful to Heinrich Müller from the University of Dortmund, and the Eurographics '97 organisers in Budapest, Gargely Krammer and Viktor Richter.

We gratefully acknowledge financial support from several funding agencies. D. Thalmann was supported by the Swiss Federal Institute of Technology and the National Swiss Foundation for Research. M. van de Panne was supported by the Natural Sciences and Engineering Research Council of Canada and the Information Technology Research Center of Ontario.

Daniel Thalmann (Co-Chair)
Swiss Federal Institute of Technology
Lausanne, Switzerland

Michiel van de Panne (Co-Chair)
University of Toronto
Toronto, Canada

Contents

1. Human Motion Capture

The Process of Motion Capture: Dealing with the Data 3
Bobby Bodenheimer, Chuck Rose, Seth Rosenthal, John Pella

A New Interface Paradigm for Motion Capture Based Animation Systems .. 19
Fernando W. S. V. Da Silva, Luiz Velho, Paulo Roma Cavalcanti,
Jonas de Miranda Gomes

2. Human Animation

A Model of Human Crowd Behavior: Group Inter-Relationship and Collision
Detection Analysis 39
Soraia Raupp Musse, Daniel Thalmann

Dynamic Analysis of Human Walking 53
François Faure, Gilles Debunne, Marie-Paule Cani-Gascuel, Franck Multon

3. Physics-based Modeling

Physically-based Wrinkle Simulation & Skin Rendering 69
Yin Wu, Prem Kalra, Nadia Magnenat Thalmann

Interactive Display and Animation of B-spline Solids as Muscle Shape
Primitives 81
Victor Ng-Thow-Hing, Eugene Fiume

An Alternative Inter-Particle Force Model for Coupled System Flexible Body
Dynamics 99
Hugh Reynolds

4. Natural Phenomena

Qualitative Simulation of Convective Cloud Formation and Evolution 113
Fabrice Neyret

Visual Model of Plant Development with Respect to Influence of Light 125
Bedřich Beneš

A Phenomenological Model of Coastal Scenes Based on Physical
Considerations 137
Jean-Christophe Gonzato, Bertand Le Saëc

Practical Experience in the Physical Animation and Destruction of Trees ... 149
Hiromi Ono

5. Collision Processing

REACT: REal-time Adaptive Collision Testing, An Interactive Vision
Approach 163
Carol A. O'Sullivan, Ronan G. Reilly

Collision and Self-Collision Handling in Cloth Model Dedicated to Design
Garments 177
Xavier Provot

Appendix: Colour Illustrations 191

1

Human Motion Capture

The Process of Motion Capture: Dealing with the Data

Bobby Bodenheimer   Chuck Rose
Microsoft Research

Seth Rosenthal   John Pella
Interactive Media Production
Microsoft

Abstract

This paper presents a detailed description of the process of motion capture, whereby sensor information from a performer is transformed into an articulated, hierarchical rigid-body object. We describe the gathering of the data, the real-time construction of a virtual skeleton which a director can use for immediate feedback, and the offline processing which produces the articulated object. This offline process involves a robust statistical estimation of the size of the skeleton and an inverse kinematic optimization to produce the desired joint angle trajectories. Additionally, we discuss a variation on the inverse kinematic optimization which can be used when the standard approach does not yield satisfactory results for the special cases when joint angle consistency is desired between a group of motions. These procedures work well and have been used to produce motions for a number of commercial games.

1 Introduction

Motion capture is a popular process for generating human animation. In this paper we describe the process whereby magnetic sensor information is transformed into an animated human figure. Our emphasis is on the data collection and processing that goes into determining an animation of a hierarchical 3D rigid-body skeleton.

Human motion capture techniques may be categorized according to the intended degree of abstraction imposed between the human actor and the virtual counterpart. Highly abstracted applications of motion capture data, analogous to puppetry, are primarily concerned with motion character, and only secondarily concerned with fidelity or accuracy. Beyond an initial calibration to insure that the 'puppet' or animated figure can be adequately manipulated, the most significant calibration takes place in the minds of the animators or puppeteers who learn to manipulate the figure indirectly as a puppet, rather than as a direct representation of themselves. Such applications commonly require the development of a unique capture procedure to take into account the characteristics of the puppet and its range of motion, and often rely on a combination of multiple actors, multiple input devices and procedural effects. Furthermore they often depend on real-time electromagnetic or electro-mechanical motion capture devices.

At the other end of the spectrum, efforts to accurately represent human motion depend on limiting the degree of abstraction to a feasible minimum. These projects typically attempt to approximate human motion on a rigid-body model with a limited number

---

Authors' address: One Microsoft Way, Redmond, WA 98052, USA. Email: {bobbyb, chuckr, sethr, johnpe}@microsoft.com

of rotational degrees of freedom. This work is not restricted to real-time systems, and is often conducted with non-real-time techniques such as optical tracking as well as with electromagnetic and electro-mechanical systems. It requires that close attention be paid to actual limb lengths, offsets from sensors on the surface of the body to the skeleton, error introduced by surface deformation relative to the skeleton, and careful calibration of translational and rotational offsets to a known reference posture.

Motion capture systems are commercially available, and the two main types of systems are optical and magnetic. At the present time neither has a clear advantage over the other, but magnetic systems are significantly cheaper. Considerable literature exists on using and editing motion capture data in animation (e.g., [1, 15, 3, 13, 14]). Motion capture for use in animation has been surveyed in [10], and various descriptions of the end product of its use have appeared (see, for example, [9, 6]) but beyond descriptions of the various algorithms for inverse kinematics such as [2, 16], there has been little attention given to processing the data for use by inverse kinematics routines. The work by Molet *et al.* [12] gives an alternative technique to inverse kinematics for going from sensors on an actor to an animated articulated figure. The goal of producing an articulated rigid body is critical if additional motions which depend on dynamics are to be added, either from dynamical simulation (e.g., [7]) or spacetime constraints (e.g., [14]); additionally, accurate motion analysis is important to the biomechanics community.

The present work deals with the data processing discussed in [12] but gives a detailed presentation of the processing techniques needed for a system which uses inverse kinematics as the base routine for producing the articulated figure. Inverse kinematic techniques are used because they have potential to avoid rotational error propagation which may result in unacceptable positions of end effectors when, for example, there is interaction with props. In the first part of our paper, we present the basic motion capture process, including sensor attachment and derivation and inference of rotational degrees of freedom (DOF). Note that this phase is accomplished in real time, so that a director can view the basic quality of the captured motion. Next we determine the skeleton lengths from the recorded data, and generate an inverse kinematic solution. In particular, we discuss our approach to the problems of noisy sensor data caused by a limited number of sensors, sensor slip, and sensor noise. We note that an advantage of our technique over many commercial systems is that it generates data which can be easily sub-sampled. Finally, we present additional steps which can be taken when our inverse kinematics optimization step fails to find a realistic or consistent solution between similar motions in a motion capture session.

2   Basic Motion Capture Process

Our motion capture data is generated from an Ascension MotionStar system and is input directly into a 3D modelling and animation program, Softimage, at capture time. Data is sampled at up to 144Hz. This high sampling rate is advisable when fast motions, such as sports motions, are captured; using slower sampling rates for such motions can often produce problems in the inverse kinematics phase, since there is less frame-to-frame coherence. Actors are suited using from 13 to 18 six DOF sensors. The typical location for the sensors of an actor is shown in Fig. 1. Our motion capture method is designed

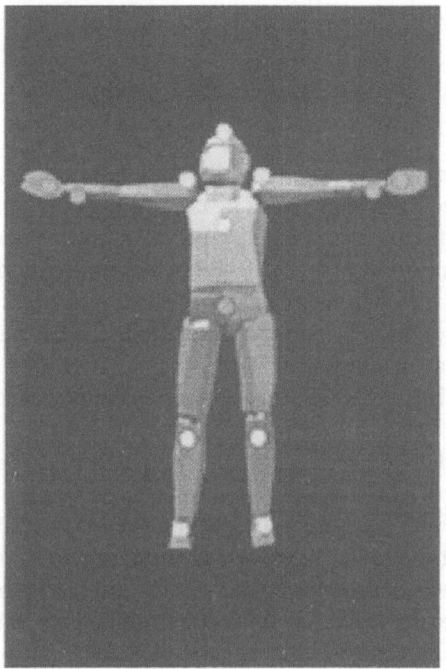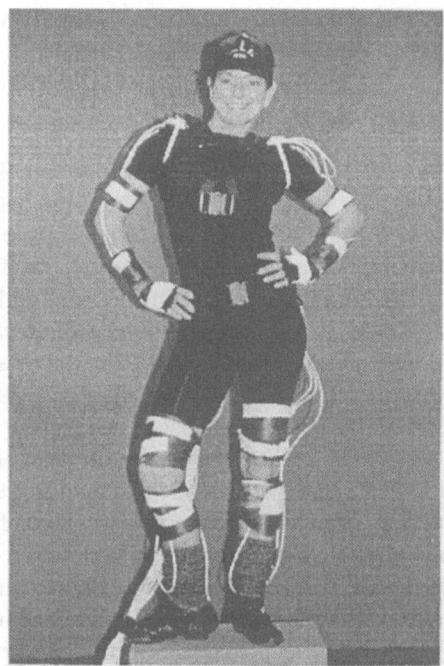

Fig. 1. Typical placement of sensors on an actor. On the left is a 13 sensor configuration; the gray dots show sensors on the back of the body. On the right is an 18 sensor configuration.

to take advantage of (a) the real-time capability of the electromagnetic capture system which allows for careful initial calibration and periodic re-calibration of sensor offsets to the virtual skeleton (i.e., the non-kinematically constrained rotation and translation data), (b) animation tools in Softimage which allow fine control over secondary structures used as a source of derived or inferred data, and (c) the ability of statistical analysis and inverse kinematics to discard gross errors and outlying data, and to fit a hierarchical rigid body with a reduced set of DOFs to the data.

2.1 Sensor Placement

Our typical capture configuration relies primarily on the pelvis, forearms, head, and lower legs; for each of these, six DOFs are captured. These body segments are chosen for the degree to which they define the position and posture of the figure and for their comparative advantages as anchor points for the sensors. The data sampled for these segments are considered *primary data*, and are not processed beyond translating their six DOFs to their respective rotation points. Data for additional body segments are considered secondary, and are inferred from the primary data. In particular, a 3D virtual skeleton is constructed that provides translational and rotational constraints enabling us to conveniently infer such things as the rotation of a virtual limb about its longitudinal axis, based on the orientation of a dependent limb.

2.1.1 Primary Data

The forearms and lower legs provide superior surfaces for immobilizing sensors relative to the skeleton. For the lower legs, the flat surface of the tibia just below the patella is used. For the forearms, the top surface of the forearm, directly behind the wrist and spanning the radius and ulna is used. The forearm is assumed to behave as a rigid body with its longitudinal axis of rotation slightly offset from the center towards the radius.

The position of the hip joints and the base of the spine are measured as offsets from a single sensor on the pelvis. The pelvic sensor is typically placed on the back of the pelvis near the top of the sacrum. The head is represented by data from a single sensor secured to a tight-fitting hat or helmet.

Jointed kinematic chains for the arms and legs are avoided at this stage for two reasons. First, capturing the global position and orientation of the lower legs and forearms localizes error and preserves primary data for the analysis and global optimization. This precludes any alteration of the orientation of the lower limbs due to migration of other sensors, as would occur if jointed kinematic structures were used in the initial skeleton (note that if this were done, the inverse kinematics would be enforced frame by frame by the modelling program). Second, at capture-time, visual cues that indicate deteriorating sensor calibration, such as excessive separation at the knee, are more valuable than real-time inverse kinematic solutions.

2.1.2 Secondary Data

Secondary data is inferred by exploiting Softimage's animation capabilities to enforce translational, rotational, directional, and up vector constraints. The up vector is commonly used to orient a virtual camera about the view direction. An up vector constraint provides a convenient method for constraining the rotation of a virtual limb about its longitudinal axis based on the orientation of a dependent limb. The up vector constraint makes use of a user-specified point to determine the resolution plane of a kinematic chain. These constraints are used to infer the rotational DOFs for the upper arms and legs, the torso, and in some cases, the neck.

The thorax is a logical candidate for treatment as a source of primary data. However, at present, the main application for our data is for real-time rendered 3D games featuring animated low-polygon humanoid characters. These characters typically represent the torso as a single rigid body with fixed shoulders. Our approach to providing data for this type of application is to infer the torso DOFs from a single segment constrained to the virtual pelvis and to the virtual nape of the neck (which is measured as an offset from a sensor on the upper back). For applications which can use more DOFs, a collarbone is added to aid in such things as shoulder shrug. The longitudinal rotation of the torso is inferred from an up vector constraint applied to the sensor on the upper back.

The upper legs and arms are difficult to capture directly with electromagnetic sensors, due to the absence of stable anchor locations. With adequate care, sensors on these body segments can be initially calibrated, but are particularly susceptible to sensor migration as a result of strenuous motions. The virtual femur is constrained by its root to the virtual hip joint and by its effector to the proximal end of the virtual tibia. The rotation of the virtual femur about its longitudinal axis is inferred from an up vector constraint applied to a contrived offset from the sensor on the lower leg. The small degree of elasticity in the virtual knee that results from the natural elongation of the actual knee in the course of flexion and any accumulated error from sources such as imperfect calibration of offsets or uncontrolled sensor migration can be removed with conventional inverse kinematics techniques, or in the global optimization phase.

The upper arm or humerus poses a more difficult challenge. Accurately representing the complex motion of the shoulder requires an impractically large number of DOFs and is complicated by the degree to which motion of the skeletal structure of the many components of the shoulder bears little relation to the motion of the surface of the body [11]. Two techniques can be used for estimating the position of the shoulder with electromagnetic sensors (other techniques are possible with optical tracking methods). First a sensor can be imperfectly immobilized to the top or back of the scapula and the position of the virtual shoulder joint can be estimated as an offset from this sensor's data. This method can be improved marginally by assuming that the direction of this estimated point from the virtual elbow is more accurate than the distance from the virtual elbow to this point. This assumption follows from observations that the direction of translational error of the shoulder sensor tends to be parallel to the longitudinal axis of the humerus. Given this assumption, the humerus can be represented by a single bone constrained at its root to the virtual elbow joint and constrained by its effector to the virtual shoulder. The proximal end of this bone is then assumed to represent the shoulder joint.

Second, the position of the shoulder joint can be estimated as an offset from a sensor on the upper arm. This method is difficult in practice due to the difficulty of immobilizing a sensor relative to the humerus. Even mildly strenuous motions can generate unacceptable variations between the DOFs recorded at the surface of the upper arm, and the actual position and orientation of the humerus. This arrangement is often acceptable for real-time puppetry-type applications but is inadequate for more exacting motion tracking applications.

As an example, the model for the arm is shown in Fig. 2. In this figure, (A) is the chain representing the upper arm, and (B) is the chain representing the lower arm. The position of the distal end of (A) is determined by the proximal end of (B). The longitudinal rotation of the upper arm needs to be inferred; (C) is the axis that controls the longitudinal rotation. (D) is an arbitrary point defined as an offset from the lower arm on a line projected back along the longitudinal axis of the lower arm. (K) is the plane defined by the root and effector of (A) and the point (D). As the effector of (B) moves through the trajectory (H), the point (D) moves through the trajectory (G). The up vector constraint applied to (A) forces (C) to lie in the resolution plane (K), thus determining the longitudinal rotation of (A). As (D) approaches the longitudinal axis of (A) the inferred rotation becomes unstable. This instability is addressed by carefully choosing the offset (D), by substituting estimated positions for (D) based on previous or subsequent frames, and, in some cases, by manually animating (D).

Finally, hand and foot motion is represented by rotational degrees of freedom from their respective sensors. Hands and feet are projected from wrists and ankles in a forward kinematic fashion. For example, the hands are not articulated but are mittens at-

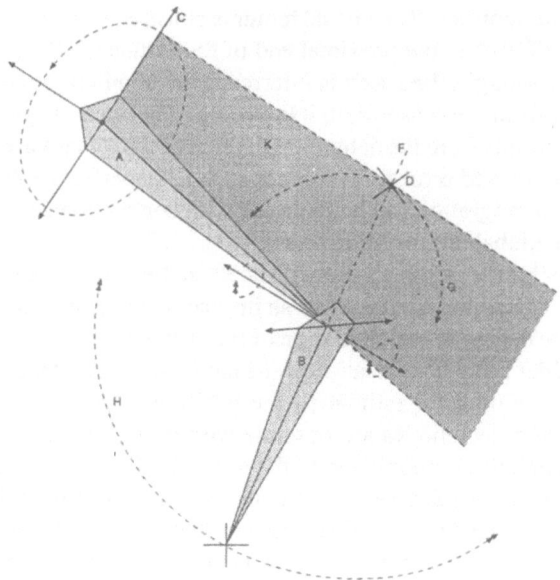

Fig. 2. Upper arm model.

tached to the wrist.

2.2 Measuring and Building the Skeleton

Our production concerns dictate that the process of preparing an actor for a capture session, and building and calibrating a virtual skeleton be as convenient as possible. Our method largely automates the process of measuring rotational offsets, and requires a comparatively small set of manual adjustments for the final calibration. It does, however, require systematic hand measurements of translational offsets for all sensors for which translation data is used. The need for such measurements can be reduced by relying on methods based solely on the rotations of sensors secured to each body segment, and a single global translation [12]. However, the tendency of rotation-based techniques to propagate error can make them unwieldy for tracking motions that rely on the precise placement of the hands and feet, such as self-referential motions and motions that depend on extensive interaction with props.

Prior to securing the sensors, the actor's limbs are carefully measured. After the sensors are in place, their translational offsets are measured according to a coordinate system based on an arbitrary reference posture or "zero position." All measurements are rounded to the nearest 0.25 inches but are assumed to be somewhat less accurate. A skeletal model based on the measured limb lengths and offsets, and posed in the zero position is then generated programmatically.

This model maps the data from each sensor to that sensor's corresponding "null model." A null model is a node in the virtual skeleton which has no geometry. Null models are used to introduce an offset between the motion of two linked objects. For each capture sensor there is a null-model that holds its rotational and translational offset to the virtual skeleton. The translational offsets are assumed to be approximately correct. The rotational offsets are arbitrary and are assumed to be wrong, as the sensors are oriented on the body according to practical concerns such as cable management and sensor stability. Before a hierarchical relationship is established between the captured input and the joint centers, a single keyframe of rotation data is recorded with the actor standing in the zero position thus setting the offset to the frame of captured data.

Fine calibration is necessary to account for any error in the measurements of the limbs and the translational offsets, and to correct for the degree to which the actor cannot perfectly assume the theoretical zero position of the skeleton. This fine calibration is accomplished by manually adjusting the translations and rotations of the null model in an interactive calibration mode, that allows manipulation of scene elements while the capture device and drivers are running. A simple set of routine motions is generally sufficient to identify any necessary refinements to the calibration; the arms may not line up, the hands may not come together, the legs may not be parallel, and so on. In practice, the fine calibration is primarily confined to the adjustments to the offsets for six sensors—those on the lower legs, the lower arms, the pelvis, and the chest. The resulting skeleton closely approximates the actor's motions and tends to localize error caused by sensor migration.

At capture time, data is recorded for the sensors and used to drive the virtual skeleton. The next stage is the optimization step. The data used in this step is not the sensor data, but data which represents the translation and rotation for each joint.

3 Optimization

Given a set of data based on the virtual skeleton described above, our goal is to construct an articulated, hierarchical rigid-body model. The model to which we will fit length and rotational data is shown in Fig. 3 and contains 38 joint degrees of freedom and six degrees of freedom at the root, located in the center of the pelvis, for positioning and orienting the entire figure. Our first task is to extract the best limb lengths from the motion capture data. Once the scale of the segments is determined, an inverse kinematics solution is calculated to determine the joint angles for the figure. Our inverse kinematics routine uses penalty functions to constrain the joint angles to approximate a human's range of motion.

3.1 Optimizing the skeleton

As mentioned previously, motion capture data is noisy and often contains gross errors. The source of the noise is primarily the magnetic sensors themselves, although we note that in our experience optical data is as noisy. We determine the size of the skeleton by determining the distances between the translated joint locations over a motion or repertoire of motions. Using the simple arithmetic mean to compute these distances results in answers unduly distorted by the gross errors, and editing the data by hand to remove outliers is impractical. As an example, gross errors in fast motions such as throwing may, for a frame or two, give a distance between the elbow and wrist of over 3 meters.

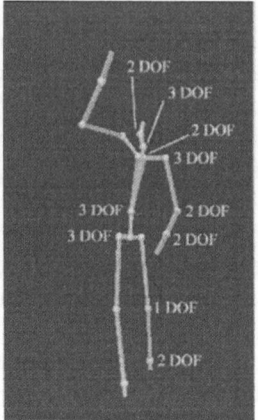

Fig. 3. Articulated body model illustrating degrees of freedom.

Thus a robust statistical procedure which can minimize or reject the influence of these outliers is employed. We have found that a one-step M-estimator [5] works well. This estimator has the form

$$T_n = T_n^{(0)} + S_n^{(0)} \frac{\sum_{i=1}^{n} \psi \left((x_i - T_n^{(0)})/S_n^{(0)} \right)}{\sum_{i=1}^{n} \psi' \left((x_i - T_n^{(0)})/S_n^{(0)} \right)}$$

where n is the size of the data set, x_i is a data point, T_n is the estimated statistic of location, $T_n^{(0)}$ and $S_n^{(0)}$ are initial estimates of the location and scale, and ψ is estimator function. In our work we use the Huber estimator

$$\psi_b = x \cdot \min \left(1, \frac{b}{|x|} \right)$$

where b is the cutoff point and is determined by the median deviation of the data. Our initial estimates of location and scale are the recommended ones for this type of estimator (see [5]), and are given by

$$T_n^{(0)} = \mathrm{median}(x_i)$$
$$S_n^{(0)} = 1.483 \mathrm{median}_i \left\{ |x_i - \mathrm{median}_j (x_j)| \right\}.$$

This estimator insures that any error, no matter how gross, has only a fixed impact on the data set.

In this phase, an outlier is defined as any data point beyond the cutoff point b, which is typically twice the median deviation (defined above for $S_n^{(0)}$). When an outlier is found, it is tagged so that during the inverse kinematics phase, data from that frame and for those joints is automatically ignored. As an example illustrating the importance of this, a short motion of a walk consisting of 508 frames of motion has 6 frames of clearly gross error. Editing these frames out by hand and computing the collarbone to shoulder length gives 13.3 cm. Our M-estimator gives 13.2 cm, but using the arithmetic means gives a length of 14.1 cm, a 6% difference. Errors of this magnitude will frequently cause difficulties in the inverse kinematics procedure, thus marking them is a valuable tool. Since the statistical estimator we are using is of the "one-step" variety, the limb length calculation is not computationally expensive.

3.2 Inverse Kinematics

Once the hierarchical model has been determined using robust statistical analysis of the data, each frame of data must be analyzed to produce a set of joint angles. Additionally, these joint angles should form reasonable piecewise-linear DOF curves which can be sampled at any time, not just the original frame times. Piecewise-linearity is extremely useful if the data is to be sub-sampled. In contrast, many commercial data sets often contain discontinuities in the rotational data from frame to frame, which make sub-sampling impossible. Our primary and secondary data yield information about many areas of the body, giving us a highly constrained kinematic problem. This problem can be solved using a non-linear optimization technique, which seeks to minimize the deviation between the recorded data and the hierarchical model. We use a modification to the technique presented in Zhao [16].

The fitness function we are minimizing is defined as

$$F(\Theta) = \sum_{j \in J} w_p \left(P_j - \tilde{P}_j \right)^2 +$$

$$w_{O_0} \left(O_{0,j} - \tilde{O}_{0,j} \right)^2 +$$

$$w_{O_1} \left(O_{1,j} - \tilde{O}_{1,j} \right)^2 +$$

$$w_c C_j^2$$

where Θ is the set of joint angles for the set of joints J. P_j is the position of the jth joint given Θ and $\tilde{P}_j$ is the recorded joint position from the capture phase. $O_{0,j}$ and $O_{1,j}$ are two vectors defining the orientation of the joint with $\tilde{O}_{0,j}$ and $\tilde{O}_{1,j}$ being the recorded orientations. Two vectors are used because, together with their cross product, they will form a right-handed coordinate system. The quantities w_p, w_{O_0}, and w_{O_1} are scalar weights that can be tuned to achieve better results. Additionally, we employ a joint angle constraint term, C_j, in the form of a penalty function. Joint angle constraints for humans have been measured and can be found in the biomechanical literature [8].

The quasi-Newton BFGS optimization technique [4] is used to solve the system and uses the gradient of the fitness function, given by

$$\frac{\partial F_j}{\partial \Theta_I} = 2w_p (P_j - \tilde{P}_j)(u_j \times d_{ji}) +$$

$$2w_{O_0}(O_{0,j} - \tilde{O}_{0,j})(u_j \times O_{0,j}) +$$

$$2w_{O_1}(O_{1,j} - \tilde{O}_{1,j})(u_j \times O_{1,j}) +$$

$$2w_c C_j$$

to produce our DOF curves in the form of piecewise-linear functions. If the data is relatively non-noisy and the skeleton is well formed, this technique will work well. It can produce poor results if these conditions are not present. Robust statistics helps to insure these conditions by making the best skeleton and by marking data points which are considered outliers. Since a hierarchical description of a skeleton is a biological simplification and since non-linear optimization is hard, the analysis can still fall into an insufficient local minima if the starting guess for the optimization is far from the desired solution.

Our internal representation of rotations is as XYZ Euler angles. This representation was originally used because it provided simplicity in our code. However, Euler angles provide only a local parameterization of the group of rotations in $\mathbb{R}^3$, and thus have singularities. While our technique works well for many motions, it cannot be denied that the use of a global parameterization, such as quaternions, would be better.

We mitigate this problem in two ways. The first technique is simple: use the result of frame i for the starting guess of frame $(i + 1)$. For many motions, this technique is perfectly valid. It suffers if the data and the skeleton are mismatched near where the skeleton goes through a singularity or where the data points are too far apart in time for a given motion's velocity. Additionally, it will suffer if it never finds a good solution for an initial frame. Over the shoulder reaching, fast motions, and motions where the arm is extended to its limit are examples. If this happens, the solution can jump over to another local minima and stay there. This behavior is not desirable.

Analyzing a walk motion of 6.7 seconds duration at 30 frames per second required 306 seconds on a Pentium 133 machine with 4389 BFGS iterations for satisfactory convergence of the solution. A selected frame showing the fit of the skeleton (yellow) to the data (black) is shown in Fig. 10 (see Appendix). Notice that the fit is extremely good and shows only a slight discrepancy in the left arm. The resulting walk motion is shown in Fig. 4.

A further refinement of the motion capture analysis presented here is to use motions to bootstrap one another by providing good starting guesses to the BFGS optimization. The assumption for this technique is that many motions of similar structure are to be analyzed, and that motions of a similar structure will have similar joint angle curves. Such a data set might include reaches, runs, walks, etc. These sets are likely to be a part of any motion capture session.

Assume there is a motion M, a set of DOF curves, for a motion of type T. If we have a motion capture dataset for another motion of this type, the joint angles for this motion will be similar to those for motion M. The main difference between the solution for the new desired motion $\tilde{M}$ and M will be a time warping to account for differences in the relative timing between M and the captured data. Thus a scaling in time on the data sets is needed. We mark a set of correspondence times, key times, in M and in the data set. We time-warp M and then use that as the starting guess for the inverse kinematics optimization described earlier.

Thus, this technique will not propagate errors, whereas in the previous technique a bad starting guess may result in a bad solution, which can propagate from frame to frame. As a result, similar motions will make similar use of their joints when analyzed. This similar joint use is important when these motions are later used in techniques like those presented in, for example, [15]. Note that this technique requires operator intervention

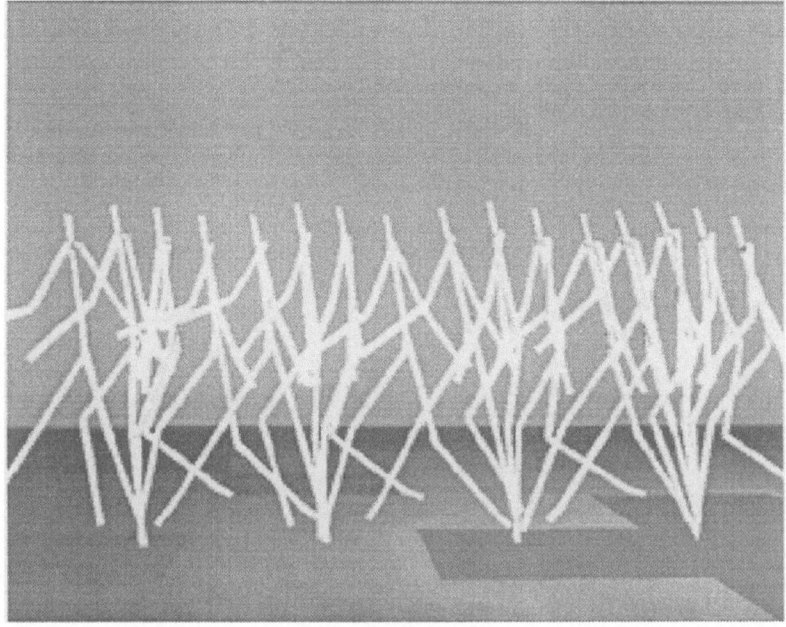

Fig. 4. Walk motion.

to mark the key times, and thus it is only employed for groups of datasets where the aforementioned method did not work.

The reach motion shown in Fig. 5 was analyzed using the same technique as the walk. Its duration is 3.8 seconds and required 1278 BFGS iterations and a total of 37.08 seconds to analyze. Unfortunately, due to noise, inadequacies in the skeletal model, and the joint angle constraints model, this method is not powerful enough to insure that it makes similar use of the joint angles as another reaching motion previously analyzed and shown in Fig. 6. Compare the shoulder DOFs shown in Fig. 7 versus those of Fig. 8. These differences would represent a fundamental obstacle if, for example, we tried to interpolate between these motions to obtain a reach motion of a different height.

Using the medium reach as a reference motion, and a time warp to align it as the starting guess for the low reach motion capture data, we can obtain a more consistent use of shoulder angles, as shown in Fig. 9. This analysis took 3295 iterations and 232 seconds. Notice that, up to a time warp, this set of shoulder angles is very similar to those for the medium reach shown in Fig. 8.

4 Conclusion

We have presented a detailed account for taking human performance sensor data and producing animations of articulated rigid bodies. Our technique involves using geometric modelling to translate rotation data to joint centers, a robust statistical procedure to determine the optimal skeleton size, and an inverse kinematics optimization to produce

14

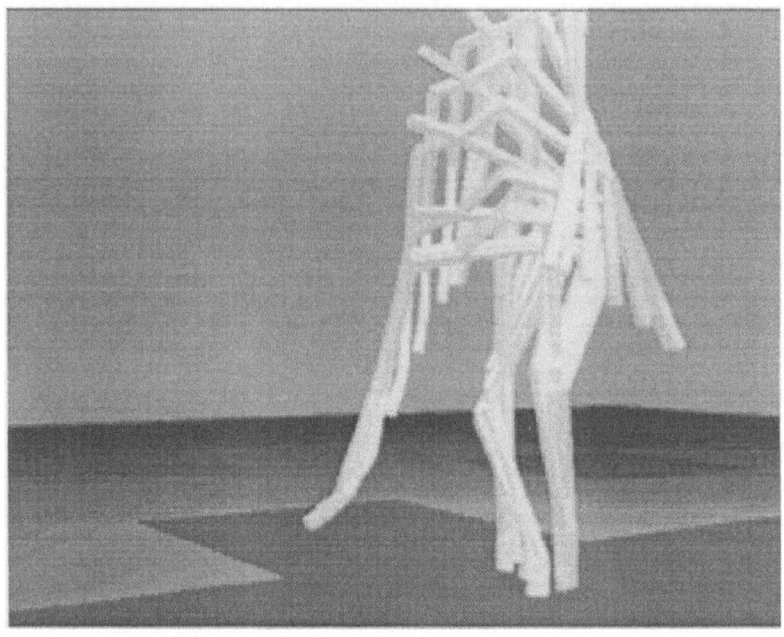

Fig. 5. A low reaching motion.

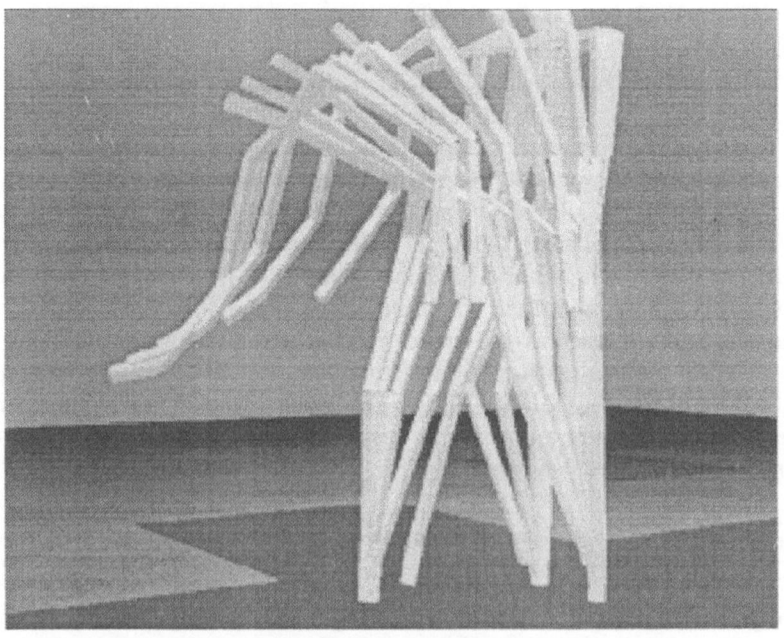

Fig. 6. A previously analyzed medium reaching motion.

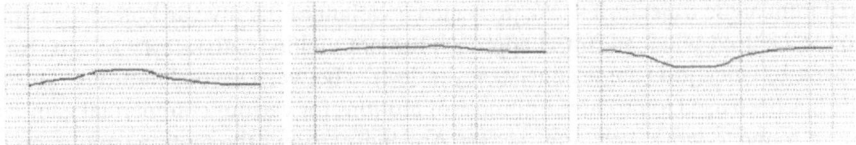

Fig. 7. Shoulder DOFs for the low reaching motion.

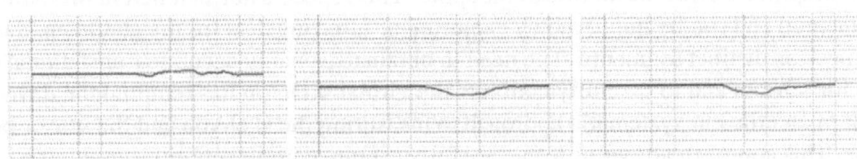

Fig. 8. Shoulder DOFs for the medium reaching motion.

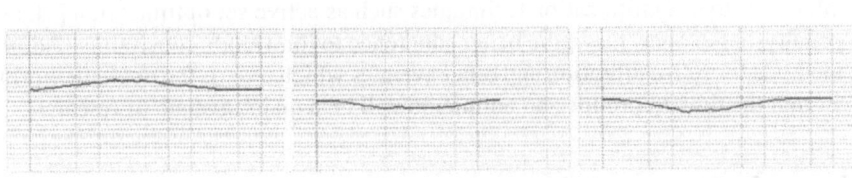

Fig. 9. Shoulder DOFs for the low reaching motion, using the medium reach as a reference guess.

desired joint angle trajectories. We presented a variant of the inverse kinematics optimization to be used when an initial approach has not yielded satisfactory results, for the special cases when joint angle consistency is desired between several motions. This procedure has been used to produce a number of motions for various commercial games and has been found to work well. Fig. 11 (see Appendix) shows the motion capture process at the various stages of processing: the first figure shows the capture phase, where an actor is interacting with a prop (a model of an Indy car); the second shows the articulated rigid body skeleton obtained after inverse kinematics optimization; the third shows this skeleton again repositioned with the prop; the fourth shows a full rendering of the character and the prop. Notice that the inverse kinematics optimization has not changed the location of the end effectors significantly, since they are still able to interact with the prop. Finally, we remark that if any animator intervention is required, this intervention will occur in a step between that of the third figure and the fourth.

The least satisfactory aspect of the motion capture method described here is the gross over-simplification of the motion of the spine. This aspect is not an inherent limitation of the method and can be improved by capturing or inferring data for the abdomen, thorax and neck as distinct segments. The need to obtain reasonably accurate translational offsets for sensors and to carefully calibrate the virtual skeleton has required the development of an efficient systematic approach to measuring the skeleton and the sensor positions. This approach allows us to successfully capture complex motions involving good registration between the virtual actor and the virtual representations of props in the capture space. However, it requires a fairly high degree of production preparedness for its efficient execution. This process is a likely candidate for a more general and robust solution.

Changing our internal representation of rotations from Euler angles to quaternions would likely help our inverse kinematics processing, particularly for fast sports motions such as throwing. Better models of the human body, including more accurate skeletons and more realistic joint angle constraints will yield better analysis of motion capture data. In the statistical analysis of the data, it is likely that a "redescending" estimator, which has the ability to reject outliers outright, would produce better results, and this will be explored further. Optimization techniques such as active set optimization [4], rather than penalty-based ones, may give better adherence to joint angle constraints. Additionally, methods for self-calibration and other avenues which reduce the operator workload and shorten the time to produce an animation will be a major avenue of research.

Acknowledgements

We are greatly indebted to Michael Cohen and Jana Wilcoxen for assistance and suggestions throughout this project. Thanks also to David Thiel and Agnieszka Morgan for help with the video and image production, respectively. Larry Frame, who designed and built Microsoft's motion capture facility, made his staff and resources readily available for our work. Hank Meuret also made numerous contributions. The IMP 3D graphics group was always eager to help, and the Simulation Games group generously allowed us to use their data. Finally, the second author thanks Princeton University, where he was a graduate student for much of this project. MotionStar is a trademark of Ascension Technology Corporation, and Softimage is a trademark of Softimage, inc., a wholly owned subsidiary of Microsoft.

References

[1] BADLER, N. I., HOLLICK, M. J., AND GRANIERI, J. P. Real-time control of a virtual human using minimal sensors. *Presence 2*, 1 (1993), 82–86.

[2] BADLER, N. I., PHILLIPS, C. B., AND WEBBER, B. L. *Simulating Humans: Computer Graphics Animation and Control.* Oxford University Press, Oxford, UK, 1993.

[3] BRUDERLIN, A., AND WILLIAMS, L. Motion signal processing. In *Computer Graphics* (Aug. 1995), pp. 97–104. Proceedings of SIGGRAPH 95.

[4] GILL, P. E., MURRAY, W., AND WRIGHT, M. H. *Practical Optimization.* Academic Press, 1981.

[5] HAMPEL, F. R., RONCHETTI, E. M., ROUSSEEUW, P. J., AND STAHEL, W. A. *Robust Statistics: The Approach Based on Influence Functions.* John H. Wiley, New York, 1986.

[6] HARS, A. Masters of motion. *Computer Graphics World* (Oct. 1996), 26–34.

[7] HODGINS, J. K., WOOTEN, W. L., BROGAN, D. C., AND O'BRIEN, J. F. Animating human athletics. In *Computer Graphics* (Aug. 1995), pp. 71–78. Proceedings of SIGGRAPH 95.

[8] HOUY, D. R. Range of motion in college males. Presented at the Conference of the Human Factors Society, Santa Monica, CA, 1983.

[9] MAESTRI, G. Capturing motion. *Computer Graphics World* (1995), 47–51.

[10] MAIOCCHI, R. 3-D character animation using motion capture. In *Interactive Computer Animation*, N. Magnetat-Thalmann and D. Thalmann, Eds. Prentice-Hall, London, 1996, pp. 10–39.

[11] MAUREL, W., THALMANN, D., HOFFMEYER, P., BEYLOT, P., GINGINS, P., KALRA, P., AND THALMANN, N. M. A biomechanical musculoskeletal model of human upper limb for dynamic simulation. In *Computer Animation and Simulation '96* (Aug. 1996), R. Boulic and G. Hégron, Eds., pp. 121–136.

[12] MOLET, T., BOULIC, R., AND THALMANN, D. A real time anatomical converter for human motion capture. In *Computer Animation and Simulation '96* (Aug. 1996), R. Boulic and G. Hégron, Eds., pp. 79–94.

[13] PERLIN, K. Real time responsive animation with personality. *IEEE Transactions on Visualization and Computer Graphics 1*, 1 (Mar. 1995), 5–15.

18

[14] ROSE, C. F., GUENTER, B., BODENHEIMER, B., AND COHEN, M. Efficient generation of motion transitions using spacetime constraints. In *Computer Graphics* (Aug. 1996), pp. 147–154. Proceedings of SIGGRAPH 96.

[15] WITKIN, A., AND POPOVIĆ, Z. Motion warping. In *Computer Graphics* (Aug. 1995), pp. 105–108. Proceedings of SIGGRAPH 95.

[16] ZHAO, J., AND BADLER, N. I. Inverse kinematics positioning using non-linear programming for highly articulated figures. *ACM Trans. Gr. 13*, 4 (Oct. 1994), 313–336.

Editors' Note: see Appendix, p. 193 for colored figures of this paper

A New Interface Paradigm for Motion Capture Based Animation Systems

FERNANDO WAGNER SERPA VIEIRA DA SILVA[1,2]
LUIZ VELHO[1]
PAULO ROMA CAVALCANTI[2]
JONAS DE MIRANDA GOMES[1]

{nando,lvelho,roma,jonas}@visgraf.impa.br

[1]IMPA–Instituto de Matemática Pura e Aplicada
Estrada Dona Castorina, 110,
22460 Rio de Janeiro, RJ, Brazil

[2]LCG - Laboratório de Computação Gráfica, COPPE - Sistemas / UFRJ
Caixa Postal 68511,
21945-970, Rio de Janeiro, RJ, Brazil

Abstract. This paper proposes a new user interface paradigm for motion capture based animation systems, providing intuitive and efficient ways to visualize the main motion capture concepts and operations. A prototype system was built, implementing the proposed interface model and supported by a flexible architecture that is suitable to work with the motion capture methodology.

keywords: motion capture, animation systems, computer animation, graphic interfaces, GUI paradigm, motion control.

1   Introduction

The Motion Capture technique has already set its place in the future of computer animation. This technique provides tools for high-quality animation, even when real-time is required.

The initial drawback of Motion Capture techniques was the lack of efficient ways to modify the captured motion, by adjusting or improving specific parts that needed to be changed, without having to repeat the entire acquisition process again.

Lately, however, several techniques were proposed to process captured data [9] [11] [12], providing tools for motion analysis, modification and reuse. This makes motion libraries more valuable for a wide class of animators.

Most of today's animation systems offer the possibility of use motion captured data to generate animations, but a great part of these systems treats this technique as an "extra tool", or even as a simple plug-in. Therefore, an effective description of motion capture basic concepts is not provided.

An interesting and alternative approach would be the construction of an animation system that uses motion capture as the kernel of the entire animation process. This leads to an unlimited range of possibilities to many animators. As an example, this motion capture based system could be integrated with high-end motion capture hardware, thus creating a powerful environment of motion acquisition and processing.

In this work, we propose a new user interface paradigm for motion capture based animation systems, supported by an extensible architecture that incorporates the "state of art" in motion capture processing techniques, and allows the use of standard animation methods, like keyframing or inverse kinematics, as powerful tools to improve system's flexibility.

The main contribution of this paper is to introduce an elegant way to describe, at the user interface level, the basic motion capture abstractions. We treat captured motion as a potentially ready animation, which can be modified with a set tools embedded in the architecture. In that way, an interface description of motion operations and associated objects is defined.

A prototype system was built, implementing the concepts described in this work. This system was used to demonstrate the potential of the proposed interface paradigm.

Section 2 of this paper introduces the basic internal structures of the prototype system, together with a brief description of its architecture. Section 3 presents the proposed interface paradigm for motion capture based systems. Finally, conclusions are given in section 4.

2   System's Architecture and Internal Structures

In this section, we present a framework for the animation system. Also, a brief description of the architecture used in the implemented system is provided. This will give a better perception of the approach used to build the proposed interface paradigm.

2.1 Basic Internal Structures

The fundamental structure used in the system is composed by two entities: an actor and motions.

The actor is treated as a skeleton. Its topology is represented by a graph formed by joints and links. Its geometry is represented by series of connected limbs (figure 1). This description is adequate to be used in a motion capture animation system, since it reflects the structure of an articulated figure. For data acquisition, markers are attached at the joints of a live performer (the real actor).

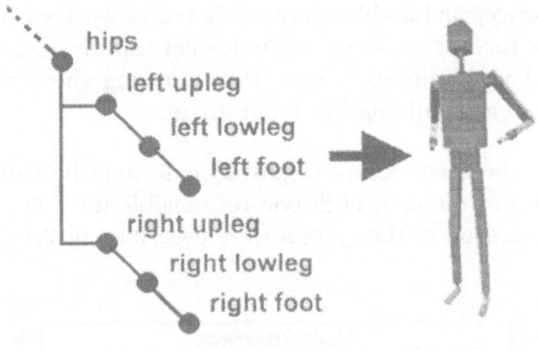

hips
left upleg
left lowleg
left foot
right upleg
right lowleg
right foot

Figure 1: Topological and geometrical description of an actor used in the system.

At the programming level, the actor is represented using a modified version of Zeltzer's APJ (*Axis Position Joint*) structure [3], adapted to work with motion captured data.

Motions are best represented as curves in time (figure 2).

Figure 2: Examples of joint motion curves.

22

Normally, the captured data consists of marker's positional and / or angular variation, sampled by the capture hardware during the number of frames required to complete the actor's performance. This description is used for each degree of freedom (DOF) of the actor.

Internally, the interaction with the user is controlled by a dynamic data structure that represents the current "state" of all windows and main data structures existing in the system.

2.2   An Architecture Focused on Motion Capture

We developed a conceptual architecture, designed to work with the motion capture paradigm. It focuses on some technological aspects and embodies several techniques to deal with captured data, thus allowing the creation of reusable motion libraries using a building block paradigm.

The framework of the architecture (figure 3) is formed by three basic modules (*input*, *processing* and *output*), each one responsible for a specific set of tasks. The data structures used in the system were described in 2.1.

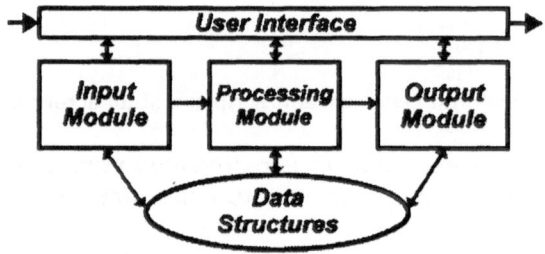

Figure 3: System's architecture.

All modules are supported by the conceptual interface that will be described in section 3. For a more detailed description of system's architecture, please refer to [4].

- **Input Module**

The input module focuses on problems concerning the interpretation and preprocessing of motion data. Skeleton definition files were created to establish relationships between the skeleton expected by the incoming data [1] and architecture's internal default skeleton definition. Also, geometrical algorithms for

---
[1] Depending on the motion data format.

3D Euler angle extraction[2], pre-filtering and hierarchical angle generation are provided in this module.

- **Processing Module**

The processing module comprises the set of tools for motion analysis, manipulation and reuse. Three basic motion operation types were defined: filtering; concatenation; and blending. Their objective is to provide efficient ways to modify the original captured data. With these tools, the user is able to generate new classes of motions, inheriting the aliveness and complexity typical of natural motion.

Filtering operations can be applied to the joint curves of a motion, to reduce noise or even modify specific components of the movement. In [9], Williams used a multiresolution filtering approach to decompose the motion in frequency bands, thus allowing modifications in a higher level of abstraction.

With concatenation operations, longer animations can be produced by combination of several motions in sequence. Smooth transitions between the combined motions can be produced using algorithms based on blending of motion parameters [4]. Spacetime constraints [12] can also be used to generate seamless and dynamically plausible transitions, with excellent results.

Blending operations are normally used to combine special characteristics of different motions. In this case, the existence of tools for motion synchronization and reparametrization is very important to help in the blending process, ensuring a coherent result.

- **Output Module**

The main objective of this module is to provide ways to store the composition created by the user, thus maintaining and expanding the existing motion library.

An universal data format was defined, embodying the main characteristics of most motion data formats available nowadays. Consequently, the system can be used as a robust conversor for motion capture data formats.

- **User Interface**

The user interface used in the system is based on a visual representation of motion capture basic concepts, as motions and operations.

---

[2]In the case of data with positional information only.

We believe that it is also interesting to supply a non-graphical user communication, using a expression language that represents all the actions that would be done using the graphical description provided in the user interface.

We are currently working on a expression language similar to that described in [12]. Using this language, the user will be able to generate complex animations with motion operations, using commands that will actually execute the callback functions supporting the user interface. These commands may be stored in a text file and can be reused or edited.

Control

A continuous loop (figure 4) verifies the status of all interface objects and windows, reporting any changes to a special function that manages those changes that actually must be done, due to user interaction.

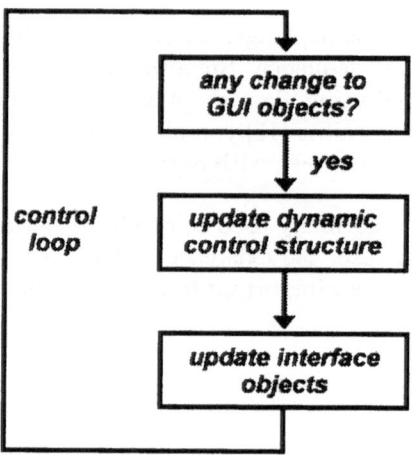

Figure 4: User interface control with a state checking loop.

3   A Graphic Interface for Motion Capture

As discussed before, our system is based on an architecture that treats the problem of working with captured motions. However, the functionality of its architecture would be shadowed by the conventional user interface paradigm used on most animation systems currently available.

Our goal is to describe the basic structures of system's architecture in a concise way, providing powerful interface tools that will make easier to execute motion editing operations. Moreover, this interface must be extensible, allowing the incorporation new operations and techniques.

We noted that each captured motion is a potentially ready animation, and therefore must be treated accordingly. After an extensive research, we decided to adopt an interface paradigm used on some post-production video workstations [10] as a starting point to our work.

In the following sub-sections, we will describe the main interface objects and concepts developed under the proposed methodology. All images presented in this section are actual screenshots of the prototype system, implemented using the concepts described in this paper.

3.1 Actor

In our interface paradigm, the actor is visualized by means of its components: the skeleton topology and geometry. The skeleton structure is shown in a window as a graph composed of joints and links (figure 5). This window displays information about each joint and the links between them. The interface allows joint selection and / or grouping.

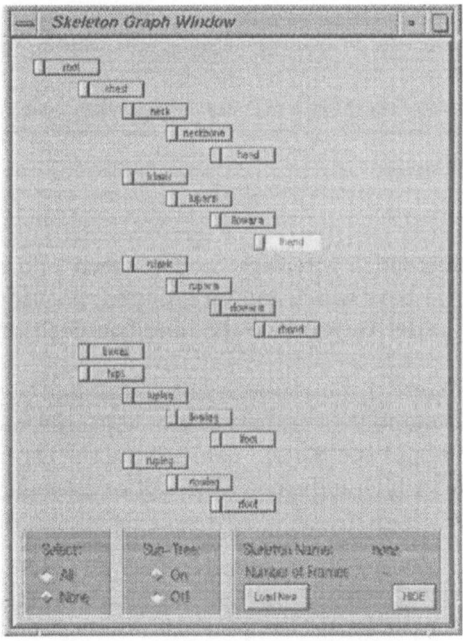

Figure 5: Skeleton graph window.

26

The representation of the actor can be visualized with different styles in the rendering window, as shown in figure 6. The selected joint in the graph window appears in different color and size in the rendering window. This selection also affects other interface objects, as will be discussed later.

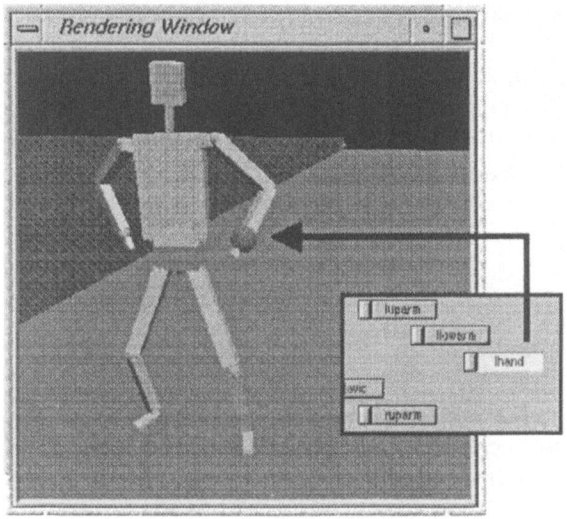

Figure 6: Joint selection (detail from skeleton graph window) and visual feedback in the rendering window.

3.2   Motions

In the post-production video interface model, video and sound sequences are visualized as horizontal bars which can be grouped, positioned and combined in a timeline canvas, in order to produce the final composition.

In our paradigm, we treat a motion as a horizontal bar (figure 7), whose width is determined by the number of frames of the captured motion. This bar also contains information about the motion name. Note the arrow marker at the right end of the motion bar, which indicates that motion resizing (reparametrization) is allowed.

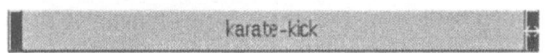

Figure 7: Motion representation as a GUI object.

We will usually visualize the motion bar using a frame ruler associated with it. This gives a more accurate temporal perception of the motion.

- **The Motion ScratchPad**

In our system, we have created an interface object whose purpose is to act as a motion organizer, providing a global perception of all motions placed on it. We called this object the Motion ScratchPad (figure 8).

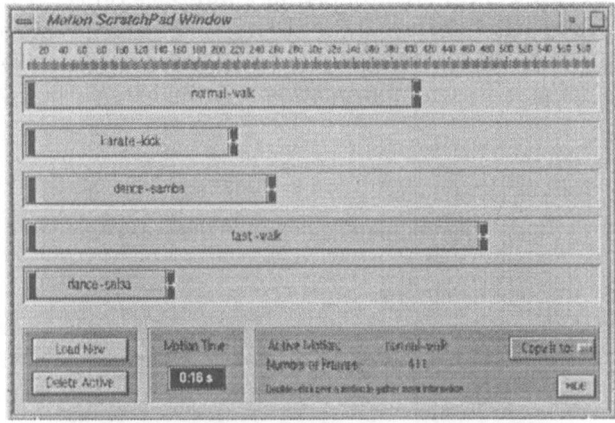

Figure 8: Motion ScratchPad - the motion organizer.

Using the ScratchPad, the user can choose several motions and organize them in the object canvas. All motions can be individually played or resized, and the user can drop them to the motion operations. The ScratchPad is actually the gateway between the input and the processing modules.

The ScratchPad is the container where motion fragments are stored, waiting to be used.

- **Joint Curves**

Joint curves are the basic components of motion. They are visually represented by an interface object that displays curve shape. It also provides numeric information about the different channels of data at each frame (i.e., x, y and z values for position and orientation, for each joint curve). The visual representation of a joint curve is shown in figure 9.

With this representation, it is straightforward to implement several curve editing techniques [9] [11], allowing a precise and interactive control of the curve shape.

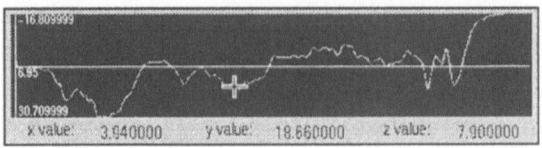

Figure 9: Visual representation of a joint curve.

For each joint of the actor, there may be several joint curves (one for each DOF) attached to it. These curves are grouped in a interface object, the Joint Curves Window, that offers a global view of the curves, and has a direct connection with the skeleton graph window. When a joint is selected in the graph window, its curves are displayed and useful information is provided, as shown in figure 10.

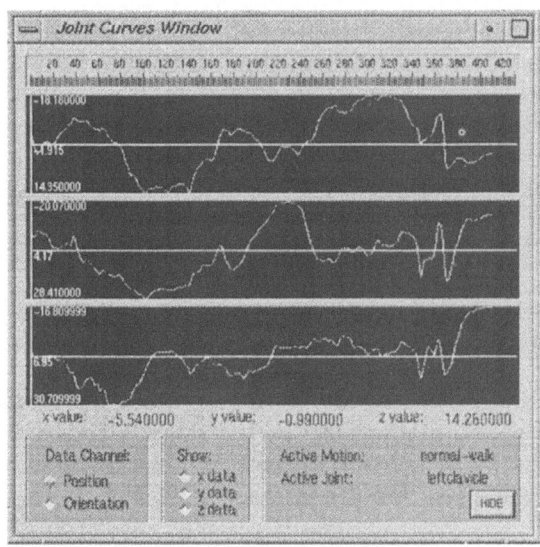

Figure 10: Joint Curves Window.

- **The Motion Window**

Finally, we decided to create an interface object that acts as a connection between motion and actor descriptions. The Motion Window (figure 11) is accessed via a double-click in a motion bar, and allows the selection (or grouping) of specific joints of the actor.

The Motion Window is composed of several bars, each one representing an actor

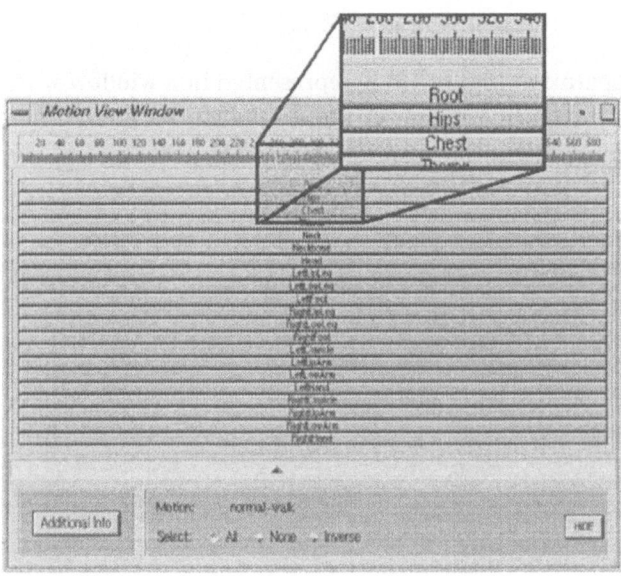

Figure 11: Motion Window - connecting actor and motion descriptions.

joint (detail in figure 11). Visually, it looks like a zoom in the motion bar. This representation was done intentionally, since the motion is formed by the curves that are attached to actor's joints.

The Motion Window will proof its utility when used in conjunction with motion operations, allowing the application of an operation to a specific set of joints of the actor.

3.3 Motion Operations

Motion operations are the most important objects in system's architecture. Therefore, they must be visualized in such a way to make the process very intuitive to the user.

In our interface paradigm, each motion operation has its own window. When requested, additional objects are used to help in the process, providing a full control of the operation parameters.

All motion operation windows have a basic set of auxiliary objects - an interactive player slider and a frame ruler. Those objects also follow the interface concepts described before.

- **Filtering**

The filtering operation (figure 12) is represented in a window with tools to allow the selection of a specific region of the motion to be filtered (⟦1⟧), and with a list of the existing filters that can be accessed by pressing ⟦2⟧.

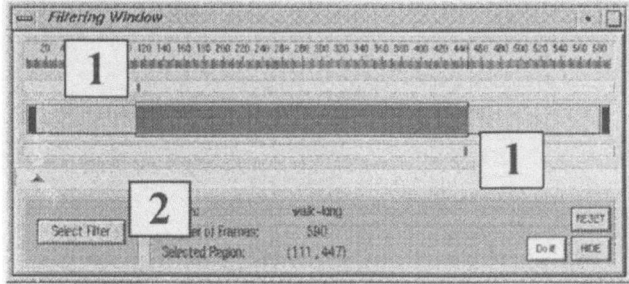

Figure 12: Filtering operation window.

- **Concatenation**

The interface object that represents the concatenation operation was designed to provide a good visual perception of the composition as a whole.

The motions selected by the user in the ScratchPad are dropped into the Concatenation Window. Initially, they are positioned in such a way to perform a direct concatenation (i.e., without blending interval), as shown in figure 13.

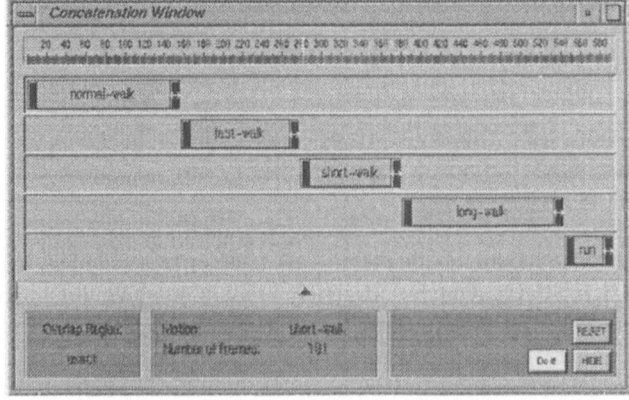

Figure 13: Concatenation operation window (initial motion arrangement).

Using the existing tools for motion positioning and reparametrization, the user can define blending intervals that will execute the smooth transition between the combined motions (in figure 14, represented by the darker regions between the motions).

However, some interface constraints were created to avoid undesirable results. These constraints ensure visual coherence and guide the user in the operation process.

The default easy-in / easy-out blending parameters can be modified by double-clicking in the desired blending interval of the Concatenation Window.

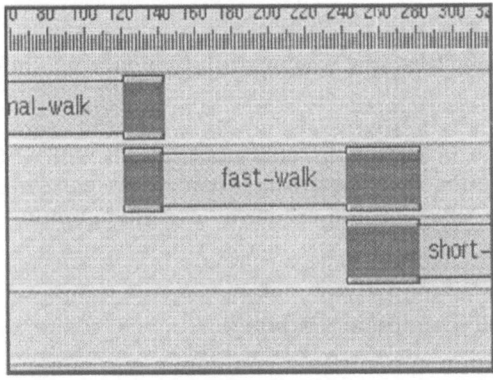

Figure 14: Blending intervals (detail from Concatenation Window).

• **Blending**

Blending is the last type of motion operation defined in the primary set of the prototype system.

As in the Concatenation Window, all motions selected by the user are placed in a canvas, providing a global view of the operation. For blending, however, new objects were introduced to assist in the specification.

These new objects are the time-markers, and their purpose is to synchronize key points in the combined motions. For example, when combining two different types of walk movements, it is desirable that the feet reaches the ground at the same instant for both motions, otherwise strange results can be produced.

Figure 15 shows a snapshot of a blending operation between three different motions. The time-markers (detail from figure 15) were used to establish a correspondence between the key steps in the combined motions.

32

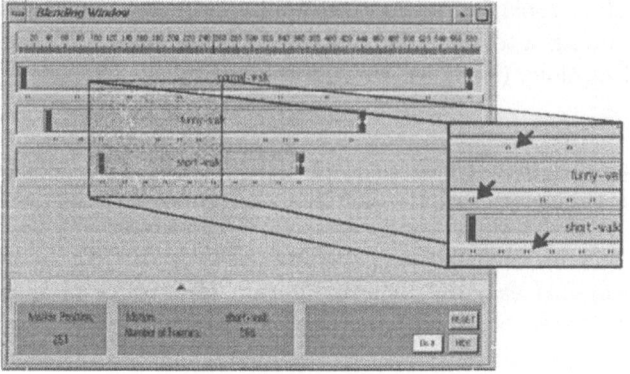

Figure 15: Blending window with time-markers (in detail).

This synchronization process will reparametrize the motions, according to the position of the time-markers, matching their occurrence in time. To do that, algorithms based on timewarping are used. A good example can be found in [9].

3.4 Higher-Level Interface Objects

To complete the interface description, we present other objects that are important to create a powerful animation environment.

- **Camera Controls**

Our system provides several tools for camera control. In figure 16, we present the Camera Control Window, with some options that allow a precise control of various camera settings.

Among these options, probably the most useful ones are: the *follow mode* - which guides automatically the camera throughout the scene, following the root joint that drives the skeleton hierarchy; the *lock joint mode* - which points the camera target to the active joint, selected in the skeleton graph window; and the *circle camera* option, which allows an interactive circular movement of the camera over the active joint, while the animation is being played.

Moreover, these camera options can be mixed, thus giving a yet more precise control of the camera motion.

Additional controls for scene lighting are also provided with the system.

Figure 16: Camera controls. From top to bottom: Zoom in, Zoom out, Follow mode, Lock Joint mode, Circle camera

- **Playback Controls**

Following the post-production video interface, we developed a control panel, which allows interactive control of animations in our system (figure 17).

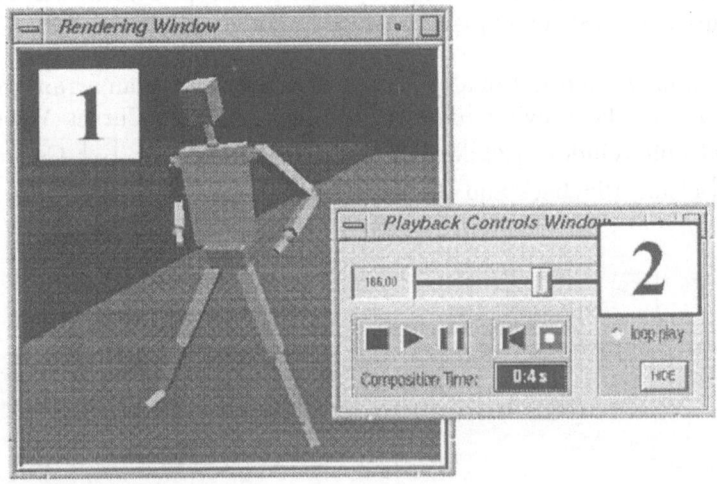

Figure 17: Playback and rendering windows.

The playback of motions or compositions produced by the user are executed in a dedicated OpenGL rendering window (in figure 17, 1). The control panel is integrated with it (in figure 17, 2), supplying a set of controls similar to those used in video recorders.

- **Objects for Other Animation Tools**

As discussed before, the architecture used in the system allows the integration of other animation techniques like keyframing, forward and inverse kinematics to help in the processing of captured motions.

In the current implementation, the system uses forward kinematics as an auxiliary tool to adjust the position of specific joints when necessary. The addition of keyframing and inverse kinematic tools is planned for future implementations.

3.5 Implementation Issues

The presented interface paradigm and prototype system were implemented in the programming language C, using a SGI Indigo 2 graphic workstation as the base platform. We employed OpenGL [14] for rendering and XForms [13] for GUI generation. The advanced GUI objects were designed and implemented separately, and then added to the forms library.

Due to OpenGL's rendering facilities and to the dynamic interface control used in the system, a real-time frame rate is achieved during the playback of animations (about 15 frames/sec in a SGI Indigo 2). The prototype system was also tested in the Linux and RISC 6000 platforms, also with good frame rates.

Figure 18 shows a snapshot of a typical system usage, with an arrangement that contain some of the previous described windows (Joint Curves Window, [1]; Skeleton Graph Window, [2]; Motion ScratchPad Window, [3]; Concatenation Window, [4] and Playback and Rendering Window, [5]).

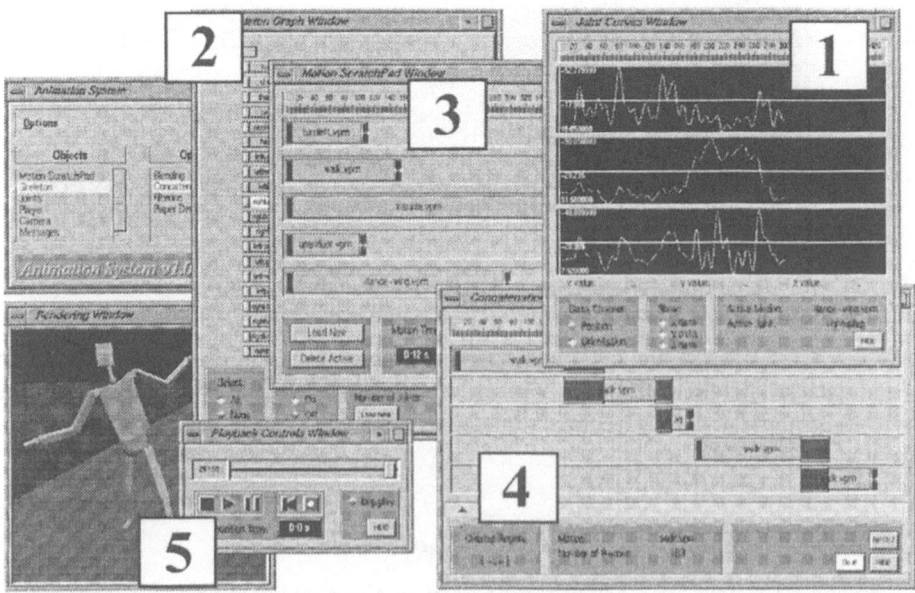

Figure 18: Snapshot of the prototype system.

4 Conclusions

In this paper, we have proposed a new user interface paradigm for motion capture based animation systems. A prototype system was built, employing the presented interface concepts and supported by a powerful architecture designed to work with the motion capture methodology.

We were very satisfied with the usability and flexibility of our system, when generating motion compositions using the proposed user interface model.

The implemented system proved to be easy and intuitive to use, with promising results that encourage us to improve it even more, with features like:

- implementation of other advanced motion operations ([9], [11], [12]), comparing their results and extracting conclusions and suggestions for improvements and / or new techniques. In this case, the system will serve as a test bed for new motion capture processing techniques.

- insertion of procedural [15] and behavioral [18] animation "plug-ins" in the system. In the first case, captured motions could act as a regent factor, guiding the procedural objects. In the second case, the behavioral functions could control the processing module, combining and modifying captured motions to improve the visual quality of the animations.

- combination of motion capture with sound. In this case, the time-markers could be used to synchronize the key moments in the motion with the temporal description of the sound.

5 Acknowledgements

This research has been developed in the laboratory of VISGRAF project at IMPA. This project is sponsored by CNPq, FAPERJ, FINEP and IBM Brasil. The authors would like to thank Viewpoint Datalabs, Inc. and Biovision, Inc. for access to motion capture data, and to the Brazilian Council for Scientific and Technological development (CNPq) for the financial support. Also thanks are due to the reviewers for their valuable comments.

6 References

[1] GINSBERG, C. M., *Human Body Motion as Input to an Animated Graphical Display*. Master Thesis, Massachusetts Institute of Technology, May 1983.

[2] MAXWELL, D. R., *Graphical Marionette: A Modern day Pinocchio*. Master Thesis, Massachusetts Institute of Technology, June 1983.

[3] ZELTZER, D. AND SIMS, F., A Figure Editor and Gait Controller for Task Level Animation. In *Computer Graphics (SIGGRAPH'88), Course Notes,* no. 4, 164-181.

[4] SILVA, F., VELHO, L., CAVALCANTI, P. AND GOMES, J. M., An Architecture for Motion Capture Based Animation. (preprint), 1997.

[5] DYER, S., MARTIN, J. AND ZULAUF, J., Motion Capture White Paper. Technical Report. Silicon Graphics, December 12, 1995.

[6] Character Motion Systems. In *Computer Graphics (SIGGRAPH'94),* Course no. 9.

[7] MULDER, S., Human Movement Tracking Technology. Hand Centered Studies of Human Movement Project, Simon Fraser University. Technical Report 94-1, July 1994.

[8] O'ROURKE, J., *Computational Geometry in C.* Cambridge University Press, 1994.

[9] WILLIAMS, L. AND BRUDELIN, A., Motion Signal Processing. In *Computer Graphics (SIGGRAPH'95 Proceedings)*(August 1995), pp. 97-104.

[10] Turbo Cube / Video Cube - User's Guide. IMIX Company.

[11] WITKIN, A. AND POPOVIC, Z., Motion Warping. In *Computer Graphics (SIGGRAPH'95 Proceedings)*(August 1995), pp. 105-108.

[12] COHEN, M., ROSE, C., GUENTER, B. AND BODENHEIMER, B., Efficient Generation of Motion Transitions Using Spacetime Constraints. In *Computer Graphics (SIGGRAPH'96 Proceedings)*(August 1996), pp. 147-154.

[13] Xforms Home Page, *http://bragg.phys.uwm.edu/xform*

[14] NEIDER, J., DAVIS, T. AND WOO, M., *OpenGL Programming Guide - The Official Guide to Learning OpenGL, Release 1.* Addison-Wesley, 1993.

[15] PERLIN, K., Realtime Responsive Animation with Personality. In *IEEE Transactions on Visualization and Computer Graphics,* Vol 1, No.1, March 1995.

[16] WITKIN, A. AND KASS, M., Spacetime Constraints. In *Computer Graphics (SIGGRAPH'88 Proceedings)*(August 1988), pp. 159-168.

[17] TERZOPOULOS, D. ET AL., Artificial Fishes with Autonomous Locomotion, Perception, Behavior and Learning, in a Physical World. In *Proceedings of the Artificial Life IV Workshop,* MIT Press (1994).

[18] COSTA, M. AND FEIJÓ, B., An Architecture for Concurrent Reactive Agents in Real-Time Animation. In *Proceedings of SIBGRAPI'96, IX Brazilian Symposium of Computer Graphics and Image Processing,* pp. 281-288. 1996.

2

Human Animation

A Model of Human Crowd Behavior : Group Inter-Relationship and Collision Detection Analysis

S. R. Musse and D. Thalmann
{soraia,thalmann}@lig.di.epfl.ch
Computer Graphics Lab. Swiss Federal Institute of Technology
EPFL, DI-LIG, CH 1015 Lausanne, Switzerland

Abstract

This paper presents a model of crowd behavior to simulate the motion of a generic population in a specific environment. The individual parameters are created by a distributed random behavioral model which is determined by few parameters. This paper explores an approach based on the relationship between the autonomous virtual humans of a crowd and the emergent behavior originated from it. We have used some concepts from sociology to represent some specific behaviors and represent the visual output. We applied our model in two applications: a graphic called sociogram that visualizes our population during the simulation, and a simple visit to a museum. In addition, we discuss some aspects about human crowd collision.

1 Introduction

There are very few studies on crowd modeling. We may mention the following related papers: *C. Reynolds* [1] developed a model for simulating a school of fish and a flock of birds using a particle systems method [2]; *D. Terzopoulos* [3] developed a model for behavioral animation of fish groups based on the repertoire of behaviors which are dependent on their perception of the environment; *S. Velastin* [4] worked on the characterization of crowd behavior in confined areas such as railway-stations and shopping malls using image processing for the measure of the crowd motion; *T. Calvert* [5] developed the blackboard architecture that allows the animator to work cooperatively with a family of knowledge based tools; *E. Bouvier* [6] presented a crowd simulation in immersive space management and a new approach of particle systems as a generic model for simulations of dynamic systems [7].

In this paper we present a new approach of crowd behavior considering the relationship between groups of individuals and the emergent behavior originated from it (i.e. the global effect generated by local rules). We treat the individuals as autonomous virtual humans that react in presence of other individuals and change their own parameters accordingly. In addition we describe a multiresolution collision method specific for the crowd modeling.

This paper is structured as follows. In section 2, we present some sociological concepts of crowd modeling which were used in our application. In section 3, we present information concerning the model : individual and group parameters, distributed group behavior and implemented sociological effects. In section 4 we present the scenarios where we have applied our model. In section 5, we describe our collision avoidance methods and we present some results and analysis of this problem in the context of crowd simulation. In section 6 we present the applied methodology. Finally, section 7 draws some conclusions about the model.

2 Some Sociological Aspects

An accepted definition of crowd is that of a large group of individuals in the same physical environment, sharing a common goal (e.g. people going to a rock show or a football match). The individuals in a crowd may act in a different way than when they are alone or in a small group [12].

Although sociologists are often interested in crowd effects arising from social conflicts or social problems [11,13], the normal behavior of a crowd can also be studied when no changes are expected.

There are, however, some other group effects relevant to our work which are worth mentioning. *Polarization* occurs within a crowd when two or more groups adopt divergent attitudes, opinions or behavior and they may argue or fight even if they do not know each other. In some situations the crowd or a group within it may seek an adversary [10]. The *sharing* effect is the result of influences by the acts of others at the individual level. *Adding* is the name given to the same effect when applied to the group. *Domination* happens when one or more leaders in a crowd influence the others.

Our goal is to simulate the behavior of a collection of groups of autonomous virtual humans in a crowd. Each group has its general behavior specified by the user, but the individual behaviors are created by a random process through the group behavior. This means that there is a trend shared by all individuals in the same group because they have a pre specified general behavior.

3 Our Human Crowd Model

This model presents a simple method for describing the crowd behavior through the group inter-relationships. Virtual actors only react in the presence of others, e.g., they meet another virtual human, evaluate their own emotional parameters with those of the other one and, if they are similar, they may walk together. As it is recognized that the model is limited in describing human relationships, only a set of criteria were defined based on the available literature.

The group parameters are specified by defining the goals (specific positions which each group must reach), number of autonomous virtual humans in the group and the level of dominance from each group. This is followed by the creation of virtual humans based on the groups' behavior information. The individual parameters are: a list of goals and individual interests for these goals (originated from the group goals), an emotional status (randomic number), the level of relationship with the other groups (based on the emotional status of the agents from a same group) and the level of dominance (which follows the group trend). As could be seen, some virtual human's parameters are totally random while others parameters follow the group trend.

All the individual parameters can be changed depending on their relations with the others. Therefore, we have defined:

i) $\underline{A}$ a virtual human from the group $\underline{GA}$ and
ii) $\underline{B}$ a virtual human from the group $\underline{GB}$.

The agents $\underline{A}$ and $\underline{B}$ have the following parameters when they are created in the initial population :

- Agent.List_of_goals = Group.List_of_goals
- Agent.List_of_interests= Group.List_of_interests
- Agent.Emotional_status= random([0;1])
- Agent.Relation_with_each_other_group *is defined by the mean emotional status value of all virtual humans from this group*
- Agent.Domination_value = Group.Domination_value

Based on these parameters, we created some situations in which the individual parameters can be changed during the simulation:

i) The virtual human $\underline{A}$ can be <u>changed from group $\underline{GA}$</u> to group $\underline{GB}$ if,

    i.1) *Relation ($\underline{A},\underline{GA}$) < Relation ($\underline{A},\underline{GB}$): if the relationship between $\underline{A}$ and GA is smaller than between $\underline{A}$ and GB.*

    i.2) *Relation ($\underline{A},\underline{GB}$) > 0.90: if $\underline{A}$ has a high value in relation to the group GB.*

  In this case, some parameters of virtual human $\underline{A}$ change according to :

- $\underline{A}$.List_of_goals = $\underline{GB}$.List_of_goals

If $\underline{A}$.Domination_value > *all_agents*.Domination_value from $\underline{GB}$, *if the domination value of $\underline{A}$ is greater than all autonomous virtual humans from group GB, then $\underline{A}$ will be the new leader of group GB and the other virtual humans from this group will have a new tendency to follow it. This represents the changes of group parameters consequent to individual changes.*

- $\underline{A}$.List_of_interests = random(each_goal)$\underline{GB}$, *meaning that the list of interests for each goal of $\underline{A}$ is generated by a random process.*

Else
- $\underline{A}$.List_of_interests = (List_of_interests) from_most_leader_ag from $\underline{GB}$, *that means $\underline{A}$ is influenced by the leader of group GB and*
- $\underline{A}$.Domination_value *is decreased.*

ii) The <u>emotional status</u> can be changed in the encounter of two autonomous virtual humans in a random process. Only when both have a high value for the domination parameter, one virtual human is chosen in a randomic way to reduce its emotional status. In this case a polarization between two leaders will follow. In any other case, both virtual humans must assume the highest emotional status between them.

iii) The <u>relation</u> of $\underline{A}$ with group $\underline{GB}$ is defined by the mean state emotional value of all $\underline{GB}$ virtual humans which have greater emotion status value than $\underline{A}$. This value must be normalized (between 0. and 1.).

$$R(\underline{A},\underline{GB})=\text{Normalized\_value} \sum_{\substack{N\_AGENTS \\ FROM\_GB}}^{i=0} (state\_emotional)ag_i > (state\_emotional)agA$$

The sociological effects modeled in the presented rules are:

i) *grouping* of individuals depending on their inter-relationships and the *domination* effect;
ii) *polarization* and the *sharing* effects as the influence of the emotional status and domination parameters; and finally,
iii) *adding* in the relationship between autonomous virtual humans and groups.

The group behavior is formed by two behaviors: *seek goal*, that is the ability of each group to follow the direction of motion specified in its goals, e.g. in the case of a visit to a museum, the agents walk in the sense of its goals (the work-of-arts); and the *flocking* (ability to walk together), has been considered as a consequence of the group movement based on the specific goals (list_of_goals) during a specific time (list_of_interests). For example, if the user chooses to have flocking in the crowd, the agents from the same group change of goal just when all the agents from this group have arrived at a same point. Thus, if one group *g* must go to goal number 2 (from the list of goals), all the agents from the group *g* must arrive before at goal number 1 (also from the list of goals).

The individual behavior is composed of three simpler behaviors. A walk, a collision avoidance (section 5) and a relationship behavior which occurs when the agents meet each other.

4 The Implemented Scenarios

We have applied our model in two situations. The first is a sociogram which means a sociological graphic representing one population, its relationships, and the different levels of domination. Figure 1 shows an example of a sociogram.

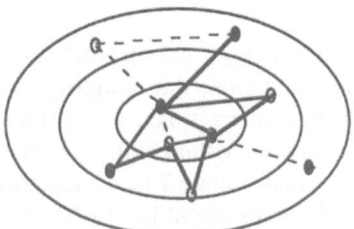

Figure 1: A sociogram

The filled circles represent the women and the empty circles the men. The dashed line represents a relationship of hostility and the full lines represent a friendly relation. In addition, this graphic represents a certain hierarchy in the group, as the individuals in the center of the sociogram have more relationships as compared to the others in the external circles [10].

In our case, we have four groups with different behaviors and parameters (does not include the gender parameter). The autonomous virtual humans walk on the limit of the circles, like in the sociogram and these circles are delimited by points which represent the goals for each group, as we can see in the next figure.

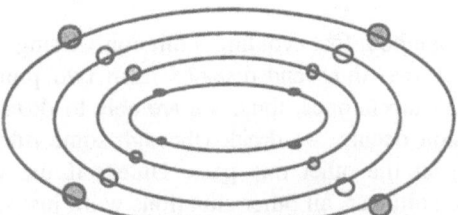

Figure 2: The sociogram in our case

The virtual humans walk in the direction of their goals. Each group has one different color allowing to show when the virtual humans change groups. We can see in the Appendix (Figures 3 and 4) some images of this simulation. Figure 3, we can see the start of the simulation where all autonomous virtual humans are in the initial (randomized assigned) positions. In Figure 4, the virtual humans walk within the limits of their group in the sociogram.

Using the parameters specified in section 3, we have modeled a sociogram including time information which allow us to see changes in crowd behavior during the simulation. In this example, the flocking behavior is represented by walking in a specific region of each group (each circle).

The second example is a crowd which visits a museum. In this simple example, the crowd is formed by different groups. In the beginning of the simulation all virtual humans of the same group visit the museum within the time of their group including, for example, the time to see a specific work of art. However, during the simulation, we can observe agents which change groups and assume the time of those from their new group to visit and walk. In this case, we consider that the virtual humans change groups as a result of both individual and group relationships.

Figures 5 and 6 (see in Appendix) show one example of this simulation. Figure 5 show is the beginning of the simulation, the virtual humans are in their randomized initial position. After one hundred interactions, the agents are gathered in groups and walk in the museum. The autonomous virtual humans of the same group look during a similar time to a specific work of art. Figure 7 (see Appendix) shows one image of this simulation integrated in a DIVE environment in COVEN Project [15].

5 Collision Analysis

The mainly question that we want to answer in this section is the possibility of using the crowd model as an advantage. That is, if we have a crowd model with many autonomous virtual humans, we may decide whether the collision is necessary or not and depending on the cases. Here, we can use some concepts of multiresolution in order to decide which method of collision must be applied. But for this, we need some information to compare different kinds of collision avoidance. Therefore, we implemented 2 types of collision avoidance which we present in this section with a comparison of the results.

5.1 Collision Avoidance Type 1

This is a very simple method for avoiding collision. Using simple mathematical equations (intersection of two lines and distance from two points) to determine the future positions from the current ones, thus, we are able to detect a possible collision event. Before the collision occurs, we decide (through some rules of priority) to stop one virtual human and let the other one pass. Unless if the vectors of the virtual humans' movements are collinear, all other situations work just with this condition.

Figure 8: Virtual human stops for the other

In the collinear cases, it is necessary one simple vector analysis to know which agent we must stop or if the agent can have its directions changed (section 5.2).

The following execution flow shows the priority rules:

> *For each pair of agents*
> > *If vectors are not collinear*
> > > *If linear velocities are different*
> > > > *Stop the slower agent*
> > > *else*
> > > > *Choose one agent in a random way*
> > *else*
> > > *If the vectors are convergent*
> > > > *Choose one agent in a random way*
> > > > *Change its movement direction*
> > > *else*
> > > > *Increase the linear velocity of the agent*
> > > > *which walks in the front of the other*

In the following images we can see some examples of the collinear cases.

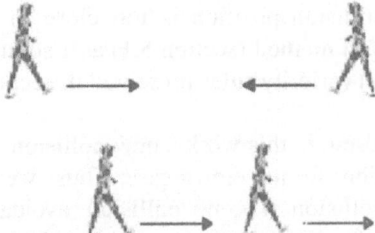

Figure 9: The special collision cases

In the situations of Figure 9, as we can see in the priority rules, it is necessary to decide which virtual human must wait or change the direction. In this latter case, we used the method which will be presented in the next section.

5.2 Collision Avoidance Type 2

This other collision method is also very simple, but it is based on the directions changes. Instead of waiting for the other one, the autonomous virtual human can predict the collision event (knowing the position of next virtual humans) through a simple geometric computing (intersection of two lines). Thus, it can avoid the collision by changing its directions through its angular velocity changes. After a specific period of time, the virtual human returns to its last angular velocity (which was stored in the data structures), and also comes back to its previous direction, it represents the goal seeking group behavior.

We assumed:
$$(ang\_vel)\underline{A} = func(position\_all\_next\_agents),$$
It means that the new angular velocity from the agent $\underline{A}$ is a function of the position vectors of the agents in a near distance.

The next images show a sequence of the collision detection method type 2. We can see the agent avoiding collision by changing his angular velocity.

Figure 10: Avoid collision sequence

Sometimes, however, the virtual human does not have enough time to modify its direction because the collision position is too close to the current position. In this case, we are using the last method (section 5.1) as a solution, that is, we decide which virtual human must wait (priority rules presented in section 5.1).

We do not intend to present in this work a new collision algorithm but just to present some useful considerations for the crowd case. Thus, we evaluated these two collision methods and a total collision (i.e, no collision avoidance). The following graphic presents the time data for ten autonomous virtual humans which start at an initial aleatory position and must arrive to a specific final position.

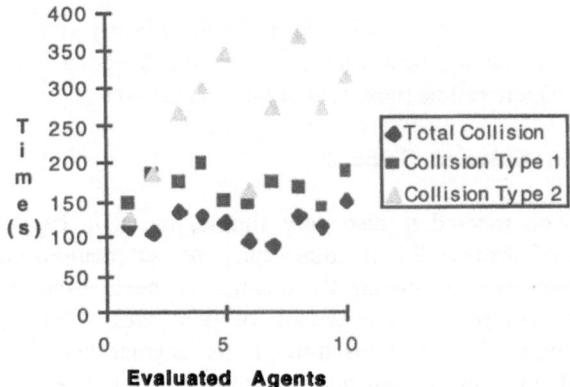

Graphic 1: Comparison of the collision methods for 10 agents

The y axis is the time spent by each virtual human to arrive to their goal. The x axis shows each evaluated agent. As their initial positions are totally random, we can explain the time spent by agent 1 (its initial position was close from its goal position, by coincidence). As the initial population and the behaviors are the same in all three cases, we can compare their time data. The next table presents some results.

Situation	Mean Time (sec)
Total Collision	117.6
Collision Avoidance Type 1	166.9
Collision Avoidance Type 2	261.8

Table 1

As it can be seen in Table 1, in terms of computational time, collision type 2 is 55% more expensive than total collision and 36% more expensive than the collision type 1.

Based on this analysis we specified our multiresolution model. We defined the position limits of the autonomous virtual humans and the collision method implemented. The next figure shows one possible model: consider the distance from the observer to the virtual humans as a high value and the three agents represent the positions limits of the different specific collision methods.

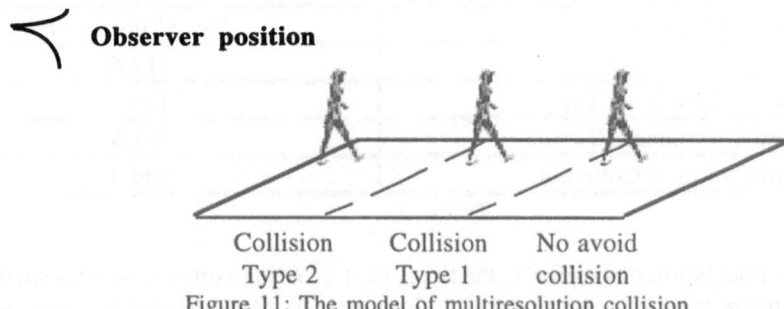

Figure 11: The model of multiresolution collision

In this case, the virtual humans that do not avoid collision must be a long distance from the viewer. We need this kind of multiresolution because we believe that when we have thousands of autonomous virtual humans, a detailed collision response may not be seen and thus become unnecessary. We must emphasize here that the dynamic movement of these three groups will be different because in case of changing trajectory or just waiting for another agent, the time and the path followed by each agent can change. In spite of this, the agents will seek their goal. We have measured the time for multiresolution collision as showed in Graphic 2 and Table 2.

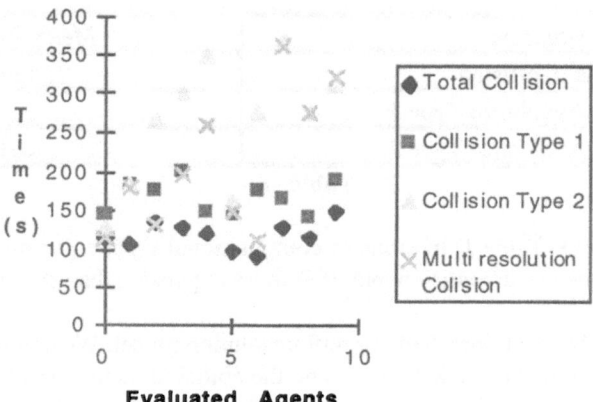

Graphic 2: Comparison with the multiresolution collision

Situation	Mean Time (sec)
Total Collision	117.6
Collision Avoidance Type 1	166.9
Collision Avoidance Type 2	261.8
Multiresolution Collision	209.7

Table 2

For the same population of graphic 1, the time spent avoiding collision is 20% smaller than the collision type 2 in the multiresolution method. We concluded that this is a good method but it will be used when we have many autonomous virtual humans, thus we can not see the collision problems originated from the totally-not-avoiding collision method even if the agents were far away.

6 Applied Methodology

Our system was developed in C Language and we have used the libraries SCENElib and BODYlib [8] dedicated to the creation of 3D objects scenes and human actors. We have also used the AGENTlib and BEHAVIORlib [9], the first one is responsible for the coordination of perception and action, and the second enables the definition of a behavior as a hierarchical decomposition in simpler behaviors performed either sequentially or concurrently. We do not use a synthetic vision approach [14] because this feature spends a lot of computational time, thus, we have used here a simple model of perception that just needs the position and orientation vectors of the autonomous virtual humans. In the next graphic (figure 12) , we show the system architecture.

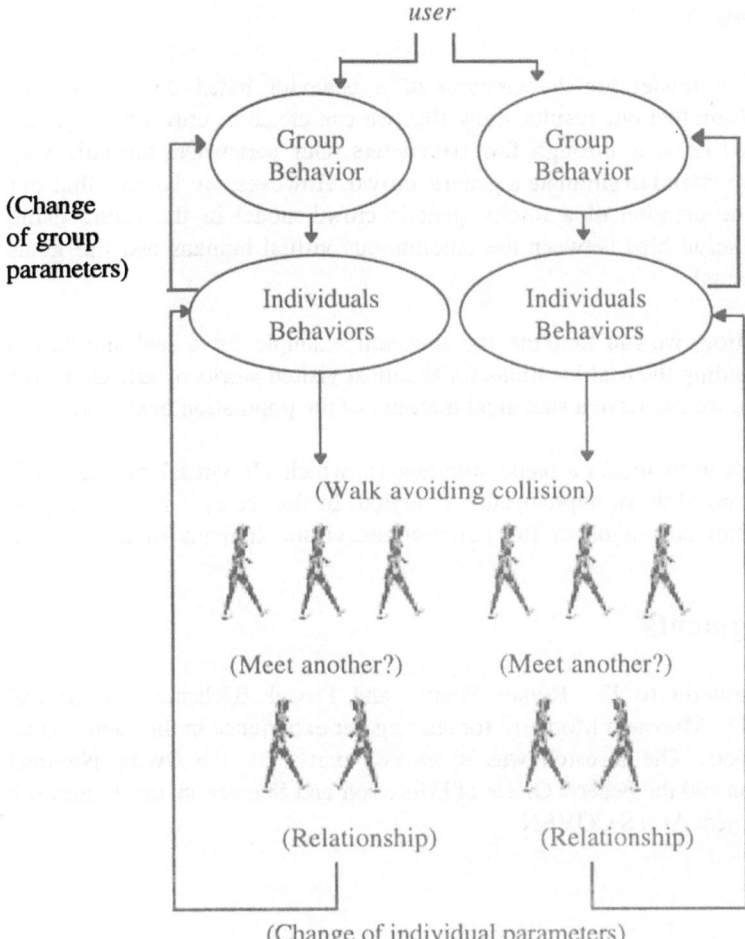

Figure 12: The system architecture

Figure 12 presented the execution flow of our system. As we could see in the last sections, the user specifies the group behavior, which is distributed to all the virtual humans creating the individual parameters. Through these parameters, each agent acts according to three possible behaviors: walk, collision avoidance and relationship with the other, for each time that one virtual human meets an other. This relationship can change the individual parameters and the group behavior, e.g., when one virtual human changes a group and becomes the leader within this new group, the other autonomous virtual humans will try to follow him. In addition, the groups seek the goals and maintain the flocking movement.

7. Conclusions

We have described a model for the creation of a behavior based on inter-groups relationships. We think that our results show that we can create a crowd through the group's behavior and drive it through few parameters. Our parameters are still very simple given that we intend to simulate a generic crowd. However, we believe that our model will allow the creation of a totally generic crowd model in the future using mainly the inter-relationships between the autonomous virtual humans and the goals schema (interest points).

As a direct application, we can imagine the museum example for a real simulation where the goal is finding the best locations for the most visited works of art. Or in the sociogram example, we can have a statistical measure of the population behavior.

In the future we intend to model a panic situation in which all virtual humans will have their goals changed to an unpredictable direction. In this case, it is necessary to have a good model of adaptation of the autonomous virtual humans in a unknown environment.

8 Acknowledgments

The authors are grateful to Dr. Ronan Boulic and Pascal Bécheiraz for fruitful discussions and to Dr. Maristela Monteiro for sharing her experience in the sociological and statistical aspects. The research was sponsored partly by the Swiss National Research Foundation and the Federal Office of Education and Science in the framework of the European project ACTS COVEN.

9. References

1. *C. Reynolds*. "Flocks, Herds, and Schools: A Distributed Behavioral Model". Proc. SIGGRAPH'87, Computer Graphics, v.21, n.4. July, 1987.

2. *W. Reeves*. "Particle Systems - A Technique for Modeling a Class of Fuzzy Objects". Proc. SIGGRAPH'83, Computer Graphics, v.2, n.2. July, 1983.

3. *X. Tu and D. Terzopoulos*. "Artificial Fishes: Physics, Locomotion, Perception, Behavior". Proc. SIGGRAPH'94, Computer Graphics, July, 1994.

4. *J.H.Yin, S. Velastin and A. C. Davies*. "Measurement of Crowd Density using Image Processing". VII European Signal Processing Conference, EUSIPCO-94, Edinburgh, UK, Sept. 1994,.

5. *T. Calvert* and et. al . "Towards the Autonomous of Multiple Human Figures". IEEE Computer Graphics & Applications, v. pp. 69-75, 1994.

6. *E. Bouvier and Pascal Guilloteau.*. "Crowd simulation in immersive space management". 3Rd EUROGRAPHICS Workshop on Virtual Environments, Monte Carlo (1996).

7. E. Bouvier, E. Cohen and L. Najman. "From crowd simulation to airbag depolyment: particle systems, a new paradigm of simulation". Journal of Electronic Imaging 6(1), 94-107 (January 1997).

8. *R. Boulic, T. Capin, Z. Huang, P. Kalra, B. Lintermann, N. Magnenat-Thalmann, L. Moccozet, T. Molet, I. Pandzic, K. Saar, A. Schmitt, J. Shen and D. Thalmann.* "The HUMANOID Environment for interactive Animation of Multiple Deformable Human Characters". Proceedings of EUROGRAPHICS'95, p.337-348 (Maastricht, The Netherlands, August 28 september, 1995).

9. *P. Bécheiraz and D. Thalmann.* "A Model of Nonverbal Communication and Interpersonal Relationship between Virtual Actors". Proc. of the Computer Animation'96, Geneva, Switzerland, pp. 58-67. May, 1996.

10. *Hellmuth Benesh.* "Atlas de la Psychologie". Librairie Générale Française, 1995, pour l'édition française.

11. *J. S. McClelland.* "The Crowd and The Mob". Book printed in Great Britain at the University Press, Cambridge. 1989.

12. *M. E. Roloff.* "Interpersonal Communication - The Social Exchange Approach". SAGE Publications, v.6, London. 1981.

13. *P. Mannoni.* "La Psychologie Collective". Presses Universitaires de France, Paris. 1985.

14. *O. Renault, N.M.Thalmann, D. Thalmann.* "A Vision Based Approach to Behavioral Animation". The Journal of Visualization and Computer Animation, v.1, n.1, pp.18-21.

15. *T. K. Capin, I. S. Pandzic, H. Noser, N. Thalmann, D. Thalmann.* "Virtual Human Representation and Communication in VLNET Networked Virtual Environments". IEEE Computer Graphics and Applications, Special Issue on Multimedia Highways, March 1997.

Editors' Note: see Appendix, p. 194 ff. for colored figures of this paper

Dynamic analysis of human walking

François Faure, Gilles Debunne,
Marie-Paule Cani-Gascuel, Franck Multon ‡

iMAGIS[†]-GRAVIR / IMAG
BP 53, F-38041 Grenoble cedex 09, France
Francois.Faure@imag.fr, Gilles.Debunne@imag.fr, Marie-Paule.Gascuel@imag.fr
‡ IRISA
Campus de Beaulieu, 35042 Rennes Cedex, France
Franck.Multon@irisa.fr

Abstract

Synthetising realistic animations of human figures should benefit from both a priori biomechanical knowledge on human motion and physically-based simulation techniques, eager to adapt motion to the specific environment in which it takes place. This paper performs a first step towards this goal, by computing and analyzing the internal actuator forces involved when the human figure performs specific walk motions. The computations rely on a robust simulator where forward and inverse dynamics are combined with automatic collision detection and response. The force curves we obtain give interesting information on the respective action of muscles in various styles of walks. Our further plans include parameterizing them and using them to control physically-based simulations of walk motions.

1   Introduction

Two main approaches have been used for generating walking motions in Computer Animation. The first one is to capture or to create several human motions and to deform or combine them in order to generate and control a large variety of virtual motions [BC93, UAT95, BW95, WP95]. However, these methods can only generate walking on a flat ground, without obstacles. The second one is to compute a physically-based simulation of the motion [BC89]. The body of the human figure is provided with actuators at hinges, which represent

---

[†]iMAGIS is a joint project of CNRS, INRIA, Institut National Polytechnique de Grenoble and Université Joseph Fourier.

simplified versions of muscles [HWBO95, LvdP96]. A controller computes the actuators actions over time, and the resulting motion is integrated according to the interactions with the virtual environment. Although such controllers could be generated from random search and optimization [NM93, vdPF93, RGBC96, LvdPF96], exploiting biomechanical knowledge on human walking seems a better approach [HWBO95]. However, this requires much skill since biomechanics analyses the kinematics of captured motion while simulators take the internal actuator forces as an entry.

In this paper, we compute and analyse the actuator forces needed for a human figure to perform different walking gaits. We first convert a priori kinematic knowledge on human walking described by biomechanics into parametrized automatons delivering angular coordinates over time for the legs of the figure. Then, we use these pre-specified relative angular motions as constraints in a dynamic simulator which handles automatic collision detection and response. During the simulation, the body copes with both unknown internal forces at hinges (due to constrained motion) and external forces such as gravity and interactions with the ground. Solving for the constraints gives us the internal actuator forces over time.

The remainder of this paper develops as follows: Section 2 reviews the informations on human walking given by biomechanics and deals with their conversion into the constrained motion of an articulated human figure. Section 3 describes the simulator we will use for internal forces computation, i.e., the way we combine collision processing with forward and inverse dynamics. Our results on the dynamic analysis of a standard walk are presented in Section 4. Analysis and validation of these results is provided in Section 5. Section 6 concludes by discussing applications and work in progress.

2 The kinematics of human walking

This section reviews results on human walking described by biomechanics, and explains how we have converted them into parametrized automata generating different walking gaits for a human figure.

2.1 Biomechanical analysis of human walking

A lot of studies on human walking can be found in bio-mechanics papers. Most of them characterize the different phases that compose the locomotion cycles. A more accurate description of these phases is provided by Nilsson [NTH85]. In particular, he identifies changes in angle trajectories between the different limbs of the legs depending on the velocity of the subject. Contrary to the other studies, he gives a locomotion sub-cycle for each articulation, by introducing phases of extensions/flexions. Each phase is defined by its position in the walking

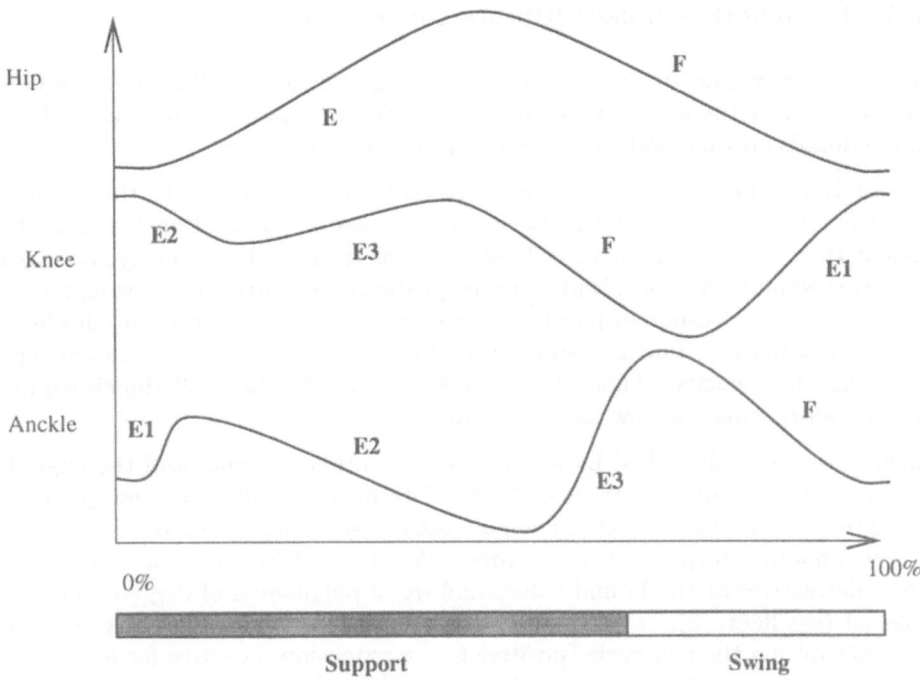

Figure 1: Angular laws of the limbs and locomotion sub-cycles during human walking.

cycle, its duration, and the associated lower and upper angle bound values. In the example of figure 1, three phases during the extension of the leg are identified for the knee (E_1, E_2, E_3). One phase during flexion of the leg (F) completes the walking cycle.

The coordination between the articulations is given by the position and duration of the sub-cycles in the entire locomotion cycle. Nilsson analyses the effects of the variations of the velocity of the walk on these coordination parameters. In practice, we use linear laws for modeling these changes.

The velocity V_G of a walker depends on the step length L_{Step} and frequency F_{Step} : $V_G = L_{Step} * F_{Step}$. So, for a given velocity, many possible step lengths and frequencies are possible. Enoka [Eno94] shows that people prefer, to a certain extend, increase their velocity by increasing L_{Step} instead of F_{Step}. Nevertheless it is possible to customize a walking gait by tuning this strategy.

2.2   Knowledge-based kinematic model

To perform dynamic analysis of human walking from the results above, we first have to convert them into a parametrized kinematic model of human walking (more details on this model can be found in [MA97]).

We use Hierarchical Concurrent State Machines (HCSM) to model the locomotion sub-cycles described by Nilsson, and to ensure coordination between the articulations. The main state machine describes the global walking cycles : each state corresponds to a specific global sub-cycle such as stance phase, swing phase, double stand, etc. *Children* parallel state machines describe the sub-cycles local to each articulation. Linear laws are used to define how these sub-cycles change depending on velocity. Thus, if a change of velocity occurs, all the states are synchronized using the new sub-cycle parameters.

Each sub-cycle is described by its dates of activation and end, and the angular values of the articulation at these times. Intermediate values are interpolated. Since the forces we are going to compute are second order derivatives of motion, a very smooth interpolation is required. We thus set to zero first and second order derivatives at the bound values and use a polynomial of degree 5 in each interval (see figure 2). This ensures that the sign of angular velocity remains constant during the sub-cycle (positive for an extension, negative for a flexion), and leads to a smooth angular motion with C^2 continuity.

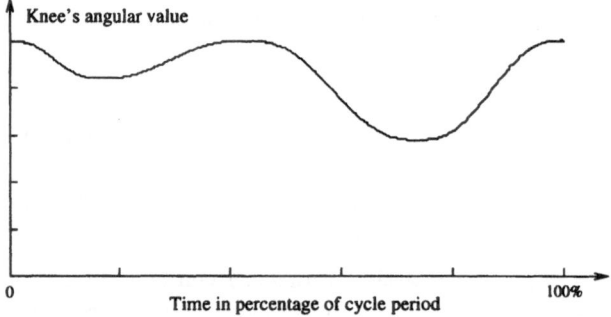

Figure 2: Approximation of the knee angle trajectory by 5-degree polynomial.

To customize the model and enable different walking gaits, we use tunable parameters for step length, step frequency and step height. Changing the step frequency simply corresponds to a change in the duration of the whole cycle whereas changing step length or height corresponds to a modification of the angular values of all the local states. This produces different walking gaits that will be analyzed in Sections 4 and 5 together with the standard gait described by Nilsson.

3   A simulator handling collisions and constrained motions

Combining the use of forward and inverse dynamics is a well known approach [IC88] but has not been applied, to the authors knowledge, to human walk including automatic collision detection and response along with a precise computation of closed loop forces and friction. Among related previous works, Boulic [BM94] performs static analyses of human postures. Ko and Badler [KB96] use an *ad hoc* inverse dynamics algorithm to modify human gaits according to force constraints, with approximate closed-loop force computation and a simplified contact model. Comparing our work with their results is not easy, since they do not provide curves of actuator forces during a walking cycle. However, our method makes no simplification for the contact (a linear displacement of the contact point on the foot was assumed by Ko and Badler), fully considering collision and friction, and handles with no simplification the calculus of torques when closed loops appear.

In order to perform a precise computation of the forces involved in a given walking gait, we use a general simulation algorithm, designed to handle arbitrarily large scenes with contact and friction. Applied to a human figure, it allows the computation of very general interactions between the figure and the universe. These interactions include frictioning contacts such as contact with the ground and collisions with arbitrary moving or stationary obstacles. Other applications of this general interaction processing include object grasping, and synchronization between several human figures (such as walking hand in hand).

3.1   Accurate closed-loop force computation

Our simulation algorithm relies on absolute coordinates for purpose of generality. A joint is represented by a set of geometric constraints on the relative motions of the bodies at the center of the joint. Each of them constrains the relative motion of the bodies along a given direction (thus, vectorial constraints are turned into sets of scalar constraints). For example, a standard revolute joint involves five scalar constraints: three orthogonal null translation constraints and two orthogonal null rotation constraints along directions orthogonal to the axis of the joint.

During the simulation, the algorithm computes the Lagrange multipliers of the constraints, i.e., scalar independent forces (or torques) associated with each independent scalar constraint. This is done in three steps:

1. we first compute the influence of inertias or external forces on the bodies by animating them while assuming null constraint forces;

2. then, we compute the constraint errors by projecting the relative motions (accelerations, velocities or linearized displacements) in the direction of

each scalar constraint;

3. finally, we reach a global solution by finding the constraint forces necessary to cancel the constraint errors.

For the third step, Baraff [Bar96] recently presented an algorithm that works in linear time on acyclic structures in absolute coordinates. An additional dense matrix solution is used for handling closed-loop constraints. We use the same linear-time solution to solve the acyclic constraints. However, since our simulator is designed for handling arbitrarily large scenes, we wish to avoid any dense matrix solution. We prefer to handle closed-loops by progressively refining a global solution, thanks to an iterative conjugate gradient-based minimization of the closed-loop constraints. It uses a Fletcher-Reeves-Polak-Ribiere method [PTVF92] to compute the closed-loop forces necessary to enforce the closed-loop constraints. This allows the time complexity to smoothly range from linear to quadratic in the number of constraints according to the number of closed-loop constraints, with a tunable precision of the computed forces.

3.2 Handling inverse dynamics in the simulation algorithm

In addition to fast forward dynamics, our simulator can be used to perform inverse dynamics (i.e., internal forces computation) on joints with pre-defined angular motions. We just have to take the desired pre-defined motion into account during the computation of the constraint errors (step 2 of the simulation algorithm above). Then, the Lagrange multipliers give us the internal forces which are necessary to meet the animation constraints.

For instance, a revolute joint with a driven rotation involves six independent constraints, including a (generally) non-null relative rotation constraint along the axis of the joint. The joint forces necessary to achieve the motion are thus computed without any change in the simulation algorithm.

3.3 Collisions, contacts and friction

We detect a sphere-plane collision when the distance between the center of the sphere and the plane is less than the radius of the sphere. The contact point is modeled by projecting the center of the sphere on the plane, and the relative velocity at the contact point is canceled using an impulsion.

We use a subclass of joints for modeling contacts. A contact joint is characterized by a constraint on the motion along the normal of the surfaces in contact at the contact point. This allows us to take the contact into account in the global force computation algorithm.

The Coulomb constraints on contact forces and motions are handled using an iterative global solution algorithm [Fau96]. The latter was initially designed

Part	Mass (% of total weight)	Length (% of total height)
Head	7.84	10.0
Trunk	53.13	28.7
Upper Arm	2.96	18.8
Lower Arm	2.20	14.5
Upper Leg	7.92	24.5
Lower Leg	4.70	24.6
Foot	1.72	8.9

Table 1: Measurements of the mass and size of the different body parts.

for dense matrix dynamics solution, but we adapted it to the sparse matrix formulation. A contact joint is destroyed when the force necessary to enforce the motion constraint corresponds to an attraction instead of a repulsion between the two solids. Then, a new force computation is performed.

4 Inverse dynamics applied to human walking

4.1 Simulating a standard gait of a human figure

The human figure model that we use is built of rigid links connected by rotational joints. Since we only have a 2D information on the walking motions (see Section 2), using joints with a single rotational degree of freedom is sufficient. The masses and sizes of the different limbs, given in table 4.1, are those of a male human adult. For each limb, the associated mass matrix is computed assuming a uniform density and a cylindrical shape of the limb.

The standard walking gait depicted in Figure 3 was generated using the angular laws described in Section 2, which define driven angular motions for the articulations of the legs. The cycle period, i.e., the interval between two consecutive stands of the same foot is one second, which corresponds to a slow walk. For the arms, we chose articular laws which gave a natural neutral swing. To position the body completely, we enforce a constant angle between the trunk and the ground. During the simulation, the human figure copes with gravity, collisions and Coulomb friction with the ground, simulated by a sphere-plan contact (see Section 3), so the driven motion of the legs makes the body move forwards.

The simulation was achieved in interactive time(2.5 frames per second) on a SGI Indigo2 Workstation. Our aim is now to analyse the torques produced at the leg joints during one cycle of this walking gait.

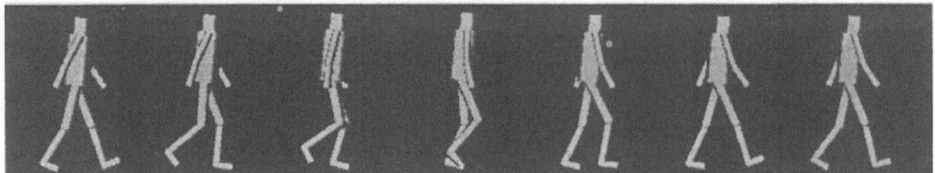

Figure 3: Snapshots of the motion, during a step. We define a step by the interval between two consecutive stands, the cycle is made of two steps.

4.2   Actuator torque curves during one step

Computations have been performed by applying our reference gait with the inverse dynamics algorithm described in Section 3.2. Played on the video, the result is an irregular gait. The character stops and starts again at each step. This is due to the difference between our angular laws and those of a real human gait. Figure 4 plots the values of the torques for the hip, the knee, and the ankle during one cycle period. We noticed that our method has a good numerical stability, as the shape of the resulting plots converged to a solution when we increased the sampling rate. Results are shown with a simulation sampling rate of 30Hz.

All the torques we computed with this gait are rather continuous, have a one second period, and only slight differences appear between two periods. The torques measured at the hip are greater than those of the knee, but their shape look alike. The torques of the ankle have lower values. This gives the first qualitative validation of our results.

We first notice the high values of the computed torques. This can be explained by the irregularity of the gait. The character stops and starts again twice a period. The total period is one second. If we approximate the velocity using lines segments, an average velocity of 1.5 $m.s^{-1}$ requires an average acceleration of $\pm 6\ m.s^{-2}$. Since the mass of the character is 80 kg and the distance between its center of mass and the ground is 1.2 m, this implies a $\pm 576\ N.m$ average torque. This is a first numerical confirmation of the visually noticeable shortcomings of the gait. Another dynamic result confirming these problems is the fact that we could not prevent the character from sliding, even with a friction coefficient as high as 1.

Interpreting the evolution of the torques according to the events appearing during walking is also important. The support phase is characterized by a negative propulsive torque, which corresponds to an acceleration of the character, followed by a positive torque, corresponding to the deceleration. The swing phase generates a lower positive torque that brings back the leg.

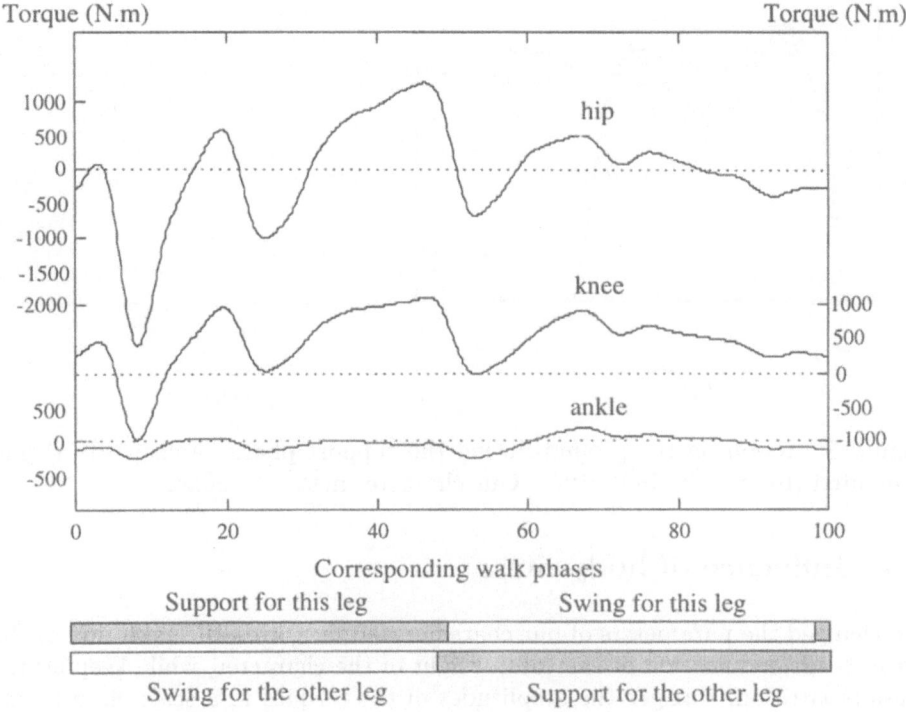

Figure 4: Computed torques for the hip, the knee and the ankle of a leg during a step. For each plot, a new zero axis is drawn, all measured in percentage of the cycle period, the scales on the ordinate are the same for the three plots, measured in $N.m$.

4.3 Biomechanical validation

Biomechanics researchers [Ped77, BLA94] have measured the interaction forces between the feet and the floor when a real subject walks. Their results are depicted in Figure 5(a).

A way to validate our computations is to compare our own results with these curves. Figure 5(b) give the vertical interaction force with the floor during our simulated walk, as ploted by our simulator. Bouncing occurs when the foot hits the ground, due to numerical instabilities. Except for the artifact due to the unwanted flying phase generated by our simulation, the curves are quite similar.

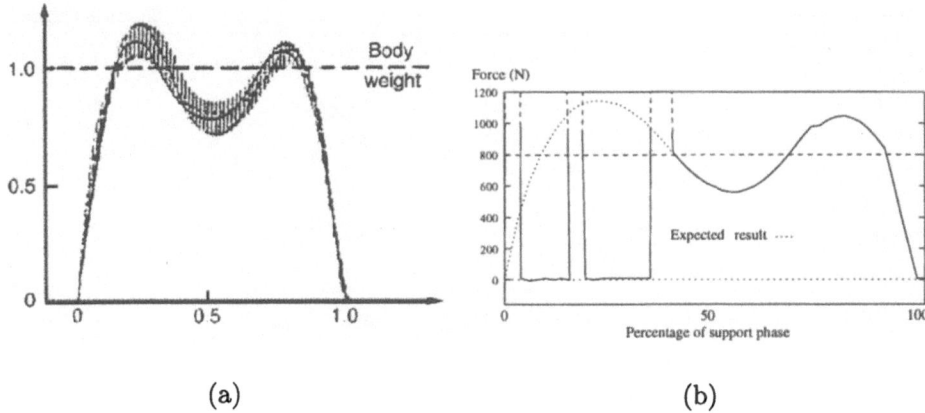

(a)   (b)

Figure 5: Action on the ground during the support phase. Measured (a) and computed (b) exhibit similarities. Our character mass was 80kg.

4.4 Influence of body mass

We changed the parameters of our character and measured the evolution of the torques. A modification of the total weight of the character, while keeping the mass repartition, changes the amplitudes of the torques in a scale close to the scale of the change of weight. The global shape remains the same. See Figure 6. Notice that this change of mass slightly changes the computed torques during the swing phase, when the leg does not support the body.

Comparison of different walking gaits

We know study the influence of the gait on our computations. We compare four different gaits including the standard one we previously studied. The three new gaits are: one with long steps (1 second period), one with short steps (0.62s period) and a walk with "goose" steps (0.82s period).

The results are plotted on Figure 7 after appropriate time scaling. As one can see, the global shape remains the same, with differences in the values. The short step gait involves the lowest torque values. On video, it is also the gait generating the most regular velocity of the character and thus, the most realistic among the four gaits.

5 Applications and concluding remarks

This paper has presented an analysis of the torques produced in the legs of a human figure during walking. Our computations are based on a kinematic description of walking gaits given by biomechanics, and on a robust simulator

Torque (N.m)

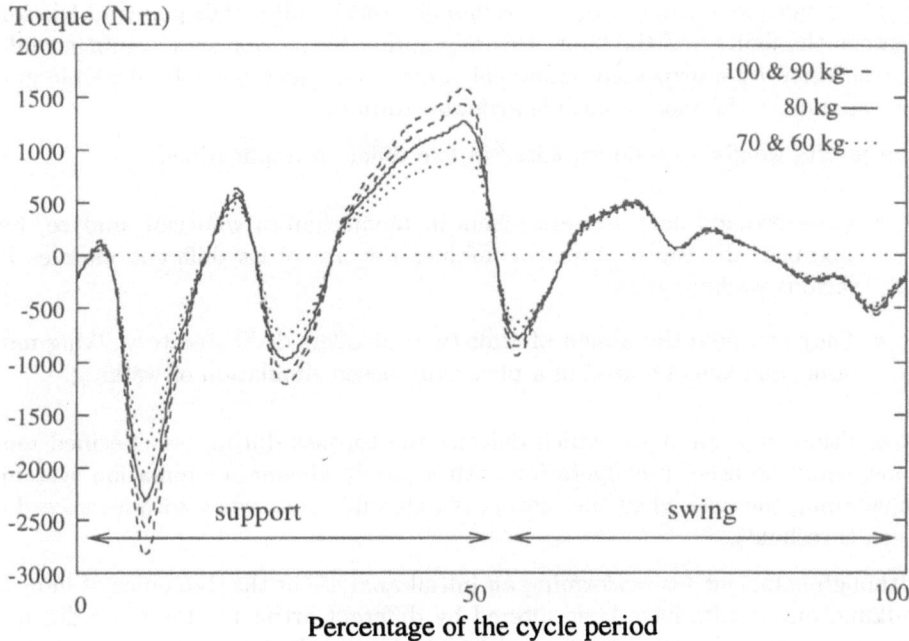

Figure 6: Influence of the mass of the human figure on the hip torques.

Torque (N.m)

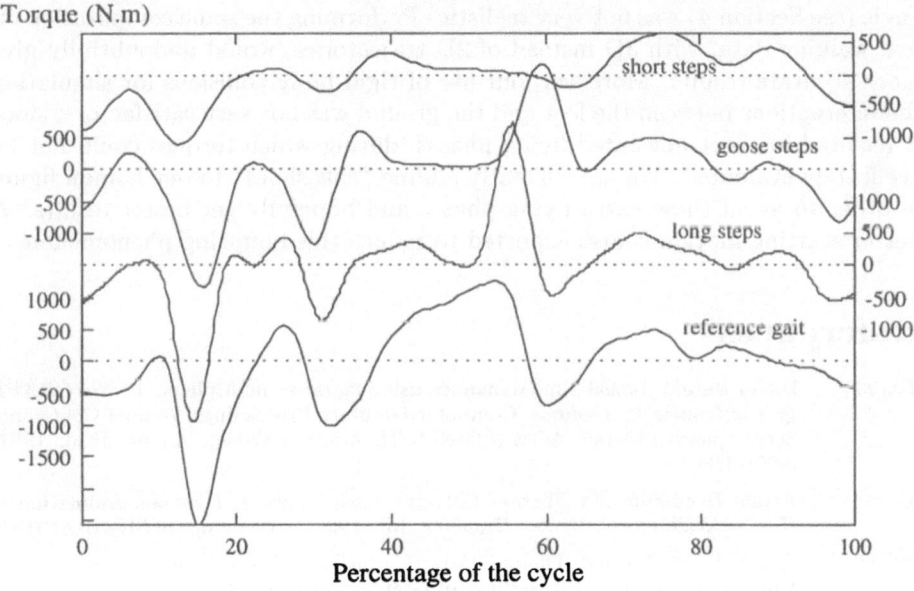

Figure 7: Comparison of the different gaits, here shown with the computed torque for the knee.

that combines forward and inverse dynamics and handles collisions and friction between the figure and the floor. Visually noticeable motion shortcomings could be confirmed by unexpected numerical values. The most visually plausible gait corresponds to the most plausible articular torques.

The results we give can be exploited in two different applications:

- They provide data to researchers in biomechanics who can analyse, for instance, the way a human combines the use of its different muscles in various walking gaits.

- They can help the design of realistic controllers dedicated to walking motions, and thus be used in a physically-based simulation of walking.

In addition, our simulator which delivers the torques during pre-specified motions, could be used in cooperation with a purely kinematic animation system, for warning the user when the motion is unfeasible (i.e., when torques exceed a given threshold).

Although sufficient for performing an initial analysis of the dynamics of human walking, our results have been altered by different artifacts. First, we did not have any captured motion to start with. The kinematic data we injected into our simulator were not very accurate, although derived from biomechanical descriptions. In particular, the variations of the angle between the body of the human figure and the world coordinate system were missing. Our choice of a constant angle (see Section 4) was not very realistic. Performing the same computation on real walking data, with 3D instead of 2D trajectories, would undoubtfully give more accurate results. Moreover, our use of rigid body collisions for simulating the interactions between the feet and the ground was not very satisfactory, since it resulted in short unwanted flying phases, during which torques could not be accurately evaluated. We are currently adding "soft shoes" to our human figure in order to avoid these extra flying phases and hopefully get better results. A better starting motion is also expected to reduce this bouncing phenomenon.

References

[Bar96]   David Baraff. Linear-time dynamics using lagrange multipliers. In *SIGGRAPH 96 Conference Proceedings*, Computer Graphics Proceedings, Annual Conference Series, pages 137–146. ACM SIGGRAPH, Addison Wesley, August 1996. ISBN 0-201-94800-1.

[BC89]   Armin Bruderlin and Thomas Calvert. Goal-Directed, Dynamic Animation of Human Walking. *Computer Graphics*, July 1989. Proceedings of SIGGRAPH'89.

[BC93]   Armin Bruderlin and Thomas Calvert. Interactive Animation of Personalized Human Locomotion. Proceedings of Graphics Interface'93.

[BLA94]   F. Barbier, P. Loslever, and J-C. Angue. Méthode informatisée de mesure et d'analyse des forces de réaction et des angles articulaires de la marche normale. *Innov. Tech. Biol. Med.*, 15(4):453–460, 1994.

[BM94]   Ronan Boulic and Ramon Mas. Inverse kinetics for center of mass position control and posture optimization. Technical report, Ecole Polytechnique Fédérale de Lausanne, September 1994.

[BW95]   Armin Bruderlin and Lance Williams. Motion signal processing. *Computer Graphics*, August 1995. Proceedings of SIGGRAPH'95.

[Eno94]   R. M. Enoka. *Neuromechanical Basis of Kinesiology (2nd Edition)*. Human Kinetics, 1994.

[Fau96]   François Faure. An energy-based method for contact force computation. *Computer Graphics Forum*, 15(3):357–366, August 1996. (Proceedings of EUROGRAPHICS'96).

[GG94]   Jean-Dominique Gascuel and Marie-Paule Gascuel. Displacement constraints for interactive modeling and animation of articulated structures. *The Visual Computer*, 10(4):191–204, March 1994.

[HWBO95]   Jessica Hodgins, Wayne Wooten, David Brogan, and James O'Brien. Animating human athletics. *Computer Graphics*, August 1995. Proceedings of SIGGRAPH'95.

[IC88]   P.M. Isaacs and M.F. Cohen. Mixed method for complex kinematic constraints in dynamic figure animation. *The Visual Computer*, 2(4):296–305, December 1988.

[KB96]   Hyeongseok Ko and Norman Badler. Animating human locomotion with inverse dynamics. *IEEE Computer Graphics and Applications*, March, 1996.

[LvdP96]   Alexis Lamouret and Michel van de Panne. Motion synthesis by example. In *Computer animation and Simulation'96*, pages 199–212. Eurograpics workshop, September 1996.

[LvdPF96] Joseph Laszlo, Michiel van de Panne, and Eugene Fiume. Limit cycle control and its application to balancing and walking. *Computer Graphics*, August 1996. Proceedings of SIGGRAPH'96.

[MA97]   F. Multon and B. Arnaldi. A biomechanical model for interactive animation of human locomotion. Submitted to the Journal of Visualization and Computer Animation, March 1997.

[NM93]   J.T Ngo and J. Marks. Spacetime constraints revisited. *Computer Graphics*, August 1993. Proceedings of SIGGRAPH'93 (Anaheim, California, August 1993).

[NTH85]   J. Nilsson, A. Thorstensson, and J. Halbertsam. Changes in leg movements and muscle activity with speed of locomotion and mode of progression in humans. *Acta Physiol Scand*, pages 457–475, 1985.

[Ped77]   A. Pedotti. A study of motor coordination and neuromuscular activities in human locomotion. *Biological Cybernetics*, pages 53–62, 1977.

[PTVF92]   Press, Teukolski, Vetterling, and Flannery. *Numerical Recipes in C*. Cambridge University Press, 1992.

[RGBC96]   Charles Rose, Brian Guenter, Bobby Bodenheimer, and Michael Cohen. Efficient generation of motion transitions using space-time constraints. *Computer Graphics*, August 1996. Proceedings of SIGGRAPH'96.

[UAT95]   Munetoshi Unuma, Ken Anjyo, and Ryozo Takeuchi. Fourier principles for emotion-based human figure animation. *Computer Graphics*, August 1995. Proceedings of SIGGRAPH'95.

[vdPF93]   M. van de Panne and E. Fiume. Sensor-actuator networks. *Computer Graphics*, August 1993. Proceedings of SIGGRAPH'93 (Anaheim, California, August 1993).

[WP95]   Andrew Witkin and Zoran Popovi'c. Motion warping. *Computer Graphics*, August 1995. Proceedings of SIGGRAPH'95.

3

Physics-based modeling

Physically-based Wrinkle Simulation & Skin Rendering

Yin Wu, Prem Kalra, Nadia Magnenat Thalmann

MIRALab, CUI, University of Geneva
email: {Yin.Wu, Prem.Kalra, Nadia.Thalmann}@cui.unige.ch

Abstract   *Wrinkle simulation with skin modeling and deformation are extremely important in enhancing the realism of human figure models. In this paper we present a model which simulates the skin deformation based on a biomechanic model and generates dynamic wrinkles rendered with texture image. The biomechanical model considers the skin as a membrane undergoing large deformations and puts the local coordinate system of each triangle element to its principal strain directions. Synthetic micro and macro structure patterns combined with real photos are employed as texture images to mimic the skin surface details. Furthermore, the potential wrinkle lines are defined , the dynamics of expressive wrinkles and aging wrinkles --their depth and fold-- is modeled based on the principal strain of the deformed skin surface and duration of deformation. Multi-layered color and bump texture mapping is used for skin rendering.*

Keywords: *Skin, Wrinkle, Aging, Texture, Deformation.*

1. Introduction

The modeling and rendering of skin is very important for human figure modeling because it greatly enhances the realism of the character animation. The skin is a continuous, protective sheet that envelops the entire body and is attached to the deeper structures by way of connecting tissues. This is the outer most visible layer of the body. At a number of places, skin adheres closely to its underlying tissue, elsewhere it glides rather freely, and at some places it becomes recessed and puckered into wrinkles [Fung, 93].

The outer skin surface consists of a geometrical structure which manifests the form of visible skin. This may look different for different parts of the body depending on its characteristics and how it is attached to the body. However, skin when observed from a close-up depicts a micro structure which is common for most parts on the body. This micro structure has a rather well defined geometrical shape and form resembling a pattern with a layered net-like structure. This structure consists of polygonal forms, most often triangles [Marks 83]. The edges of the triangular forms define the location of furrows or micro lines, and the curved surface surrounded by furrows define the ridges. On the other hand, the visible lines, patterns, creases and folds constitute a distinct structure which may be specific to one part; this structure we refer to as a macro structure. The macro structure defines the characteristic features of skin associated to a region of the body such as visible deep flexure lines and potential wrinkle lines. The macro lines form deeper and wider furrows and creases as compared to the micro lines. The micro and macro structures over skin constitute major elements affecting its visual appearance.

Skin mainly consists of collagen and elastin fibers whose combined effects decide skin's mechanical properties. Skin is usually considered as an incompressible and anisotropic material that has a visco-elastic behavior and becomes plastic with time. Two types of wrinkles appear with skin deformation: expressive wrinkles and wrinkles due to age (particularly for the face). Expressive wrinkles appear on the face during expressions at all ages and may become permanently visible over time. Skin changes with age. More lines and wrinkles emerge and with time the general appearance and texture of the skin become pronounced and rough. In addition to their visual effects, wrinkles indicate the age of a person, and expressive wrinkles act as an important factor for understanding and interpreting facial expressions.

Varied models are used to simulate skin deformation for different purposes. There are geometric models, physically-based models and biomechanical models using either particle system or continuous system. Many geometrical models have been developed. For examples, Parke [74, 82] used parametric models; Waters [87] and Magnenat-Thalmann [88] proposed models based on muscle actions of the face. There are also different kinds of physically-based models. Platt [81] proposed a tension-net model for facial animation. Terzopoulos [90] and Lee[95] used a three layered deformable lattice structure for facial tissues. Finite Element Method is also employed for more accurate calculation, especially for medical applications such as plastic surgery [Larrabee 86, Pieper 92, Koch 96].

Many research efforts have been undertaken for generating skin textures for animal as well as human skin. Bump and color mapping techniques as well as texture synthesis language are used to simulate reptile skin pattern [Miller 88, Kaufman 88]. Nahas et al. [90] proposed a method for obtaining the skin texture by recording the data of a human face. Ishii et al. [93] also proposed a geometric model for skin micro structures which applies a curved surface on a based polygon for expressing folds and ridges. There also exist a few commercial softwares (such as Alias-Wavefront) which include texture mapping features, where a photograph can be mapped on a 3D object. Most of these softwares do not impose position correspondence for the features in the model and the image [Kalra 93]. Furthermore, there does not exist yet a method where the texture image is modified as a function of skin deformation.

There have been a few efforts for the dynamic wrinkles with skin deformation. Viaud et al. [92] have presented a geometric hybrid model for the formation of expressive wrinkles, where bulges are modeled as spline segments. Terzopoulos and Waters's model [90] produces some of the expressive wrinkles during the skin deformation. A simplified facial model with a two dimensional lattice skin surface is proposed to simulate expressive wrinkles in facial animation and the aging process [Wu 1994].

However, the present models do not provide a unified framework to generate different kind of wrinkles with animation. Texture mapping offers a good simulation of static wrinkles, but it is difficult to mimic the wrinkle dynamics during animation by a purely geometric model with texture mapping. A physically based approach can offer a better simulation of wrinkle formation, but if it requires geometrical modeling of all the wrinkles it may be expensive. Therefore, in our model, the deformation of skin is motivated by a simulated muscle layer and decided by a biomechanical model while the wrinkle formation and rendering nuance are reflected by several layers of color, bump or displacement texture mapping. The texture images consist of synthetic patterns as well as real photos. The influence of the skin deformation to wrinkle formation is affected by controlling their bulge depth according to the principal strain at the skin surface points.

The paper is organized as follows. In Section 2, we give an overview of the skin deformation and wrinkle simulation mechanism. Section 3 describes the muscle design process in which muscles are simplified as B-spline patches. In Section 4, a biomechanical skin model is presented, which employs a biaxial plane-stress elastic constitutive relationship to the membrane undergoing large deformations. In addition, a linear plastic process is applied to form permanent wrinkles. Section 5 presents wrinkle simulation and its rendering with texture images. Finally, we give some concluding remarks in Section 6.

2. Overview

The skin is attached to the underneath muscle and subcutaneous layers by connective tissues. A three layered structure: an outer layer of skin with two inner layers of muscles and connective tissues, is used for skin deformation (See Figure 1). The skin surface is represented as a triangle mesh, having material properties associated with triangles but kinematical features with vertices. During animation, muscle contractions apply tension to the skin surface through insert points while the connective tissues constrain the skin deformation through connective points [Wu 94].

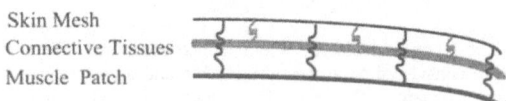

Skin Mesh
Connective Tissues
Muscle Patch

Figure 1: Layered structure for skin deformation

Figure 2 shows the overview of our wrinkle simulation prototype. In our facial model the skin's geometrical structure is defined as a triangle mesh. Facial muscles are designed as B-spline patches according to the nature and direction of muscle fibers. The skin surface is deformed using a biomechanical model following muscle contractions. Patterns for static wrinkles are represented in texture images. The dynamics of wrinkle simulation is computed using the strain measures of skin deformation of the 3D facial model. The wrinkle formation information modifies the corresponding synthetic wrinkle pattern texture image. Final rendering may combine texture mapping of real photos and synthetic skin texture using a layered rendering process of RenderMan[Upstill 89].

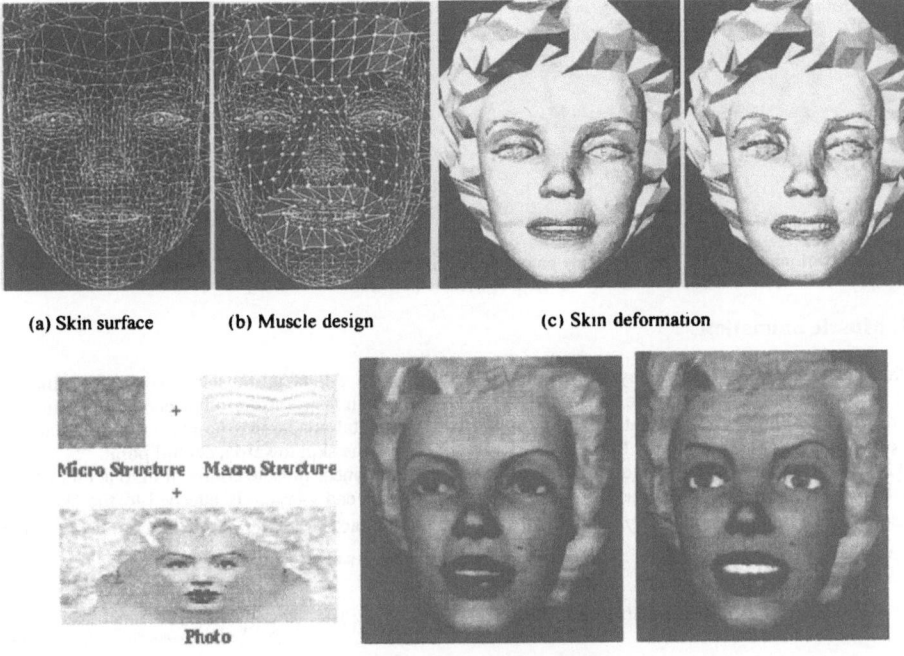

(a) Skin surface   (b) Muscle design   (c) Skin deformation

Micro Structure   Macro Structure

Photo

(d) Wrinkle formation and rendering

Figure 2: The overview of skin deformation and wrinkle simulation process

3. Muscle design

Muscles are principle motivators of skin deformation so that when a muscle contracts, it attempts to draw its attachment together. Though muscles have a large variety of sizes, shapes and complexity, they are essentially bundles of fibers lying and operating along some direction in unison. In this section, we will discuss simplified facial muscle design which produces reasonable results.

3.1. Muscle patches

Facial muscles mostly consists of cluster of fibers with a rather flat structure so that surface models can be used to simulate muscles instead of volume models. A muscle has a biaxial structure and behavior because of its fiber configuration. Due to the biaxial nature along its two parameters, B-spline patch is chosen for muscle representation in our model.

The facial muscles are classified into two main types: linear muscles and sphincter muscles. A linear muscle contracts toward the static attachment on the bone such as the frontalis major muscle which raises the eyebrows. A sphincter muscle contracts around an imaginary central point such as the obicularis oris muscle which draws the mouth together [Waters, 87]. Open B-spline patches are used to simulate the linear muscles while the B-spline patches closed in one parametric dimension are employed to imitate the sphincter muscles. Figure 3 shows the two types of muscle patches.

To construct the muscle patch, a mesh of key points is interactively defined on the skin surface which briefly describes the shape of the muscle as well as its fiber orientation. These points are shifted with an inward offset which indicates the distance between the skin and muscle. Through these displaced points, a B-spline patch $S(u,v)$ is built by interpolation. The v parameter direction approximates the muscle fiber orientation, and intuitively, the transverse parameter dimension u indicates the potential wrinkle locations with skin deformation. The attached end of a muscle is fixed inward to the skull while the insertion end is connected outward to the skin surface by springs. Figure 2(b) presents some of the muscle patches designed on a face.

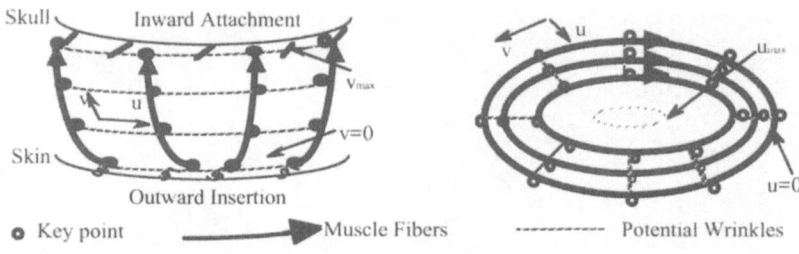

(a)Linear muscle: Open B-spline patch   (b)Sphincter muscle: Close B-spline patch

Figure 3: Muscle patches

3.2. Muscle animation

A facial expression is conducted by a set of muscle contractions. All facial muscles except the orbicuris oris are attached to the skull at one end while inserted into the skin fasica at the other end. These muscles are described as linear muscles that pull the skin toward the skeletal attachment points. On the contrary, the orbicuris oris are embedded in the skin soft tissues and draw the skin toward a central point.

Let $S(u,v)$ be a muscle patch at the initial time. To simulate the linear muscle contraction, one end of the patch $S(u,v)|_{v=0}$ is inserted to the skin surface while the other end $v=v_{max}$ is attached to the skeleton. Muscle contraction is simulated by adjusting the v parameter at each time step. For a relax muscle point $S(u,v)$, the contracted muscle position at time t, $r^t_{muscle}(u, v)$, is represented as,

$$r^t_{muscle}(u, v) = S(u, v') = S(u, v\lambda_t + v_{max}(1-\lambda_t)), \quad 0 < \lambda_t \le 1 \quad \dots\dots\dots\dots\dots\dots(1)$$

where λ_t is the muscle contraction rate at current time, which equals I at time 0 and reaches minimum at maximum muscle contraction.

To simulate the sphincter muscle contraction, the whole B-spline patch is connected to the skin surface. The muscle contraction is simulated by adjusting the u parameter at each time step. The deformed muscle is calculated as,

$$r^t_{muscle}(u, v) = S(u', v) = S(u\lambda_t + u_{max}(1-\lambda_t), v), \quad 0 < \lambda_t \le 1 \quad \dots\dots\dots\dots\dots\dots(2)$$

where u_{max} specifies a central region limits the sphincter muscle contraction.

The tension from muscle to skin is simulated by the Hookean spring which connects the skin surface vertices to muscle patches.

4. Biomechanic skin model

Different types of models such as geometric models and physically based models are used for skin deformation. In order to produce more accurate skin deformation with wrinkles and provide a potential for medical applications, we employed a biomechanical model. Moreover, a linear plastic model is extended to calculate the permanent skin deformation which provides measures of wrinkle formation due to aging.

4.1. Elastic membrane model

Different biomechanical models of skin have been proposed in the literature [Lanir 87]. For our purpose, we consider skin to be biaxial and incompressible. The skin can not support negative stress, and hence buckles easily [Danielson 75].

As skin is thin and quite flexible, a plane stress elastic model is applied for each triangle. Each triangle employs a local coordinate system (X,Y) according to skin's biaxial behavior. Generally, the Y direction corresponds to the direction of muscle contraction, and X to the potential wrinkle. These two directions are usually perpendicular to each other. The potential wrinkle direction of each triangle is obtained by mapping the u direction of the closest muscle patch to the skin surface while the muscle contraction direction is set to be vertical to it (see Figure 4).

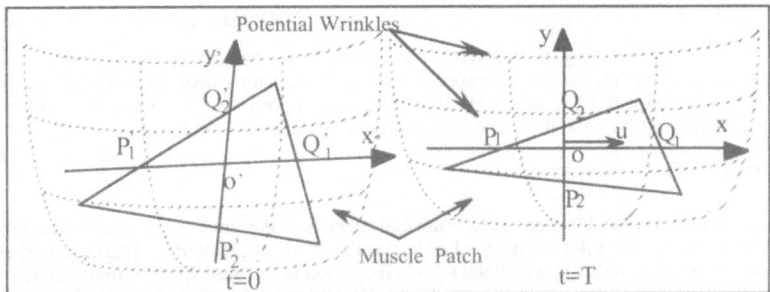

Figure 4: Local coordinate system for a triangle

In case of small deformation, any three measurements in the triangle can be used to calculate the components of strain $(\varepsilon_x, \varepsilon_y, \gamma_{xy})$. Usually, the three measurements are strains along three lines defined on the triangle along the three edges of a triangle. The strain value for a line at an angle θ with X axis is given as [Timoshenko 82].

$$\varepsilon_\theta = \varepsilon_x \sin^2\theta + \varepsilon_y \cos^2\theta + \gamma_{xy} \sin\theta\cos\theta \quad\dots\dots\dots\dots\dots\dots\dots\dots\dots\dots\dots(3)$$

However, in the case of large deformation, this method is no longer valid and may produce unreasonable deformation. The general theory of large deformation is rather complicated to apply. Nevertheless, the incompressibility of skin simplifies the problem. As the model only supports non-negative stress, skin at a particular region deforms along a rather uniform direction controlled by muscle contractions. Therefore, the shear strain is quite small and the principal strain direction (the direction with no shear strain component) approaches to the potential wrinkle line. We can assume that the potential wrinkle line remains vertical to the muscle contraction direction in the deformed state. In this configuration, we directly calculate the strain components by measuring strain along the coordinate axis.

As the forces are calculated referring to current state, at each step T, the coordinate system is first set in the deformed triangle (Figure 4). The X direction is set along the potential wrinkle segment P_1Q_1, the Y coordinate is set vertical to X direction along P_2Q_2 segment which approximates the muscle contraction direction.

At original state, segment $P_1'Q_1'$ is along the potential wrinkle direction, and $P_2'Q_2'$ corresponds to P_2Q_2 respecting that P_1, Q_1, P_2, Q_2 and P_1', Q_1', P_2', Q_2' separate the edges with the same ratio. The stretch strain components are calculated as,

$$\varepsilon_x = \frac{P_1'Q_1' - P_1Q_1}{P_1'Q_1'}, \qquad \varepsilon_y = \frac{P_2'Q_2' - P_2Q_2}{P_2'Q_2'} \quad\dots\dots\dots\dots\dots\dots\dots\dots\dots (4)$$

while the shear strain component is obtained by,

$$\gamma_{xy} = (\frac{\pi}{2} - \phi)\big/\phi \quad\dots\dots\dots\dots\dots\dots\dots\dots\dots\dots (5)$$

where ϕ is the angle between segments $P_1'Q_1'$ and $P_2'Q_2'$, and $\pi\big/2$ is the approximation of the angle under the deformed state.

Hook's law is used for computing the stress components on the triangle. To filter the negative stress component, principal stress directions (directions with no shear stress) are computed. Let α be the angle between the principal stress direction and X axis, we have the relation:

$$\tan 2\alpha = \frac{2\tau_{xy}}{\sigma_x - \sigma_y} \quad\dots\dots\dots\dots\dots\dots\dots\dots\dots\dots(6)$$

where τ_{xy} is the shear stress component, σ_x and σ_y are normal stress components. The principal stress components are calculated along the two vertical directions [Timoshenko 82]. The negative component is neglected in our model while the other components are then used for calculating the in-plane force along triangle edges. Each edge force is finally distributed to its two vertices. Therefore, the in-plane stress of triangles is finally contributed to the vertices as a force component.

4.2. Plastic model

Plasticity causes the irreversible atom dislocation and permanent deformation beyond certain force limits. Skin's remaining deflection after the removal of load is the result of plasticity. Shanders [73] proposed a plasto-visco-elastic skin model in which the total deformation is the sum of an initial elastic response, a viscous component and a plastic component. In the case of certain deformations the plastic component linearly depends on the load duration. We extend it to present the sum of plastic deformation after a deformation process,

$$V_p = a \int_0^T V_e(t)dt$$

....(7)

where V_p is the permanent deformation after animation, $V_e(t)$ is the deformation at time t during the animation, T is the animation duration. In our model, the plastic deformation is applied to wrinkle bulge height in the synthetic texture image to form wrinkles due to age. We will discuss the modification of texture image in the following section.

5. Wrinkle simulation

According to the characteristics of the skin, we classify two types of wrinkle models: static and dynamic models[Wu 96]. For the static model we define the shape and form of the wrinkles or other macro lines as geometrical structures on the planar skin surface which do not change with skin deformation. The dynamic wrinkle model is based on the biomechanical skin model and accounts for the changes in the form and shape over time. The following sections present the static and dynamic models.

5.1. Static model

The physiology of wrinkles demonstrates that one needs to consider the micro and macro structure of the skin surface for modeling the geometrical features of the skin texture. For the static model, the location and the form of the wrinkles or other lines are established on the structure of the skin surface. Real photos hold more skin details including micro and macro structure, which can be used combined with a synthetic skin structure. In the following sections, we describe our method of modeling and rendering the geometrical features in the micro and macro structure of the skin.

5.1.1. Micro structure

The micro structure appears to be a layered net-structure which is determined by two major factors: the furrow pattern and the ridge shape. A close look at this structure shows a triangular mesh pattern with several layers of furrows. This suggests applying a hierarchical triangulation to a skin region to obtain geometrical patterns for the micro structure. A ridge surface is defined as a function on the triangle base.
The furrow pattern is generated by a Delaunay triangulation [Farin 90] for each skin region. Given the texture image boundary corresponding to the 3D object, the Delaunay triangulation divides the 2D texture image plane into a triangle mesh where the edges represent the furrows. By imposing some conditions such as edge size or angle constraints, different kinds of triangle mesh can be produced.

The ridge shape is defined on the triangle base. The height of the ridge increases while going from the edge to the centre of the triangle. Figure 5 shows a ridge shape model: C is the centre of the triangle, P is any point inside the triangle, $H(C)$ and $H(P)$ are their corresponding ridge surface heights. The value of basic shape function $f(P)$ is zero at the edge, and reaches unity at the centre. Sharper or flatter bulges can be obtained choosing different shape functions.

Micro furrows present a hierarchical structure: there are smaller ridges inside a small ridge. Thus, the Delaunay triangulation is repeated until the desired layer is achieved. The shape function of the hierarchical structure is recursively defined. Figure 6 shows close up of micro structure rendering using bump texture mapping.

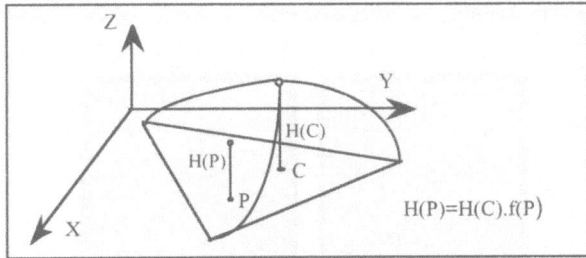

Figure 5: Ridge shape model

Figure 6: Examples of micro structure rendering

5.1.2. Macro structure

In addition to micro furrows all over the body, macro furrows such as palm lines and potential flexure wrinkle lines exist in some skin regions. These are modeled as the macro structure. An array of points on the skin model surface is defined interactively to locate the position of the macro furrows. A B-spline curve is then obtained by interpolation or approximation through the defined points. This 3D curve is mapped to a polyline on the 2D texture image using cylindrical or planar projection. As the macro lines are always along the furrows of micro lines, a constraint Delaunay triangulation is employed to generate the skin pattern so that the edges on the micro structure are retained. For more natural visual effects, a random deviation is added to the furrow.

Macro lines bulge between the furrow lines. The bulge region can be defined in the 2D texture image space (S, T) as a quadrilateral mesh along the polyline (see Figure 7). The bandsize –defined as an offset– of the wrinkle gives its neighboring points along the bulge direction. We use bilinear interpolation parameters (u, v) in each quadrilateral to define the bulge function.

The bulge shape is defined as a height function H of band width. The (u, v) values of an inside point P are used as parameters to obtain the height value. The band width for the shape function is computed as the linear distance ratio of P along the isoparametric line for a given u. Different kind of shape functions can be used for simulating the bulge shape.

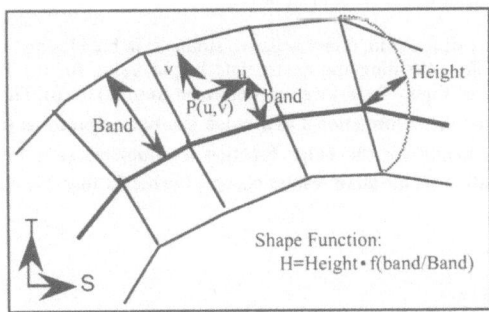

Figure 7: Macro wrinkle band

Figure 8 shows some skin rendering examples combined with macro and micro structures with different bulge shape functions.

Figure 8: Macro structure of skin

5.1.3. Real photo image

Real photos capture all skin details including micro and macro structure. Manipulating a 3D model of a face in conjunction with a real photo by texture mapping gives the realism to the character animation. However, the real photo carries only the skin details of the person whose photograph is used. Furthermore, it does not reflect the change of the same human model at different ages. In our model, synthetic texture patterns are combined with the real photo image, adding new features of skin or forming wrinkles due to facial animation or aging.

An interactive tool is used to match features from a 3D face model to a 2D photo image by selecting 3D feature points and projecting them to a 2D photo image. The texture coordinates of other vertices are obtained by using linear interpolation in a triangular domain[Kalra 93].

To apply synthetic texture patterns to the real photo, feature points in the skin surface are projected to the photo image. For a key point inside a triangle of the 3D model, its location in the 2D texture image can be achieved by linear interpolation of the vertex texture coordinates using barycentric coordinates. The synthetic patterns are constructed through the key points in the 2D photo image.

5.2. Dynamic model

It is quite expensive to geometrically model all the wrinkles on the 3D skin surface. This would require very fine skin surface resolution resulting in enormous computation. Thus, we deform the skin mesh according to the biomechanical model as described, and form the wrinkle bulges by deforming a synthetic bump texture image. The bulge parameters are determined by skin deformation. In the next sub-sections we describe the deformation parameter mapping to the texture image for expressive and aging wrinkles.

5.2.1. Expressive wrinkles

Expressive wrinkles are usually transverse to the muscle fibers whose actions are active during the facial animation. In our model. They are defined as curves on skin along the potential wrinkle lines which are determined by muscle patches. The wrinkles are then mapped to the texture image as macro line (Section 5.1.2). To get the deformation information, each point on the wrinkle polyline in a texture image has the corresponding triangle reference of the 3D skin surface.

Due to the incompressibility of the skin, under negative strains skin buckles and bulges appear. A simple mapping approach is used for obtaining the appropriate height value for the bulge function from the deformation or strain value ε. Figure 9 shows a line deformed from (a) to (b). The original length is $2l_0$; after deformation it is $2l$, and the deformation d as a bulge can be computed as (assuming linear case for bulge) $l_0^2 = l^2 + d^2$. The height for the bulge function is computed as a function of strain and the bandsize. During the animation, as the strain values change, the height function changes accordingly.

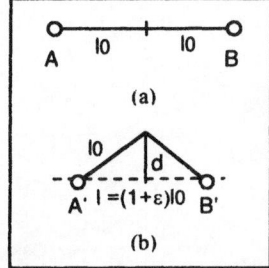

Figure 9: Approximation for the height of bulge

5.2.2. Age wrinkles

Age wrinkles are visible after repeated skin deformation over time. The deformation during facial expression is recorded by the measure of wrinkle bulge d. The bulge measure of a permanent wrinkle. d_p, is calculated as the deformation V_p in the plastic model described in Section 4.2,

$$d_p = a \sum_i d_i \Delta t_i \qquad \qquad \qquad (8)$$

where d_i is the bulge height at each step with time duration Δt_i. a controls the degree of permanent deformation. The Bulge height function flatter than expressive wrinkles are employed. The bulges around the furrow are more recessed rather than pronounced, while random noises are added to the bulge furrow to obtain natural appearance.

5.3. Rendering

In our model, different skin surface details and their deformations are stored in texture images. This prompts us to use a renderer that supports different types of mapping (color mapping, displacement or bump mapping) and can compose multiple levels of details. RenderMan is chosen because it provides the facility to define our own rendering shaders satisfying the multi-layered texture mappings. BMRT (Blue Moon Rendering Tools) is the specific renderer employed in our animation production[Gritz, WWW site]. We demonstrate our model with some examples. Figure 10 (see Appendix) presents a close up of a man and a baby face. It is produced by texture mapping of real photo and synthetic micro structure of different roughness. Figure 11 (see Appendix) shows an aged face applying age wrinkle formation after skin deformation.

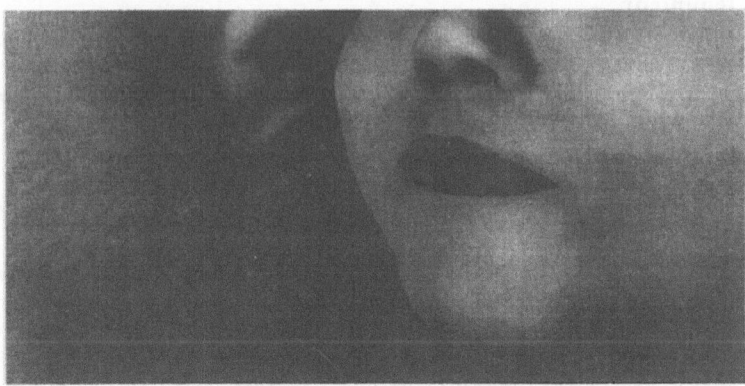

Figure 10: A man kissing a baby

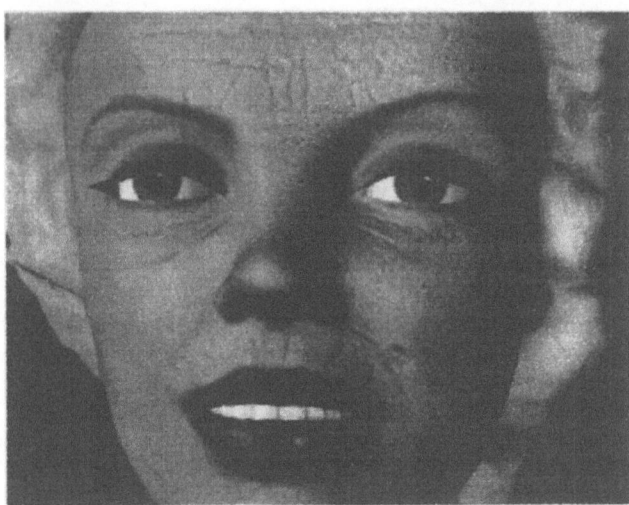

Figure 11: Old wrinkled Marilyne

6. Conclusion

In this paper we have presented an approach for simulating wrinkles during deformation on human skin. There are three major modules in the whole process: Muscle Design. Skin Deformation and Wrinkle Simulation. In this approach the static model of wrinkles considers the rendering of the geometrical structure and other details of the skin, while the dynamic model employs biomechanical deformation information. The models are applied for different cases: general surface details of skin, expressive wrinkles and aged wrinkles on the face. In the static model, synthetic micro and macro structure are combined with real photos to create realistic pictures. The dynamic model is used for expressive and age wrinkles. As wrinkles are induced by facial animation, they are defined according to the muscle anatomy and contraction. More specifically, the position of the wrinkle is defined on the muscle in its transverse direction. An expressive wrinkle is generated as a direct mapping from muscle patch contraction. The bulge generated along the wrinkle line is decided by the skin deformation during animation. A multilayered renderer is used to combine different kinds of skin detail in the same region.

Solid modeling of the human body based on actual medical data and a biomechanical skin model with finite element analysis would offer the foundation for wrinkle formation and growth, but it would be computationally intensive. Thus, our approach simplifies the process and combines biomechanical deformations with rendering nuances by layered texture mappings.

Acknowledgment

This research is supported by Le Fonds National Suisse pour la Recherche Scientifique (FNRS). The authors would like to thank Larry Gritz for providing BMRT. We also thank Gael Sannier for useful discussions concerning texture mapping. Many thanks to Nabil Sidi-Yacoub for his help in producing the final rendered images.

References

Danielson D A and Natarajan S (1975), "Tension Field Theory and the Stress in Stretched Skin," J. Biomechanics, Vol .8, pp. 135-142.

Farin, G (1990), Curves and Surfaces for Computer Aided Geometric Design, A Practical Guide. Academic Press, Second Edition.

Fung, Y C, (1993), "Bioviscoelastic Solids," in Biomechanics: Mechanical Properties of Living Tissues. Springer Verlag.

Ishii T, Yasuda T, Yokoi S and Toriwaki J (1993), "A Generation Model for Human Skin Texture." Proc. of CGI '93, pp. 139-150.

Gritz L, BMRT Home Page:http://www.seas.gwu.edu/students/gritz/bmrt.html.

Kalra P and Magnenat-Thalmann N (1993), "Simulation of Facial Skin using Texture Mapping and Coloration," Proc. ICCG'93, Bombay India, in Graphics, Design and Visualization, pp. 247-256.

Kaufman A (1988), "TSL- a Texture Synthesis Language," The Visual Computer, Vol. 4, No. 3, pp. 148-158.

Koch RM, Gross MH, Carls FR, Von Buren DF, Fankhauser G and Parish YI(1996), "Simulation Facial Surgery Using Finite Element Models," Proc. of SIGGRAPH'96, Computer Graphics, pp. 421-428.

Lanir, Y (1987), "Skin Mechanics," in Ed. Skalak, R. Handbook of Bioenginering, Mc GrawHill Book Company.

Larrabee WF(1986), "A Finite Element Method of Skin Deformation: I.Biomechanics of Skin and Soft Tissues," Laryngoscop, 96: 399-405.

Lee Y and Terzopoulos D(1995), "Realistic Modeling for Animation," Proc. of SIGGRAPH'95, Computer Graphics, pp. 55-62.

Magnenat-Thalmann N, Primeau E, Thalmann D (1988), "Abstract Muscle Action Procedures for Human Face Animation," The Visual Computer, Vol. 3, No. 5, pp. 290-297.

Marks R (1983), "Mechanical Properties of the Skin," in Ed. Goldsmith L, Biochemistry and Physiology of the Skin, Oxford University Press.

Miller, G (1988), "The Motion Dynamics of Snakes and Worms," Proc. of SIGGRAPH'88, Computer Graphics, Vol. 22, No. 4, pp. 169-178.

Nahas M, Huitric H, Rioux M and Domey J (1990), "Facial Image Synthesis Using Skin Texture Recording," The Visual Computer, Vol. 6, pp. 337-343.

Parke FI(1974), "A Parametric Model for Human Faces," Ph. D Dissertation, University of Utah.

Parke FI(1982), "Parametric Model for Facial Animation," IEEE Computer Graphics and Applications, Vol. 2, No. 9, pp. 61-68.

Platt S, Badler N(1981), "Animating Facial Expressions," Proc SIGGRAPH'81 Computer Graphics, Vol. 15, No. 3, pp. 245-252.

Pieper S(1992), " CAPS: Computed-Aided Plastic Surgery," Ph.D Thesis, MIT, Media Arts and Sciences, Cambridge, MA.

Shanders R(1973), "Torsional Elasticity of Human Skin in Vivo," Pluegers Arch., No.342, pp. 255-260.

Terzopoulos D, Waters K(1990), "Physically-Based Facial Modeling and Animation", Journal of Visualization and Computer Animation, Vol. 1, pp. 73-80.

Timoshenko, S.P. and Goodier, J.N. (1982), Theory of Elasticity, McGraw-Hill.

Upstill S(1989), The RenderMan Companion, Addision-Wesley.

Viaud M, Yahia H (1992), "Facial Animation with Wrinkles," 3rd Workshop on Animation, Eurographics'92, Cambridge.

Waters K(1987), "A Muscle Model for Animating Three Dimensional Facial Expression," Proc SIGGRAPH'87, Computer Graphics, Vol.21, No. 4, pp. 123-128.

Wu Y, Magnenat Thalmann N and Thalmann D (1994), "A Plastic-Visco-Elastic Model for Wrinkles In Facial Animation And Skin Aging," Proc. Pacific Conference '94, pp.201-213.

Wu Y, Kalra P and Magnenat Thalmann (1996), "Simulation of Static and Dynamic Wrinkles of Skin," Proc. of Computer Animation'96, Geneva, Switzerland, pp.90-97.

Interactive display and animation of B-spline solids as muscle shape primitives

Victor Ng-Thow-Hing and Eugene Fiume

University of Toronto, Dynamic Graphics Project
10 King's College Circle,
Toronto, Ontario, M5S 3G4, Canada
{victorng,elf}@dgp.toronto.edu

Abstract.

We argue that B-spline solids are effective primitives for the animation of physically-based deformable objects. After reviewing the mathematical formulation of B-spline solids, we describe how to quickly display and modulate their shapes. We apply our ideas to muscle modelling and provide techniques for initial shape definition and subsequent shape deformation. Data-fitting techniques are developed to build muscles from profile curves or from contour data taken from medical images. By applying a spring-mass model to the resulting B-spline solid, we have transformed a static model to a deformable one. The 3-D parameterization of the solid allows us to model microstructures within the solids such as fibre bundles in a muscle. B-spline solids are powerful and versatile deformable shape primitives that can be used in practical settings, such as the building-blocks of a muscle-based modeller and animation system for anatomical design.

Keywords: deformable objects, muscle, B-spline solid, free-form deformations, anatomy

1 Introduction

Since the beginning of computer graphics, geometry has played an essential role in the modelling and animation of physical objects in virtual worlds. Solid shapes are predominantly described with boundary representations such as polygons and parametric surfaces, which are literally superficial representations of the solid, physical objects they are depicting. The last few years have witnessed the application of techniques originally created for CAD design of mechanical vehicles to the modelling and animation of living animals. In contrast, sculptors often study anatomy to shape body parts using knowledge of the underlying skeleton and muscles. The figure is built layer by layer with pieces of clay until the desired form is achieved. To motivate the construction of animals with solid deformable components, this paper introduces the use of B-spline solids as first-class primitives that can be used to model muscles as well as other structures. We intend to use these primitives as important components of an anatomical modeller and animation system for animals. The 3-D parameterization of B-spline solids allows us to define continuous fields within the solid. This feature can be used to eventually transform muscles modelled with B-spline solids into active force generators that can be used in articulated figure animation.

Despite the added dimensionality, we will show that it is possible to quickly display and manipulate B-spline solids in real-time, making them feasible primitives for animation. We provide solutions to two common tasks: *1) How do we initially define a shape?* and *2) How can we modify and animate an existing shape?* These ideas of interactive modelling will be illustrated by showing how B-spline solids can be used to design skeletal muscles.

2 Previous Work

Solids are traditionally modelled using boundary representations of geometry such as polygons or tensor product spline surfaces. Polygons can be quickly rendered using specialized graphics hardware, but can leave a faceted appearance depending on how close the viewer is to the object. Tensor product spline surfaces offer parameterizations that define every point on a surface, providing information for tessellation and texture mapping. In addition, the control point handles associated with spline surfaces allow local control over shape. Specialized spline surfaces such as Bezier triangular patches [HL89] and generalized cylinders [SH94, Sha84] have been created to provide better inherent topologies for body segment modelling than the traditional rectilinear patch representation of B-spline surfaces.

Implicit surfaces such as blobbies and metaballs [Bli82] have also been used to model body parts. They have the advantage of being mathematically conditioned to produce smooth blends between themselves and have convenient formulations for determining point inclusion. They often are modelled as iso-level surfaces of a three-dimensional field function. These formulations usually require nonlinear root-finding searches to find and render a particular iso-level surface [Bli82]. To model irregular shapes, multiple algebraic implicit functions must be combined. The combination of these two factors makes rendering implicit surfaces currently non-interactive while quicker wireframe or skeletal preview modes [BW90] of objects obscure or poorly approximate the final, desired global shape. However, newer methods that generate moving particles constrained to the iso-level surface [WH94] can provide faster previews of implicit object shapes.

Implicit representations do not easily yield ways to systematically evaluate the surface in the same manner as parametric surfaces. Parameterization of implicit objects is thus necessary. Since there exist implicit functions that cannot be globally parameterized, a piecewise parameterization step is often used instead [Ped95].

There are a few examples of multivariate spline formulations being used in computer graphics. Multivariate polyhedral splines have been applied to analytic antialiasing in [McC95] and tensor product solids have been used in free-form deformation (FFD) lattices [SP86, LW94]. The FFD lattice defines a three dimensional space that is warped as the control points of the lattice are moved. Typically, geometry such as spline surfaces or polygons are embedded in the space so that the vertices or control points undergo a transformation that can roughly follow the shape of the warped space. Rappoport et al. [RSB95] have demonstrated a method for preserving the volume of free-form deformations. Surprisingly, there has been little exploration of the direct rendering of these lattice solids themselves. In [HL89], tensor-product Bezier and B-spline solids and their mathematical properties are described in detail.

The majority of attempts to model muscles focus primarily on the geometric aspects of muscle and their role in creating deformations in the surrounding skin. Muscles have been modelled directly with generalized cylinders and spline surfaces [Sch96, SH94]. Wilhelms [Wil97] has used ellipsoids for muscle and tendon to deform a surrounding polygonal skin mesh. Shen and Thalmann [ST95] use a hybrid model of metaballs and B-spline surfaces to deform and model human leg deformation. In all of this work, the muscle is deformed as a result of joint motion in the skeleton. In reality, muscles are force actuators that also create the motion in the skeleton, motivating the need to develop physical models for muscle force production. There have been relatively few attempts to model the physical forces of muscle in computer animation. Chen and Zeltzer [CZ92] use a finite element model to simulate muscle contraction using biomechanical muscle models based on work by Zajac [Zaj89]. We introduce the use of B-spline solids as primitives that can model both the geometric and physical aspects of muscle. After reviewing the mathematical formulation of a B-spline solid, we will outline a procedure for defining an initial shape using data-fitting techniques and the subsequent modification and animation of these shapes.

3 Model

A B-spline solid is represented by the following equation:

$$\mathbf{V}(u, v, w) = \sum_{i=0}^{l} \sum_{j=0}^{m} \sum_{k=0}^{n} B_i^u(u) B_j^v(v) B_k^w(w) \mathbf{C}_{ijk} \tag{1}$$

where each $\mathbf{C}_{ijk} \in \mathcal{R}^3$. The set $\mathbf{C} = \{\mathbf{C}_{ijk}\}$ of points form a control point lattice which will influence the shape of the B-spline solid (Figure 1A). $\mathbf{V}$ describes a parametric solid given by the tritensor product of these B-spline basis functions (in this case, the polynomials $B_i^u(u)$, $B_j^v(v)$, $B_k^w(w)$) with the control points in $\mathbf{C}$. We can substitute the control points $\mathbf{C}$ with other vector or scalar values to define other continuous fields or functions within the solid such as continuous internal forces. The basis functions for each parameter need not all have the same order and each basis function family is indexed depending on the size of its associated knot vector, U, V or W. In all the following figures, we use degree 2 basis functions. Although higher degree solids are possible, using the lowest possible degree can eliminate unwanted surface oscillations that may accompany higher order B-spline solids. The B-spline basis functions are used as weights that determine the influence of the control points $\mathbf{C}$ on the solid's shape. For a more detailed description of the properties and evaluation of B-spline basis functions, please refer to [HL89].

3.1 Control Point Lattice Design

The control point lattice determines the shape of the B-spline object. The coordinate system used to represent and position control points will determine the space in which the object will be displayed. Although any three-dimensional coordinate system can be

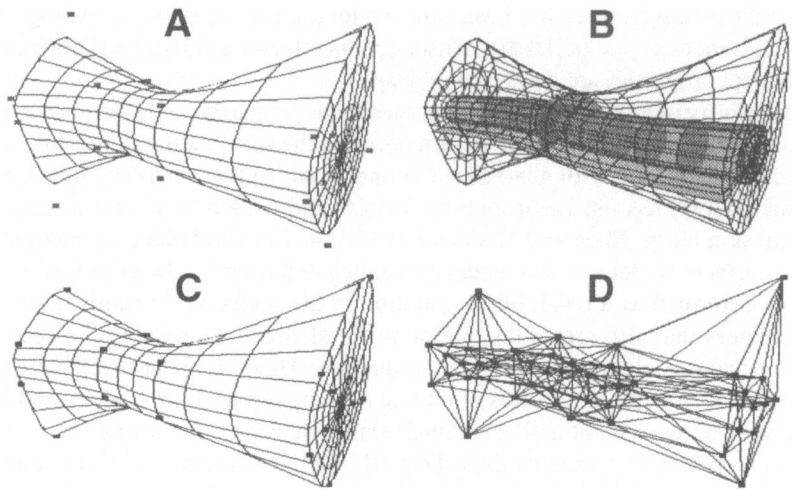

Figure 1: Features of B-spline solids. (A) B-spline solid with control points. (B) Iso-parameteric surfaces of a B-spline solid. (C) B-spline solid with sample points. (D) Sample points are connected with a spring-mass network.

used for solids, we chose the cartesian coordinate system to represent geometry for 3-D graphics.

The topology of the lattice defines the topology and the control point indexing of its associated B-spline solid. Therefore, the design of the control point lattice is influential in creating the user interface handles that can be used to modify the object's shape [Coq90]. The indexing of control points will affect the interpretation of the solid's iso-parametric surfaces or curves when one or more parameters are held constant (see Figure 1B).

The choice of control point lattice should depend on the type of object being modelled. Since we are interested in modelling muscles, we choose a natural cylindrical-type indexing that allows us to retain the basic cylindrical topology of muscle-like bundles after shape deformations. This allows us to model fusiform muscles. To model multiple-belly muscles, we would need to model each belly as a separate solid. Similarly, solids can be combined together to create other shapes with different topologies. The topology of a cylindrical lattice is actually the same as a tube since there are outer and inner surfaces, with the main axis corresponding to the inner surface where all the surface points are coincident on the axis curve (see Figure 2).

3.2 Interactive Display of B-spline Solids

For the purposes of animation, we need to quickly display and update the changing shape of B-spline solids. A key advantage of using a solid formulation instead of a surface parameterization is that the solid produces a unified model that allows us the flexibility of displaying arbitrary isosurfaces within the solid. It is possible to display subvolumes within the solid (Figure 1B) by displaying different iso-parametric surfaces. To visualize

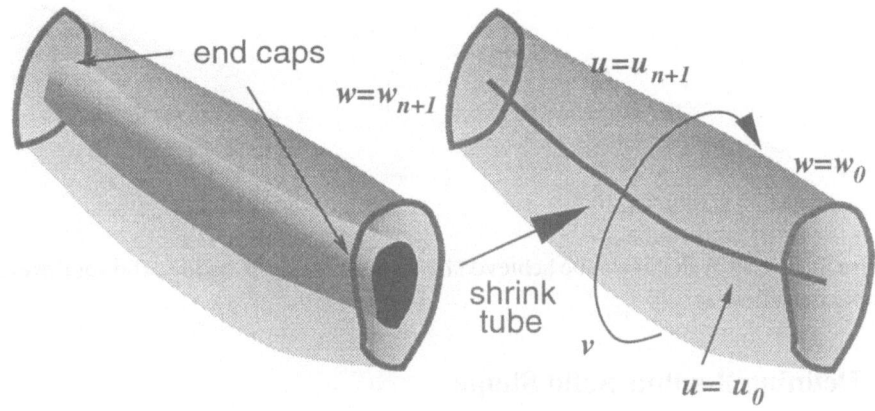

Figure 2: The parameterization of the cylindrical B-spline solid. The topology of the solid is actually the same as a tube.

the closed outer surface of the solid, we simply draw iso-parametric surfaces (holding one parameter constant while varying the other two over their respective domains) that correspond to the boundary of the parameter domains. Although it is possible to create a closed cylindrical surface with a single B-spline surface, duplicate control points or additional knots must be inserted to create discontinuities at the edges between the caps and the outer shell of the cylindrical shape.

Due to the use of multiple knots in the u and w parameter domains, the control points on the convex hull are solely responsible for the shape of the solid's boundary since the internal basis functions evaluate to zero at the boundaries. Consequently, the outer surface of a B-spline solid is equivalent to a standard B-spline surface [HL89], making it possible to apply standard acceleration techniques to interactively update and display B-spline solids. To take advantage of graphics hardware, it is necessary to tessellate the B-spline solid surfaces. By pre-evaluating the B-spline basis functions at tessellation points and storing these basis function values in a table, we can quickly update a pre-existing tessellation whenever a control point is changed. A given control point will affect only a finite set of tessellation points which correspond to the parameter values of u, v, and w where $B_i^u(u) B_j^v(v) B_k^w(w) \neq 0$ for a control point C_{ijk}. By storing the non-zero $B_i^u(u) B_j^v(v) B_k^w(w)$ for each control point, we can achieve fast incremental updates of the solid deformations at interactive rates. Choosing the density of tessellation points allows us to produce different levels of detail of each model (Figure 3), which will be needed to display very complex scenes with hundreds of these solids in them.

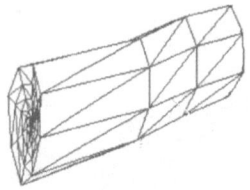 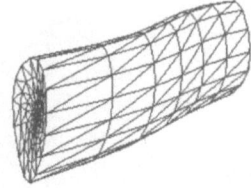 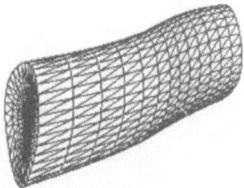

Figure 3: Levels of detail can be achieved by re-tessellating B-spline solids at different sample densities.

4   Defining B-spline Solid Shapes

With the mathematical formulation of the B-spline solids described, it is important to develop data-fitting techniques that can specify the initial locations of control points to define the solid's shape. Manually adjusting control points on an individual basis is a tedious process and is complicated by the fact that we will need to modify the points in three dimensions, requiring us to frequently switch to different viewpoints to move the point accurately in 3-D space.

We have developed a methodology that uses a *sampling function* that allows us to retrieve samples from a specially designed 3-dimensional vector function, GC. These sample points are subsequently used in a data-fitting process which determines the positions of control points that allow the B-spline solid to interpolate these sample points. These same sample points can also be used instead of control points to directly manipulate the solid's shape.

4.1   Creating the Sample Function

The purpose of the sample function is to convert a high-level user specification of the shape which is usually a set of discrete curves to a continuous 3-D volume function that interpolates the original curves. This function can be used to extract sample points for data-fitting. The high-level user specification can be thought of as a sketch for the general desired shape of the solid. We have implemented methods for building the sample function from two types of curve sets: *profile curves* and *contour curves*. Profile curves can be used by a modeller to quickly define shapes based on a few curves, avoiding the need to specify the position of every control point manually. Contour curves can be extracted from cross-sections of real muscles (like in the Visible Human Dataset [oM96]), to build a library of muscle shapes based on real human anatomy.

4.2   Muscles from Profile Curves

Skeletal musculotendons typically have two areas of attachment to bone located at the ends of the musculotendon. Previous methods for muscle modelling have used line segments [DLH+90] or generalized cylinders [SH94]. Both of these previous techniques model the areas of insertion and origin of muscle attachment and force application as single points. In reality, the tendon portion of a musculotendon structure often attaches over wide surface areas of the bone. This motivates the need to design a way of quickly building muscle shapes by allowing the modeller to sculpt two curves that will define the regions of attachment on a bone's surface and to sketch a third curve which would represent the main muscle's axis. We have developed a set of skeletal editing curves to quickly sketch out the desired muscle shape given three B-spline profile curves with parameter domain $[0, 1]$: an axis curve, and two end cap curves. These curves are useful for modelling muscle shapes as the end cap curves can correspond to the insertion and origin muscle attachment area boundaries (see Figure 4A). Once this initial shape is defined, intermediate control points can be adjusted to modify the shape further.

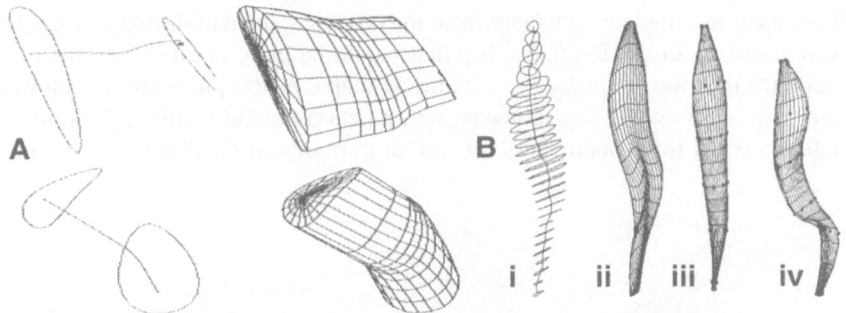

Figure 4: A. Profile curves and their corresponding B-spline solids. B. Contour curves (i) are used to create an initial solid shape (ii). A spring-mass lattice is applied (iii) which is used to deform the solid's shape (iv) by dragging on the sample points.

From these curves, a 3-D parameterized scalar function is created that represents the solid spanned by the interpolation of these curves:

$$\mathbf{GC}(\tilde{u}, \tilde{v}, \tilde{w}) = (1 - \tilde{u})\mathbf{axis}(\tilde{w}) + \tilde{u}[(1 - \tilde{w})\mathbf{cap}_1(\tilde{v}) + \tilde{w}\mathbf{cap}_2(\tilde{v}) + \mathbf{axis}(\tilde{w})], \quad (2)$$

where $\tilde{u} = \frac{u}{u_{n+1}}$, $\tilde{v} = \frac{v}{v_{n+1}}$, and $\tilde{w} = \frac{w}{w_{n+1}}$ are normalized versions of the parameters $u, v,$ and w. This reference function is used to sample any number of points necessary to define the B-spline solid shape.

4.3 Muscles from Medical Contour Data

If we need to model muscles accurately for virtual surgery or biomechanical applications, we need to create a library of muscle shapes based on real anatomy. Fortunately, the Visible Human dataset [oM96] has been created to provide a vast amount of information about the human body. The data consists of a collection of cross-sectional slices along the transverse axis of a human body. We have used a portion of these slices to reconstruct a muscle with a B-spline solid. B-spline solid muscles can later be deformed for animation purposes.

4.3.1 3-D Parameterization Construction

Like profile curves, we need to build a reference function parameterized by three variables from these stacks of cross-sectional slices. Afterwards, this reference function can be substituted for GC and used to generate samples for data-fitting. We can isolate a set of slices that contain a muscle and extract the boundary of every slice in the set using an active contour (*snakes*) image processing program [KWT87]. Once an active contour has locked itself onto a muscle outline, the next image slice can be presented and the previous contour is deformed to the new outline position from its previous state. This allows corresponding points between adjacent contours to be located closely together. From this process, we obtain a set of planar contours with each contour being represented by a set of vertices that form a closed piecewise line-segment curve in 3-D space.

If we were to sample exclusively from the contours, the data-fitting process would produce isocurves in the B-spline solid that would be more aligned with the original data contours than the orientation of the muscle shape. A new parameterization was developed to produce evenly distributed isocontour curves on the resulting B-spline solid. We define a set of three parameters $\tilde{u}, \tilde{v}$ and $\tilde{w}$ to represent the distance from the cen-

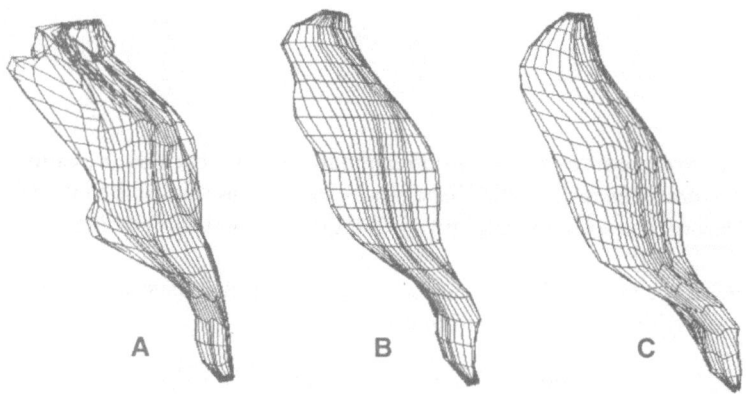

Figure 5: Sources of distortion in data-fitting. Process A and B did not have twist-correction and isocurve alignment about the axis respectively. In process B, the isocurves are aligned with the original planar data curves which does not flow with the overall shape of the muscle. Process C has corrections for both twisting and isocurve alignment.

tral axis, the distance around the axis, and the distance along the axis respectively. We first compute a set of centroids from each data contour and interpolate a spline through these points to produce **axis**$(\tilde{w})$. A normalized arclength parameterization[1] for **axis**$(\tilde{w})$ allows samples to be evenly distributed along the muscle's axis.

To minimize twisting distortion around the muscle axis, we remap $\tilde{v}$ to the angular domain $[0, 2\pi]$. By inducing a polar coordinate system with the centroid of each contour being the origin, we can find a point on the contour that corresponds to the correct angle

---

[1]The full arclength of the curve corresponds to $\tilde{w} = 1$.

specified by $\tilde{v}$. This is achieved by calculating the angles of each point in the piecewise line segments of the extracted contours and interpolating between these angles when necessary. Another arclength parameterized B-spline curve, **outer**$(\tilde{v}, \tilde{w})$, is created to interpolate through each of the contour samples with the same $\tilde{v}$ value. The choice of arclength parameterization tends to produce isocurves that are evenly distributed around the muscle's axis and along the muscle's length (Figure 5). The final parameter $\tilde{u}$ is used to linearly interpolate between **axis**$(\tilde{w})$ and **outer**$(\tilde{v}, \tilde{w})$ to generate the desired sample point, $\mathbf{GC}(\tilde{u}, \tilde{v}, \tilde{w})$. Figure 4B illustrates the various stages of the data fitting process with the final produced shape.

5   The Data Fitting Process

With the creation of the continuous function $\mathbf{GC}$, we are free to sample any number of points anywhere within the domain of $\mathbf{GC}$. However, we restrict the number of samples we wish to take to be equal to the number of degrees of freedom (control points) in our B-spline solid. This allows us to create a set of linear systems through which we can solve for the control points efficiently. In contrast to Hsu *et al.* [HHK92], who developed a general direct manipulation interface for any point within a free form deformation lattice, we restrict manipulation to the original sample points used for data fitting.

The control points cannot all be solved for in a single large linear system containing the sample points. This is because linear dependencies arise due to multiple knot vectors occurring at the boundaries of the B-spline solid's knot vectors. For example, the control points around the outer ring of an end cap of a cylindrical B-spline solid is sufficient to completely specify the shape of the cap's boundary. Including these control points in a larger linear system would overconstrain the problem and create a singular matrix. The solution is to solve a sequence of linear systems that partition the unknown control points into solvable sets. The boundary conditions of the solid are solved first. These boundary control points can then be used to solve for the internal control points within the solid. Figure 6 illustrates the sequence that the various sets of control points must be solved in. The general form of these linear systems is:

$$\mathbf{Bc} = \mathbf{s} - \mathbf{b}$$

where $\mathbf{c}$ are the control point components to solve, $\mathbf{s}$ are the sample points to fit, and $\mathbf{B}$ is a matrix where each row is made up of the evaluated basis functions at the parameter values assigned to the sample point stored in the same row of $\mathbf{s}$. In cases where the boundary control points have been solved, $\mathbf{b}$ will store the product of these solved control points and their corresponding evaluated basis functions which will be subtracted from $\mathbf{s}$ to maintain an independent set of equations.

In some cases, the data fitting matrices, $\mathbf{B}$, for two systems are identical due to symmetries in the boundary conditions of the solid. This allows us to solve two simultaneous systems in one pass. In all cases, we perform an LU factorization of the matrix $\mathbf{B}$ and use the factors to solve two simpler linear systems with triangular matrices to significantly accelerate the solution of the linear systems. Since we must repetitively solve the system each time the sample points are moved, the acceleration technique is very important. These factors can be stored and reused to recompute the new control points for

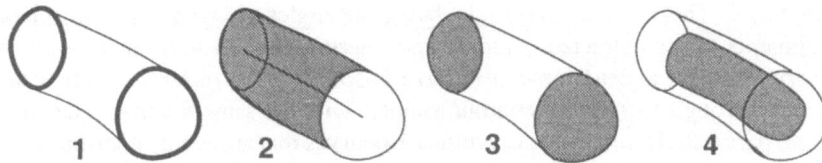

Figure 6: Proper sequence for solving all the control points for a B-spline solid. 1. Cap rings. 2. Outer shell and inner axis. 3. Inner caps. 4. Remaining region between the outer shell, axis and caps.

an animated set of sample points very quickly without the need to expensively compute inverse matrices.

The choice of sample points and their corresponding parameters within the B-spline solid determines how the shape will change as sample points are moved. We choose sample point parameters that locate the maximum of each basis function of the B-spline basis for each parameter dimension. This adjusts the weighting of control points that must be moved to interpolate the sample point so that the corresponding control point of the basis function has the greatest influence on the sample point. Forsey and Bartels [FB88] use a similar formulation for direct manipulation of hierarchical B-spline surfaces. They avoid solving linear systems by restricting the manipulation of sample points to only one at a time.

Sample points are an effective alternative to control points because they allow the user to specify the exact placement of the solid in space. The use of sample points becomes very useful when fitting a spring-mass system over these points instead of the control points. Springs between sample points create direct correlations between actual points in the solid. In contrast, springs acting between control points can create undesirable deformations in the underlying solid shape.

6 Animation Techniques for B-spline Solids

A key difference between solids and surfaces in computer graphics is that a solid's interior is just as much a part of the object as its outside surface. Pure mathematical spline surfaces are infinitesimally thin membranes. Cutting through a closed surface object would produce a cross section consisting of a boundary curve instead of a solid face.

The challenge for manipulating B-spline solid shapes is to create tools that conveniently specify new positions for the control points of the solid. The number of control points can be an order of magnitude larger for solids than for surfaces. Although the external control points are the only ones really needed for the visible surface, proper location of internal control points is necessary for the distribution of matter within the solid.

The obvious approach would be to click and drag control points using a pointing device. Unfortunately, this can be time-consuming to achieve a desired shape while producing a good distribution of control points. Some deformations require a coordinated movement of control points. This is difficult to achieve if the sculptor can only move one point at a time. If we know something about the types of objects we will manipulate, we can constrain the manipulation of control points. We have developed two interactive tools for animating deformations of B-spline solids.

6.1 Anchored and Constrained Fields

Using insights and ideas from a classical sculptor, Alexander Moyle, we designed a simple modelling tool called the *anchored field* that creates a limited force field by specifying the radius of influence of a field and constraining the distance the point source of the field can travel with respect to an anchor point (Figure 7). A spring-damper system is placed between the anchor point **a** and the field source **p** which has a mass of m:

$$m\ddot{\mathbf{p}} + d\dot{\mathbf{p}} + k(\mathbf{p} - \mathbf{a}) = \mathbf{0}. \tag{3}$$

The interaction of the mass m and the spring and damping constants dictate whether the oscillation behaviour between the two points is underdamped, overdamped or critically damped[Ste87]:

$$
\begin{aligned}
d^2 - 4mk < 0 & \quad \text{underdamped.} \\
d^2 - 4mk > 0 & \quad \text{overdamped.} \\
d^2 - 4mk = 0 & \quad \text{critically damped.}
\end{aligned}
\tag{4}
$$

The spring-damper system animates the force field in a manner that can simulate stretch and squash effects in the B-spline solid.

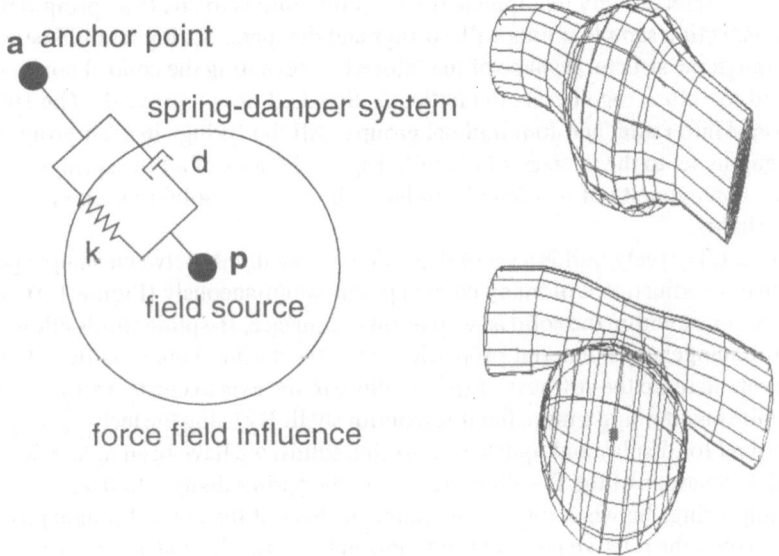

Figure 7: The anchored field is used to modulate a B-spline solid.

If we want the field's effects to be temporary so that the object deforms gracefully back to its original shape when it is outside the influence of the field, we can create a vector of displacements that are added componentwise to each control point. To ensure a gradual transition so that the object's surface does not abruptly bounce back once the object is out of the field's influence, it is important that the field's force smoothly decreases to zero from the source centre to the radius of influence. Whenever the field is moved, the displacement vector is recalculated to show the new positions. The user can interactively change the radius of the field, the relative positions of the anchor point and field sources, or the spring-damper characteristics of the connection between the two points (Figure 7). We have created variants of the anchored field that constrain the position of the anchor point a to isocurves within the solid by using the internal parameterization of the solid. In particular, we can constrain the anchor point to stay on the axis of the B-spline solid to restrict the field's influence to the vicinity of the solid. This effectively reduces the degrees of freedom of the tool to a single meaningful slider that is customized to the solid's shape and simplifies the three-dimensional use of the tool.

The key differences of the anchored field and free form deformations (FFDs) are in the domain of influence of each tool. The user has control over the radius of influence and the strength of the force field using anchored fields. For FFDs, the entire object is constrained to be embedded within the lattice at all times. To increase the range or amount of deformation with FFD lattices, one must manually manipulate or define high order operations to coordinate the modification of several control points of the lattice. Consequently, anchored fields can also be applied to FFD lattice points.

6.2 Spring-Mass Lattices

Another way to interactively manipulate the B-spline solid is to create a spring-damper lattice by connecting sample points with springs and dampers. Springs should be added to help maintain the structural shape of the lattice by preventing the control points from being forced too close together as the lattice is stretched or compressed. The springs are partitioned into radial and longitudinal groups. All the springs in each group have their rest lengths set to the average of the initial spring lengths of all the springs in each group. This homogeneity of rest lengths induces the B-spline solid to seek symmetry-preserving shapes.

The lattice effectively builds a set of dependency constraints between sample points to allow the easy adjustment of many control points simultaneously (Figure 1D). Since sample points exist within the solid as well as on the surface, B-spline solids allow us to design non-homogeneous material properties using the spring-damper lattice. For example, we can increase the stiffness of springs close to the axis to create a strong core to the solid while maintaining a more flexible exterior shell. By using the techniques previously described for display and update of B-spline solids, we have been able to achieve real-time deformations of the B-spline shape with the spring-damper lattice.

Applying springs between the sample points instead of the control points provides more control over the relative positions of points in the solid. In contrast, control points can be situated arbitrarily far away from the actual solid shape, providing a poor correspondence between their positions and the solid portions they influence. This is especially evident when we try to animate a spring-mass system on a muscle defined from contour curves from medical images. During data fitting, control points can be positioned far away from the surfaces they influence. In a spring-mass system using control

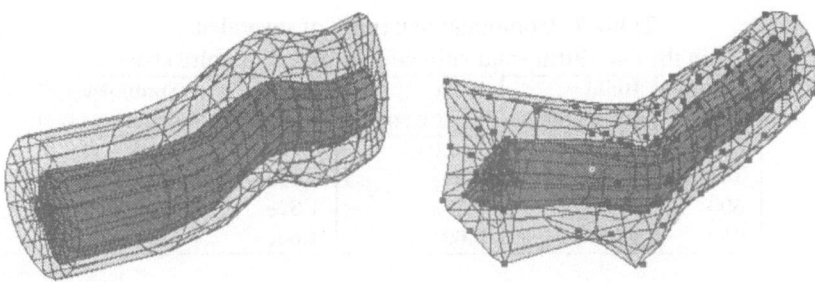

Figure 8: A b-spline is embedded in another b-spline solid which is being used as a free-form deformation. Internal geometry can be animated as the b-spline solid is deformed.

points as the mass points, changing the control point positions can distort the underlying B-spline solid shapes. In contrast, when we use sample points with springs, there is a direct spatial relationship between sample point positions and the solid portions they will deform, creating stable deformations as neighbouring sample points are pulled closer or pushed farther away from each other. Within the solid, sample points can be evenly distributed, providing better isotropic behaviour in contrast to the corresponding control point distribution which may be unevenly arranged.

6.3 Nested B-spline Solids and Free-form Deformations

The parameterization of B-spline solids becomes important when we wish to model internal structures within the solids. In the case of muscles, there is a hierarchy of anatomical structure within the muscle belly and deep fascia tissue that binds internal bundles of muscle fibre together[Gol91]. Since the movement of these internal bundles is restricted to be within the envelope of the outer deep fascia tissue, it makes sense to model this situation by embedding geometry that represents the solids within a larger B-spline solid. As the B-spline solid deforms, the internal bundles deform with it (Figure 8). Fortunately, the B-spline solid also can be used as a specialized freeform deformation lattice. The embedding process where one determines the parameter coordinates of the internal geometry relative to the B-spline solid's domain is complicated by the fact that the enveloping solid may already have been deformed and therefore its parameter axes of the 3-D space may not be aligned with the world space. This necessitates the use of non-linear equation solving techniques to find the parameterization of a given point in world space.

We use the Levenberg-Marquardt[DS83] nonlinear least squares technique to find the closest parameters for a given point. Using a least square technique has the nice property that if the point lies outside a solid, the solver will produce the closest point on the solid's surface to the given point. This iterative method attempts to find a reliable model of the local region of the current iterate to restrict the search step size and allow a solution to be found (*a trust region algorithm*).

The Levenberg-Marquardt method makes uses of the Jacobian which can be calculated using the B-spline basis functions, resulting in locally quadratic convergence in its

Table 1: Computational times of several stages
in the data-fitting and animation of B-spline solid shapes.

Control points	Build LU matrices	Solve control points	Initial tessellation	Spring-Mass update
60	0.01s	< 0.01s	0.26s	0.01s
144	0.05s	0.01s	0.42s	0.02s
600	3.32s	0.17s	1.32s	0.2s
960	57.76s	0.60s	1.66s	0.64s

iterative search. This local convergence property makes it important to choose an initial guess for the iterative search that is reasonably close to the correct parameterization or convergence will not occur. From the sample points with their known parameterizations, we can find the closest sample point to the query point and use this as the starting guess for the search. We avoid using sample points on the inner axis of the solid because these points lie on the boundary of the parameterization domain and have been constrained to be coincident, producing unreliable derivative values that will confuse the nonlinear least squares solver which is designed to work on continuous domains with well-behaved derivatives. In the event that the nonlinear least squares solver fails to converge, we can adjust the initial step size for the iterative search. This method of freezing a solid within an already deformed lattice allows the enveloping B-spline solid to tightly bound the objects within it, producing a better correspondence between lattice and embedded object deformations.

7 Results

We have implemented and timed these animation tools for B-spline solids on an Indigo2 Impact graphics workstation with a 250 MHz processor (see Table 1). Interactive graphics were displayed with OpenGL and numerical routines were implemented with Matlab[Gra94]. The matrix library we used did not have sparse matrix storage, so performance can be improved further.

From the timings in Table 1, it is recommended to minimize the number of control points to allow interactive updates of the solid's shape as well as allowing more solids to be moving in the scene. The number of internal control points should be reduce to only the minimum necessary to satisfy the modelling requirements of the internal volume. Fewer control points can provide a smaller set of handles for manipulating larger portions of the solid. In addition, using a smaller number of control points can filter out unwanted detail when we desire only the general form of the shape.

Although the time to build the LU matrices may be relatively long, the computed L and U factors can be reused to significantly increase the speed of solving the control points. Similarly, most of the time for creating the initial tessellation is used in the evaluation of the B-spline basis functions. This step is only done once and subsequent updates of single control point changes are very fast (< 0.01s). The local properties of a control point modification only require a few tessellation points to be updated.

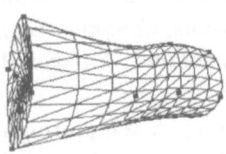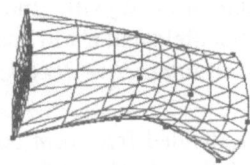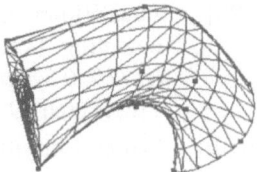

Figure 9: By animating control points or sample points on a B-spline solid, we can deform its shape over time.

8 Conclusions

We have outlined and demonstrated a technique for building and animating muscles modelled as B-spline solids. To quickly display and animate muscles, we can use standard tessellation techniques and precomputed basis function values to allow changes in the shape to be visualized at interactive rates (Figure 9). We have developed data fitting techniques to induce a B-spline solid to interpolate points throughout the solid, allowing precise control of matter distribution. In addition, the sample points from the data-fitting process can be used as a direct manipulation interface for modifying the solid's shape either manually or with a spring-mass lattice. Finally, a solid can be used as a free-form deformation lattice to embed internal geometry to achieve greater detail in solid models that may have interesting internal structure. We have used these tools to create deformable muscles from static data in the Visible Human Dataset.

As part of ongoing research, we intend to use the B-spline solids as building block primitives for muscles in an anatomical modeller for creating animals that have deformable body parts. We intend to further develop these B-spline solid primitives to conserve volume as they deform and to collide with each other as well as other surfaces. We believe that an important first step is the choice of B-spline solids as primitives that can be deformed and can specify a wide variety of shapes. Furthermore, a three dimensional solid formulation can be used for physical modelling or for deforming internal geometry when developing detailed anatomical representations of muscle.

Acknowledgements

Thanks to Alexander Moyle who participated in many insightful discussions about modelling shapes from a sculptor's perspective and who inspired the idea of an anchored field. The authors are grateful to the Information Technology Research Centre of Ontario and to the Natural Sciences and Engineering Research Council of Canada for funding our research. The ongoing support of Alias|Wavefront is also greatly appreciated.

References

[Bli82]   James F. Blinn. A generalization of algebraic surface drawing. *ACM Transactions on Graphics*, 1(3):235–256, July 1982.

[BW90]   Jules Bloomenthal and Brian Wyvill. Interactive techniques for implicit modeling. In Rich Riesenfeld and Carlo Sequin, editors, *Computer Graphics (1990 Symposium on Interactive 3D Graphics)*, volume 24, pages 109–116, March 1990.

[Coq90]   Sabine Coquillart. Extended free-form deformation: A sculpturing tool for 3D geometric modeling. In Forest Baskett, editor, *Computer Graphics (SIGGRAPH '90 Proceedings)*, volume 24, pages 187–196, August 1990.

[CZ92]   David T. Chen and David Zeltzer. Pump it up: Computer animation of a biomechanically based model of muscle using the finite element method. In Edwin E. Catmull, editor, *Computer Graphics (SIGGRAPH '92 Proceedings)*, volume 26, pages 89–98, July 1992.

[DLH+90]   Scott L. Delp, J. Peter Loan, Melissa G. Hoy, Felix E. Zajac, Eric L. Topp, and Joseph M. Rosen. An interactive graphics-based model of the lower extremity to study orthopaedic surgical procedures. *IEEE Transactions on Biomedical Engineering*, 37(8):757–767, 1990.

[DS83]   J. E. Dennis Jr. and Robert B. Schnabel. *Numerical Methods for Unconstrained Optimization and Nonlinear Equations*. Prentice-Hall, Inc., 1983.

[FB88]   David R. Forsey and Richard H. Bartels. Hierarchical B-spline refinement. In John Dill, editor, *Computer Graphics (SIGGRAPH '88 Proceedings)*, volume 22, pages 205–212, August 1988.

[Gol91]   Eliot Goldfinger. *Human Anatomy for Artists*. Oxford University Press, 1991.

[Gra94]   Andrew Grace. *Optimization Toolbox User's Guide*. The MathWorks, Inc., Natick, Mass., 1994.

[HHK92]   William M. Hsu, John F. Hughes, and Henry Kaufman. Direct manipulation of free-form deformations. In *Computer Graphics (SIGGRAPH '92 Proceedings)*, volume 26, pages 177–184, 1992.

[HL89]   Josef Hoschek and Dieter Lasser. *Fundamentals of Computer Aided Geometric Design*. A K Peters, 1989.

[KWT87]   Michael Kass, Andrew Witkin, and Demetri Terzopoulos. Snakes: Active contour models. *International Journal of Computer Vision*, 1(4):321–331, 1987.

[LW94]   Henry J. Lamousin and Warren N. Waggenspack Jr. Nurbs-based free-form deformations. *IEEE Computer Graphics and Applications*, pages 59–65, November 1994.

[McC95]   Michael D. McCool. Analytic antialiasing with prism splines. In *Computer Graphics (SIGGRAPH '95 Proceedings)*, volume 29, pages 429–436, August 1995.

[oM96]   U.S. National Library of Medicine. The visible human project. `http://www.nlm.nih.gov/research/visible/visible_human.html`, October 1996.

[Ped95]   Hans Kohling Pedersen. Decorating implicit surfaces. In *Computer Graphics (SIGGRAPH '95 Proceedings)*, volume 29, pages 291–300, 1995.

[RSB95]   Ari Rappoport, Alla Sheffer, and Michel Bercovier.   Volume-preserving free-form solids. In *Solid Modelling '95*, pages 361–372, 1995.

[Sch96]   Coenraad Frederik Scheepers. *Anatomy-Based Surface Generation for Articulated Models of Human Figures*.   PhD thesis, Ohio State University, 1996.

[SH94]   Sudhanshu K. Semwal and John J. Hallauer. Biomechanical modeling: implementing line-of-action algorithm for human muscles and bones using generalized cylinders. *Computers and Graphics*, 18(1):105–112, 1994.

[Sha84]   Uri Shani. Splines as embeddings for generalized cylinders. *Computer Vision, Graphics and Image Processing*, 27:129–156, 1984.

[SP86]   Thomas W. Sederberg and Scott R. Parry. Free-form deformation of solid geometric models. In David C. Evans and Russell J. Athay, editors, *Computer Graphics (SIGGRAPH '86 Proceedings)*, volume 20, pages 151–160, August 1986.

[ST95]   Jianhua Shen and Daniel Thalmann. Interactive shape design using metaballs and splines. In *Implicit Surfaces '95*, pages 187–193, 1995.

[Ste87]   James Stewart. *Calculus*. Brooks/Cole Publishing Company, 1987.

[WH94]   Andrew P. Witkin and Paul S. Heckbert.   Using particles to sample and control implicit surfaces. In Andrew Glassner, editor, *Computer Graphics (SIGGRAPH '94 Proceedings)*, volume 28, pages 269–278, 1994.

[Wil97]   Jane Wilhelms. Animals with anatomy. *IEEE Computer Graphics and Applications*, 17(3):22–30, 1997.

[Zaj89]   Felix E. Zajac. Muscle and tendon: Properties, models, scaling, and application to biomechanics and motor control. *Critical Reviews in Biomedical Engineering*, 17(4):359–411, 1989.

An Alternative Inter-Particle Force Model for Coupled System Flexible Body Dynamics

Hugh Reynolds
(hugh.reynolds@tcd.ie)

Image Synthesis Group,
Department of Computer Science,
Trinity College Dublin

Abstract: We present a modified coupled particle system for the animation of flexible body motion, deformation and breakage. The standard Lennard-Jones model of inter-particle potential is replaced by a little known potential theory originally formulated by Fr. Roger Boscovich in 1765. This, multi rest-point, approach yields elegant solutions for problems which have proved difficult to address using alternative inter-particle potentials (e.g. permanent plastic deformation). Experimental simulation, results and analysis are presented which validate the approach.

Keywords : Particle Models, Physics, Deformations, Dynamics.

1 Introduction

Some of the most influential work in the field of discrete systems has been that of Donald Greenspan, [Gre73, Gre74]. Greenspan argues that the traditional "discrete observation → continuous law → discrete prediction" model is only one, of many, possible ways to look at the world around us. As an alternative view he proposes a purely discrete approach reasoning that the concepts of derivative, integral and limit are not helpful when modeling physical concepts. In particular Greenspan stresses that such concepts are not useful for modeling non-linear phenomena.

Within the computer graphics community this alternative, discretised, view of the modeling process has proved especially popular [Bli82, Ree83, Sim90]. The application of discrete systems that we focus on in this paper is that of structural animation.

Traditional engineering techniques such as the Finite Element Method have been used extensively within the computer animation field [MTT85, BB88, TF88]. Despite this widespread use some difficulties exist with these types of approach. Changes in topology pose a substantial problem when using the FEM, or any global solution approach. Once the shape of a FEM mesh is established, altering it during simulation proves difficult perhaps even necessitating the fusion of separate simulation approaches [TPF89]. Discrete system techniques, such as spring-mass networks [NTB+91, BHW94] or force-field mass networks [MP89, LJR+91, Ton91, DG95, LP95], present a more unified framework for animating highly non rigid objects.

In this paper we discuss the origins and operation of the force-field particle system approach in more detail. We highlight an alternative to the traditional Lennard-Jones force-field model and describe the advantages such an alternative provides.

2 Background and previous work

2.1 Spring mass particle systems

Consistently robust and innovative results have emerged from researchers working on the topic of flexible body animation with behavioural and particle system techniques. Norton *et al.* [NTB+91], used pre-structured shapes made up of spring-mass cubic lattices, to demonstrate fracture effects based on macroscopic limits of elasticity. Deussen *et al.* [DKT95] working in a similar area adapted coupled spring-mass networks to model specific real-world material properties. The spring mass approach can deal with breakage and general elastic deformation but if more general behaviour is required then a more general inter-particle force than a linear spring is desirable.

2.2 Pseudo molecular particle systems

To create a more general system than the spring-mass network a force-field function is frequently modeled around each particle. One of the most commonly used functions is the Lennard-Jones 12-6 potential, [TPF89, Ton91, ST92, DG95]. Numerous variants and approximations exist but typically the energy between each pair of particles, a distance r from each other, is taken as

$$\phi(r) = \frac{B}{r^{12}} - \frac{A}{r^6} \tag{1}$$

where A and B are constants. Inter particle force is therefore

$$f(r) = -\frac{d\phi(r)}{dr} \tag{2}$$

The force between any two particles is repulsive at very small distances, zero at equilibrium distance and attractive at greater distances. This attraction quickly decays to simple gravitational attraction.

A comparable force function, derived from a global hydrodynamics approach, has been proposed by Desbrun & Cani-Gascuel [DG96]. This formalism improves both the coherency and stability of the technique but problems, inherent in the simple attraction-repulsion model, still remain.

Difficulties with the Lennard-Jones model

The Lennard-Jones type force model is binary in nature. A pair of particle are either linked or completely separate. The force curve is well suited to elastic deformation or complete fracture but it lacks an ability to describe permanent, pair-wise, plastic deformation. Such a description would allow transitory forces to alter the shape of a structure and leave it in equilibrium after deformation.

In the next section we present an alternative to the Lennard-Jones force model and show how it addresses this problem in a simple and physically plausible fashion.

3 Boscovichian Physics

In 1763 Fr. Roger Boscovich S.J., then Professor of Natural Science at the Gregorian University in Rome, [Why61], published his most famous work entitled "A Theory of Natural Philosophy Reduced to a single law of the Forces existing in Nature" [RB22]. In this work Boscovich proposed a comprehensive model of matter composed of elemental points.

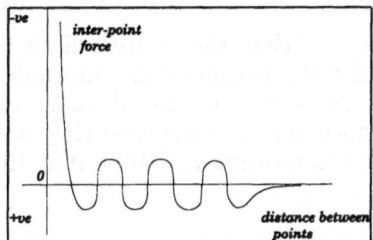

Fig. 1. Boscovich's Law of Force reproduced from the 1763 edition

The forces between these elemental points are

> ... repulsive at very small distances, and become indefinitely greater and greater as the distances are diminished indefinitely, in such a manner that they are capable of destroying any velocity, no matter how hard it may be, with which one point may approach another, before ever the distance between them vanishes. [RB22, Art. 10]

As the distance between the two points increases there exist

> ... attractive forces... which... at first increase then diminish, vanish, & become repulsive forces, which in the same way first increase, then diminish, vanish & become once more attractive & so on, in turn, for a very great distance, until finally... they begin to be continuously attractive & approximately inversely proportional to the squares of the distances. [RB22, Art. 10]

This law can be represented by a single continuous curve (e.g. see Figure 1). Boscovich's work predates all of our modern concepts of atomic structure yet remains relevant even in the light of contemporary quantum theory. It has served as an inspiration and basis for many physicists. J.J. Thomson who deduced the existence of electron orbitals did so directly from Boscovich's theory and even the atomic model of Niels Bohr is itself a linear descendant of that of Fr. Boscovich [Fey70].

Boscovich's single fundamental physical theory together with a little physical chemistry can model all of the familiar pseudo-molecular particle system behaviours such as elasticity and fracture. In addition it can model inelasticity, fatigue and creep.

To demonstrate the generality of this approach and clarify its operation we look at a number of phenomena in detail.

3.1 Elasticity & Plasticity

Neighbouring points generally exist at a distance from each other so that forces of attraction and repulsion are balanced. So long as the distance between two points corresponds to a stable distance or orbital then the configuration is at rest. If the inter point distance changes then forces manifest themselves and attempt to return the configuration to a stable state (see Figure 2(a)). Locally this behaviour will be Hookean and, provided that the deflections from the stable orbital remain small, the system will return to its initial configuration when the deforming influence is removed. In the words of Boscovich,

> If our points are... so that the nearest limit-points are very distant... they may, under the action of an external force causing either compression or tension, be reduced... to a distance, either less, or greater, than the original distance in such a way that they will always strive however to revert to their old position... [RB22, Art. 198]

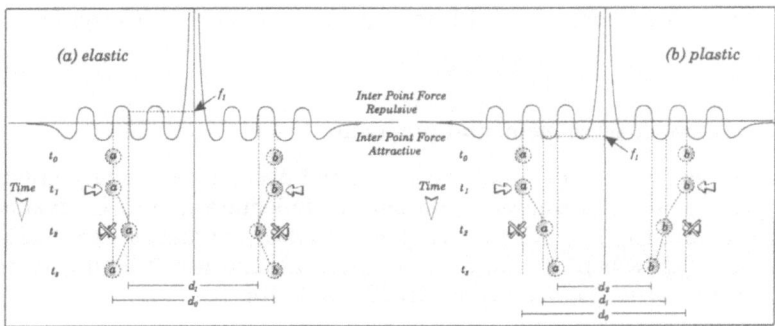

Fig. 2. Inter-point elastic and plastic response to applied forces

Initially the two points which we are focusing on are a distance d_0 apart, (Figure 2(a)). At time t_1 a stress is applied. This stress gradually forces the points together. They reach an inter-point distance of d_1 at time t_2. At this time the constraining energy barrier has not been overcome, (f_1 is still repulsive), and the mutual repulsion between the two points balances the applied stress. When the stress is removed the points repel each other returning to their initial equilibrium separation of distance d_0 at time t_3. This micro-mechanical process when distributed throughout an object gives familiar macroscopic elastic behaviour.

If the deformation of a bond is large enough to counter the forces maintaining an orbital then the bonding pair will attempt to find a new equilibrium state by moving to the nearest available stable orbital. When the deforming influence is removed the bond remains at this new orbital giving a permanent change in the bond shape (see Figure 2(b)). This process is described by Boscovich in the following way :

> ... if... the limit points on either side occur at very frequent intervals; then indeed, after compression, or separation, caused by an external

force,... the points... may stop at a much less or a much greater, distance apart, & still be at a distance equal to that of another limit-point of cohesion, without there being any endeavour to revert to their original position. [RB22, Art. 199]

3.2 Fracture

The Boscovichian potential model further postulates that there exist only a finite number of stable orbitals between bonding points. If a bond is stretched to such an extent that no nearby stable orbital remains then the bond has broken and when the forces which caused the displacement are removed each point experiences negligible influence from its former partner—fracture has occurred (see Figure 3).

this force... having overcome the maximum repulsive force of the further arc as it recedes, would carry off the particles forming the mass to those distances, at which there is no sensible force, but the arc of exceedingly small amplitude corresponding to gravity... [RB22, Art. 416]

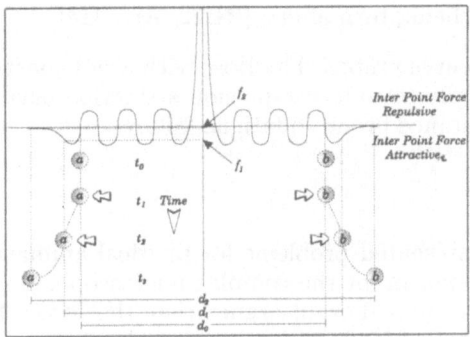

Fig. 3. Fracture in the Boscovich model.

3.3 Creep

As ambient temperature is raised, materials, under loads which cause no permanent deformation at room temperature, start to creep. Creep is a slow, continuous deformation with time. Strain, ε, instead of depending only on stress, σ,

$$\varepsilon = f(\sigma) \qquad (3)$$

now depends on time, t, and temperature, T, also,

$$\varepsilon = f(\sigma, t, T) \qquad (4)$$

The creep mechanism becomes noticeable at temperatures of approximately $T > 0.4T_M$ where T_M is the materials melting temperature in degrees Kelvin.

Physically, creep occurs because atoms, even in a solid, are able to move and potentially jump from one atomic site to another. Using the multi rest-point Boscovich model, slow thermal expansion is possible. On each simulation cycle the locations of selected particles are randomly perturbed. The number and magnitude of these oscillations is proportional to the temperature. If the local energy potential is reduced after the movement then the particle remains in its new location. A molecular jump is assumed to have taken place. If the potential has increased then the particle is returned to its original location to avoiding undue oscillation.

3.4 Fatigue

If a component or structure is subjected to repeated stress cycles it may fail at stresses well below its tensile strength and often below its yield strength. In the Boscovichian model alternating cycles of compression and extension produce non-symmetric behaviour.

> a sufficient number of jutting particles, pushed out beyond the distances corresponding to those of the limit-points, at which they previously cohered, give rise to a repulsion of such sort as prevents the other particles from approaching to the distances of the limit-points, at which they were before being torn apart. [RB22, Art. 414]

As the original force curve proposed by Boscovich is not constrained to be regular or symmetric we simply introduce repulsion-attraction asymmetry in the force curve to make a substance prone to fatigue failure.

3.5 Friction

Friction has always presented problems for physical animation. Finding a useful mathematical formalism for the complex microscopic interaction has proved difficult. Richard Feynman [Fey70] argues that the forces between atoms are "the ultimate origin of friction". Reasoning that the static\dynamic friction distinction is unnecessary he goes on to describe a unified, point based, model of friction which closely resembles our point wise surface interactions.

Each contact force effects the acceleration of only a single particle at any instant in time. Since each particle's acceleration normal to the collision is unaffected by any friction forces present neither inconsistency nor indeterminacy are possible [Bar92].

4 Implementation Overview

4.1 Force Profile Representation

Boscovich's family of forces were originally defined geometrically and hence have no corresponding defining equation. In our implementation we represent each profile as a piecewise cubic spline, using a lookup table to access spline parameters during simulation. This representation allows simple, intuitive, adjustment of the curve.

Our curve representation allows us to easily adopt the methods proposed by Lombardo and Puech [LP95] to alleviate the problem of stiffness near particle rest points. To achieve this we simply alter the classical Boscovichian force curve to have a near zero slope at each equilibrium distance. A typical Boscovichian curve used in our test-bed is shown in Figure 4

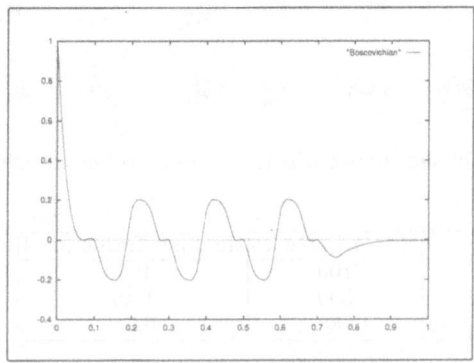

Fig. 4. Boscovichian curve used to create the animation of Figure 8

4.2 Object Creation

The distribution of molecules within a compound has a huge impact on the properties (rigidity, pliability etc.) of an object made from that substance. Within material science crystalline configurations are described using a unit cell shorthand notation. Specific regular crystalline configurations (e.g. carbon in diamond) can give exceptionally strong structural strength. Other non-crystalline (amorphous) substances are not so regular. The examples we present in Section 5 fall largely into this latter category. In our implementation we use constructive solid geometry and superquadrics, (see Figure 5), to define a volume into which Boscovichian points are stochastically seeded. Further geometric transformations on the space to be occupied allow arbitrarily complex objects to be created.

Each point is given a valence, n, i.e. an ability to bond with some finite number of its neighbours, and initially examines its locality and establishes Boscovichian bonds with the n nearest points. This initial state is taken to be a stable orbital.

4.3 Simulation of Solution through time

Each point experiences forces arising from its neighbours plus forces from external sources, (constraints, gravitational pull etc.). These force interactions are summed and the point system is advanced through time. We have implemented both Euler integration with adaptive time step control and adaptive Runge-Kutta integration and give some sample timings from the former in Table 1.

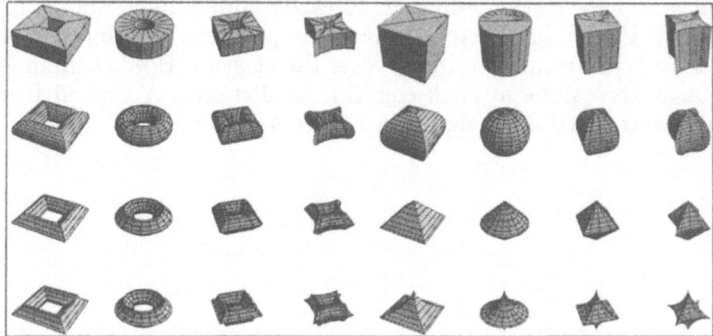

Fig. 5. Examples of the shapes which can be represented using superquadrics.

Animation	No. of Particles	time per frame (sec)	iterations per frame
Steps	100	0.4	20
Trampoline	300	1.45	15
Plastic deformation	180	0.75	20

Table 1. Calculation times for 16fps Simulation on Pentium 133Mhz PC

4.4 Interactions with rigid bodies

Collision resolution between points and rigid bodies in our test-bed was a secondary issue and hence is treated in a relatively elementary fashion. The points occupy only a position in space and have no orientation. Boscovich's law states by definition that any two points will be prevented from touching irrespective of the velocity with which they initially approach each other. This asymptotic potential implies a possibly infinite force, i.e. an impulse. Equal and opposite impulses can be easily calculated to avoid inter-penetration between each point and each rigid body [Hah88, Bar92].

4.5 Self-interaction and interaction with other flexible bodies

Detecting interactions with non-neighbour particles could potentially be an $O(n^2)$ problem. The problem can be addressed by maintaining a spatially sorted list (e.g. Hilbert R-tree, linear Quadtree etc.) and checking for interactions only with relatively near points. Using this method interaction detection is reduced to $O(n \log n)$ [Sam89, KF94]. The method we adopt is that proposed by van der Stappen and Overmars [VO94] for "fat" objects (i.e., objects roughly spherical in nature). Using this approach $O(n)$ collision detection can be achieved.

4.6 Visualisation

The particle models described here exist within a finite energy field in three dimensional space. Using the *soft object* concept as discussed by Wyvill *et al.*,

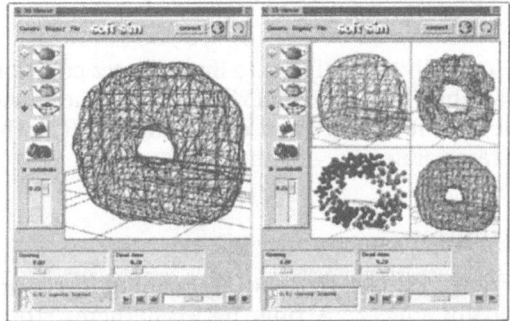

Fig. 6. Assorted *soft object* representations of the same squashed doughnut.

[WMW86], we describe the "shape" of this field by wrapping it in a skin of arbitrary tightness. A polynomial density function is placed around each individual particle p_i. If each particle has a sphere of influence, (proportional to the average field function rest length), of radius r_i then the density function at any point a distance d from p_i is given by

$$density_i = \begin{cases} -\frac{4}{9}\frac{d^6}{r_i^6} + \frac{17}{9}\frac{d^4}{r_i^4} - \frac{22}{9}\frac{d^2}{r_i^2} & d \leq r_i \\ 0 & d > r_i \end{cases} \tag{5}$$

The influence of all the particles are summed and an iso-surface formed which contains all points whose density is equal to some specific threshold value [MP89, TPF89, Ton91]. By adjusting the point's sphere of influence and the iso-surface threshold value we can move all the way from a convex hull representation to completely disjoint points (see Figure 6). We are currently working on integrating the implicit collision surface technique developed by Desbrun and Cani-Gascuel [Gas93, DG95] with our Boscovichian model.

5 Experimental results

Simulations of a wide variety of test cases have been conducted. Control issues remain a topic of further study but the underlying model behaves robustly and intuitively. The simulations are easily manipulated using constraints to move or stretch objects, to fix objects in place or maintain inter-object relationships. A number of examples will illustrate the model in action.

5.1 Soft–Hard interaction

In Figure 8, (see Appendix), we show a semi-flexible cylinder being dropped onto a stair structure. The cylinder bends, stretches and flips its way downstairs to the floor where it comes to rest. On the way it exhibits many of the kinds of motion necessary for aesthetically pleasing computer animation [Las87]. Figure 9, (see Appendix), illustrates the pattern of localised stress wave creation and dissipation as the tube tumbles over the top step.

5.2 Soft-Soft interaction

In Figure 10, (see Appendix), we illustrate inter-object collision, action and reaction. A relatively hard ball falls onto a flexible trampoline causing the trampoline to stretch. The ball loses its energy and comes to rest. It is then thrown up and eventually off the trampoline.

5.3 Object deformation

In the example in Figure 11, (see Appendix), bending forces are applied by three rigid bars which slowly squeeze a tube between them, stop, and then slowly release it. When the forces are removed the object springs back to its original shape.

By bending our object a little more, (Figure 12 (see Appendix)), some of the particle pairs move into new adjacent rest states. The macroscopic interpretation of this microscopic effect is that the elastic limit of the substance being modeled has been exceeded and the deformation becomes permanent. When the deforming influences are removed the object retains its new shape.

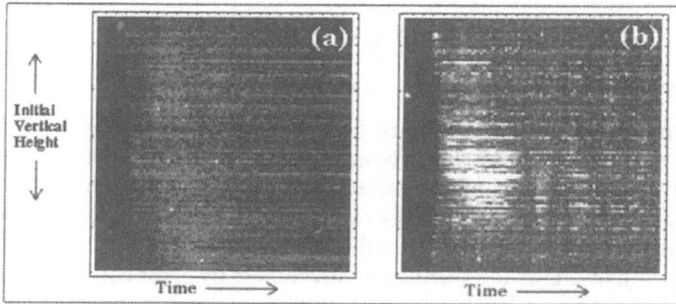

Fig. 7. Evolution of internal stress for elastic and plastic deformation respectively.

It is interesting to examine the internal forces generated during these two simulations. In Figure 7 we see the stress on each particle during the progression of the two simulations. In this graph black indicates low stress, white high stress. Before the simulation begins the individual particles are sorted into a vertical slice. Each subsequent slice shows how the stress on each particle evolves over time. In the elastic case the stress is distributed evenly throughout the tube and it dissipates fully when the tube is released. In the example which shows permanent deformation, the stress is absorbed more locally, mainly at the center. On release the stress again dissipates leaving the tube in a stable state despite having a new shape. Figure 13, (see Appendix), illustrates the stable nature of the new shape.

6 Summary

The model presented in this paper is innovative in its use of a multiple rest point inter-particle force profile for structural animation. The approach is based on a valid, though little known, unified physical theory. Using this Boscovichian profile allows us to create particle systems which incorporate a coherent model for permanent plastic deformation.

7 Future work

The Boscovichian model presented in this paper is spherical in nature corresponding to the covalent model of chemical bonding. Extensions to more directed ionic type bonding are planned. Work is also planned to investigate more appropriate physical constraints to replace the existing geometric ones and to explore more complex non-homogeneous compounds with unit cell distributions.

8 Acknowledgments

The research presented here was supported by Eolas applied research grant AS/92/027 and Trinity College Dublin.

Images and animations : `http://isg.cs.tcd.ie/hrynolds/egcas97.html`

References

[Bar92]   David Baraff. *Dynamic Simulation of Non-Penetrating Rigid Bodies*. Ph.D. thesis, Cornell University, Ithaca, NY, March 1992.

[BB88]   Ronen Barzel and Alan Barr. A modeling system based on dynamic constraints. In *Proc. SIGGRAPH '88*, pages 179–188. ACM, Academic Press, August 1988.

[BHW94]   David E. Breen, Donald H. House, and Michael J. Wozny. Predicting the drape of woven cloth using interacting particles. In *Proc. SIGGRAPH '92*, pages 365–372. ACM SIGGRAPH, ACM Press, July 1994.

[Bli82]   James F. Blinn. Light reflection functions for simulation of clouds and dusty surfaces. In *Proc. SIGGRAPH '92*, pages 21–29. ACM, Academic Press, July 1982.

[DG95]   Mathieu Desbrun and Marie-Paule Gascuel. Animating soft substances with inplicit surfaces. In *Proc. SIGGRAPH '95*, pages 287–290, Los Angeles, August 1995. ACM, Academic Press.

[DG96]   Mathieu Desbrun and Marie-Paule Gascuel. Smoothed particles: A new paradigm for animating highly deformable bodies. In *Eurographics Workshop on Animation and Simulation '96*, 1996.

[DKT95]   Olivier Deussen, Leif Kobbelt, and Peter Tücke. Using simulated annealing to obtain good nodal approximations of deformable bodies. In *Eurographics Workshop on Animation and Simulation*, pages 30–43, 1995.

[Fey70]   R.P. Feynman. *The Feynman Lectures on Physics*. Addison Wesley Publishing, fifth edition, 1970.

[Gas93]   Marie-Paule Gascuel. An implicit formulation for precise contact modeling between flexible solids. In *Proc. SIGGRAPH '93*, pages 313–320. ACM, Academic Press, August 1993.

110

[Gre73]   D. Greenspan. *Discrete Models*. Addison-Wesley, Reading, Massachusetts, 1973.

[Gre74]   D. Greenspan. *Discrete numerical methods in physics and engineering*. Academic Press, London, New York, 1974.

[Hah88]   James Hahn. Realistic animation of rigid bodies. In *Proc. SIGGRAPH '88*, pages 299–308. ACM, Academic Press, August 1988.

[KF94]   Ibrahim Kamel and Christos Faloustsos. Hilbert r-tree: An improved r-tree using fractals. Technical report, University of Maryland, Department of Computer Science, College Park, MD 20742, 1994.

[Las87]   John Lasseter. Principles of traditional animation applied to 3D computer animation. In *Proc. SIGGRAPH '87*, volume 21, pages 35–44, July 1987.

[LJR+91] A. Luciani, S. Jimenez, O. Raoult, C. Cadoz, and J. Florens. An unified view of multitude behaviour, flexibility, plasticity, and fractures: balls, bubbles and agglomerates. In *IFIP WG 5.10 Working Conference*, Tokyo, Japan, April 1991.

[LP95]   Jean-Christophe Lombardo and Claude Puech. Oriented particles: A tool for shape memory objects modelling. In *Proceedings of Graphics Interface '95*, pages 255–262, May 1995.

[MP89]   Gavin Miller and Andrew Pearce. Globular dynamics: A connected particle system for animating viscous fluids. *Computers and Graphics*, 13(3):305–309, 1989.

[MTT85]   N. Magnenat-Thalman and D. Thalman. *Computer Animation*. Springer Verlag, 1985.

[NTB+91] A. Norton, G. Turk, B. Bacon, J. Gerth, and P. Sweeney. Animation of fracture by physical modelling. In *The Visual Computer*, 7(4):210–219, July 1991.

[RB22]   S.J. R. Boscovich. *A Theory of Natural Philosophy, Put Forward and explained by Roger Joseph Boscovich, S.J.,*. Open Court Publishing Company, first lat.-eng. edition, 1922. with trans. by J.M. Child from 1st Venetian ed.(1763).

[Ree83]   William T. Reeves. Particle systems - a technique for modelling a class of fuzzy objects. In *ACM Transactions on Graphics*, volume 2, pages 91–108. ACM, Academic Press, April 1983.

[Sam89]   Hanan Samet. *The Design and analysis of spatial data structures*. Addison-Wesley Publishing Company, Inc, Reading, Massachusetts, 1989.

[Sim90]   Karl Sims. Particle animation and rendering using data parallel computation. In *Proc. SIGGRAPH '90*, pages 405–413. ACM, Academic Press, August 1990.

[ST92]   Richard Szeliski and David Tonnesen. Surface modeling with oriented particle systems. In *Proc. SIGGRAPH '92*, volume 26, pages 185–194, July 1992.

[TF88]   Demetri Terzopoulos and Kurt Fleischer. Modeling inelastic deformation: Viscoelasticity, plasticity, fracture. In *Proc. SIGGRAPH '88*, pages 269–278. ACM, Academic Press, August 1988.

[Ton91]   David Tonnesen. Modeling liquids and solids using thermal particles. In *Proceedings of Graphics Interface '91*, pages 255–262, May 1991.

[TPF89]   Demetri Terzopoulos, John Platt, and Kurt Fleischer. Heating and melting deformable models (from goop to glop). In *Proceedings of Graphics Interface '89*, pages 219–226, June 1989.

[VO94]   A. Frank van der Stappen and Marc H. Overmars. Motion planning amidst fat obstacles. In *Proceedings of the Tenth Annual Symposium on Computational Geometry*, pages 31–40, Stony Brook, New York, June 1994. ACM.

[Why61]   Lancelot L. Whyte, editor. *Roger Joseph Boscovich, S.J., F.R.S., 1711-1787, Studies of His Life and Work on the 250th Anniversary of His Birth*. London, 1961.

[WMW86]   B. Wyvill, C. McPheeters, and B. Wyvill. Animating soft objects. In *The Visual Computer*, volume 2, pages 235–242. CGS, Springer International, 1986.

Editors' Note: see Appendix, p. 197 f. for colored figures of this paper

4

Natural phenomena

Qualitative Simulation of Convective Cloud Formation and Evolution

Fabrice Neyret

DGP - University of Toronto

SF 4306-C, 10 Kings College Road

Toronto, Ontario, M5S 3G4, Canada

Fabrice.Neyret@inria.fr   http://www.dgp.toronto.edu/people/neyret

Abstract.

Cloud simulation models are rare in computer graphics, although many rendering algorithms have been developed to evaluate the illumination and the color of gaseous phenomena. The laws of fluid mechanics used for physical simulation require a fine resolution in space and time, and solving the Navier-Stokes equation in 3D is in general quite costly. However, many heuristics, dealing with various scales, can be used to describe the evolution of the shape of convective clouds such as cumulus. These go beyond the classical equations governing the motion of each element of fluid volume. Physicists characterize the identity and behavior of phenomena such as bubbles, jets, instabilities, waves, convective cells, and vortices. Moreover, the shape of a convective cloud can be considered as a surface, so that we only require detailed information near the periphery of the cloud volume.

A guiding principle in our ongoing research is to take advantage of this type of high level knowledge available at various scales in order to obtain a simulation of convective clouds that may not be physically-accurate, but that will be perceptually convincing.

Keywords: clouds, simulation, natural phenomena

1 Introduction

Atmospheric convective phenomena such as cumulus clouds and billowing smoke are important natural phenomena that often occur in outdoor scenes. However, few animated clouds or smoke generators are available for computer graphics. The evolving fractal shapes of clouds are difficult to model, because what we see is the large scale result of complex non linear physical phenomena, combining the effects of fluid mechanics and thermodynamics. Moreover the numerical values of some of the real parameters required in numerical models (e.g. turbulent viscosity) are not readily known. Real boundary conditions such as heat and moisture generation on the floor are also not well understood. Furthermore, the Eulerian schemes used to solve the equations require a grid having at least the resolution of the smallest detail we wish to see, while the volume of the desired scene may be quite large. Thus, a physical cloud simulation using local equations is a task that is especially consuming in terms of memory and time !

By using a macroscopic approach, atmospheric physicists have characterized many specific structures appearing in fluid phenomena, whose evolution, properties, and interactions can be measured. Some of these structures are as follows (some are shown in Figure 1):

- *Rayleigh-Taylor instability*: when a dense (cold) fluid layer lies on a light (hot) one, bulbs appear at the interface, rising to become 'atomic mushrooms', then becoming *bubbles* once they take off.
- *bubbles*: their ascending velocity, rate of expansion, and cooling through mixing can all be estimated.
- *jets* or *columns*: bubbles often 'drip up' along a vertical chimney. When a train of decelerating bubbles collides, the bubbles merge in a column having more intense behavior because the mixing with background air is less important.
- Once a bubble reaches the dew point, the water vapor it contains starts condensing and makes the rising bubble visible. The release of latent heat of condensation boosts the rising motion, and is the driving force for cumulus phenomena.
- Without mixing, a bubble's temperature decreases by 10 degrees per kilometer until reaching the dew point altitude, and then becomes 6 degrees per kilometer. This is different than the ambient air temperature, whose usual vertical thermal profile decreases by 6.4 degrees per kilometer. Near the floor, this variation is logarithmic, positive in summer and negative in winter. Convective motions can thus only start around summer.
- *Turrets*: bubbles are also born and rise on the top and from the sides of clouds, for the same reasons as near the floor, i.e. difference of density between two layers. The balance of forces tend to make them move in a direction that is halfway between the vertical and the cloud surface normal [14] (see Figure 4).
- *Kelvin-Helmholtz instability*: on the boundary of fluids having different velocities (e.g. a bubble top surface, see D on Figure 2), *waves* appear.
- These waves amplify and turn into *vortices*.
- On the top of a rising bubble (e.g. on a cloud surface), the balance between the mixing and the shearing in the surface layer produces waves with a characteristic size [5, 6] (about 1/10 of the bubble radius).
- *Vortices* tend to break into smaller vortices, up to the quasi-molecular size where the energy can be dissipated as heat. This transfer of energy among vortices of different scales is known as *Kolmogorov cascade*, and its power spectrum can be estimated.
- *Benard cells*: inside a fluid layer with a hot bottom surface and a cold top surface having a Rayleigh number in the correct range, regular convective cells appear. These usually are hexagonal in shape, with the fluid rising at the middle and sinking at the borders.
- Under specific wind conditions, the cells turn into ribbons, orthogonal or parallel to the wind direction depending of the wind velocity.

A classical survey about atmospheric structures can be found in [15]. More about convective clouds is explained in [8]. Advanced topics about plumes and thermals are presented in [1]. Interesting information concerning air motion below and around natural clouds can also be obtained from experienced paragliders [11].

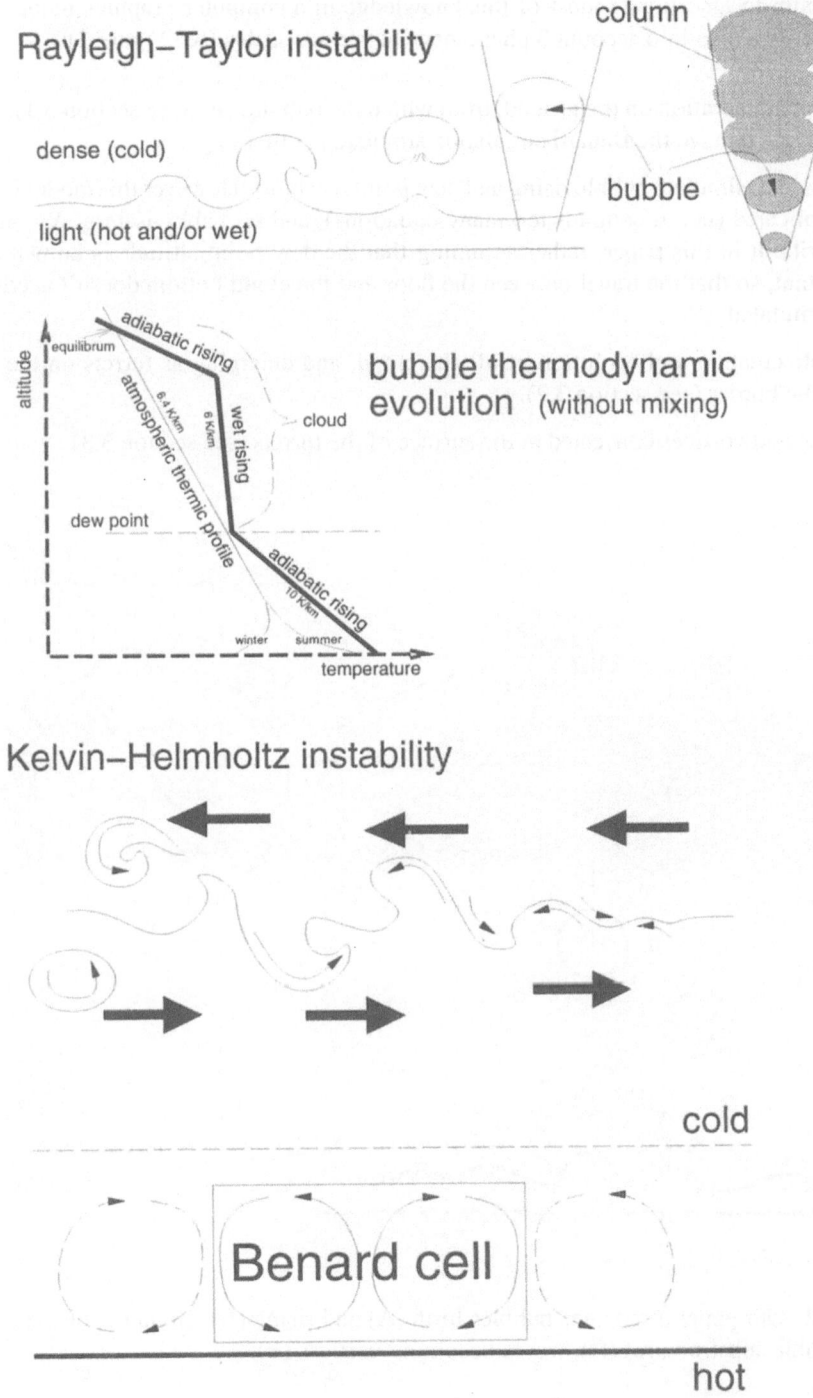

Figure 1: Some macroscopic structures in fluid motions.

We aim to incorporate most of this knowledge in a computer graphics model. In this paper, we take into account 3 phenomena at various scales (see Figure 2):

- hot spot generation on the ground, from which the bubbles rise (see section 3.1). We also hope to have the Benard circulation simulated at this stage.

- we used to simulate bubble rising and dew point reaching. However this model is too complicated (i.e. it contains too many equations), and probably useless. We don't describe it in this paper, rather assuming that the dew point altitude is known and constant, so that the travel between the floor and the cloud bottom doesn't needs to be simulated.

- bubble creation and evolution inside the cloud, and emerging as turrets on the top and the border (see section 3.2).

- waves and vortices convected at the surface of the turrets (see section 3.3).

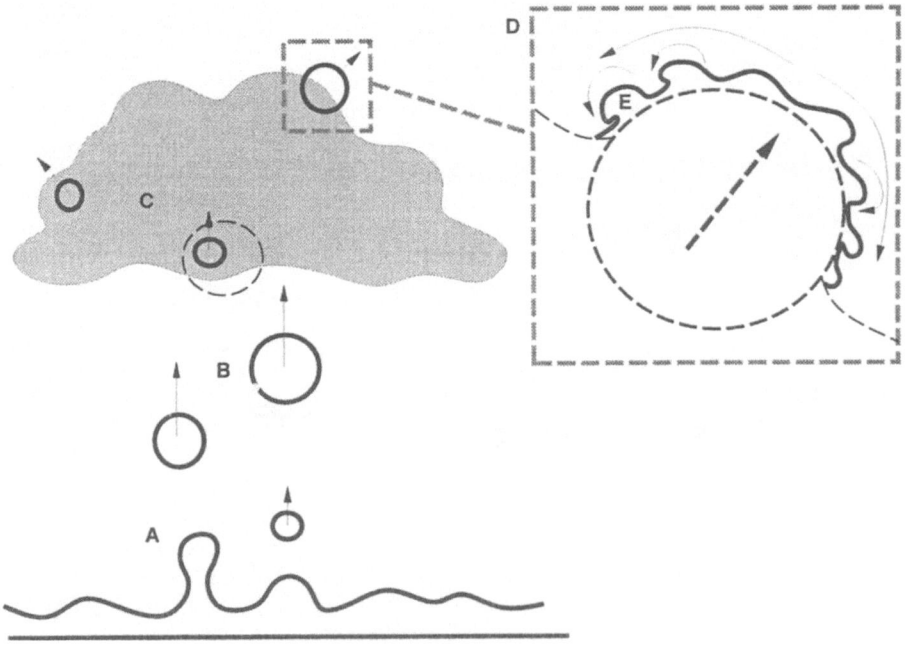

Figure 2: Our general scheme: bubbles birth (A) and rising (B), cloud bubbles motion (C), bubble substructures (D), waves becoming vortices (E).

2 Previous Work

Many physical simulation techniques exist, most of which are not used to produce images. Few physicists are really interested by the shape of the clouds. Instead, they are interested by the heat field, the velocity field, and the formation of rain drops. Simplifications are commonly assumed for efficiency, e.g. 2D vertical simulation, axisymmetric simulation. In our work we are not interested by such costly simulations which are not particularly tuned for providing a shape.

In 1984, Kajiya proposed a model to achieve some clouds simulation [9]. These equations are very close to the physical models, so that the affordable resolution is very low (10x10x20).

Two papers simulate fluids in the context of computer graphics, and with an appropriately-high resolution [2, 10]. However, these deal only with the 2D case. Alas, not only there is a cost gap between 2D and 3D, but 2D and 3D fluids motions are qualitatively different in nature.

Several computer graphics models exist to produce cloud shapes using various kinds of procedural noise, possibly generating an explicit volumetric density field. Some fractal models exist as well. However, none of these models deal with the growth and animation of the cloud, which is the main goal of our work. We would like to consider that the shape is the consequence of the movment.

In [3, 4], Garner proposes an interesting primitive, the textured ellipsoid, covered with a procedural noise opacity which fades on the horizon of the shape so that one cannot see the elliptical border. In the 1985 paper, he describes how this ellipsoid can rise from the soil and grow, then becomes visible and stabilizes at a given altitude. While the images are detailed and interesting, the animation on the ellipsoid surface is simply obtained using an offset for the Perlin noise, which doesn't correspond to any real convection effect.

In [12, 13], Stam uses white noise filtering to generate a wind field with a mass conservation property and having defined statistical properties. Smoke, flames and cloud shapes are achieved by combining spheres warped by the wind field. The wind model provides for very fluids-like motions, but cannot generates real vortices, because these cannot be described by the second order statistical moments of the fluid velocity.

A new approach is thus required !

3 The proposed model

3.1 Bubble generation

In summer, the sun intensely radiates the surface of the earth. Depending of the type of soil (earth, water, concrete), orientation and vegetation (barren, grass fields, forest), the ground heats the bottom layer of air and provides moisture[1], so that the bottom layer becomes lighter than the neighboring air layers above. At the hottest points above the floor, the air begins to rise, and in doing so, sucks the hot air from the surrounding terrain. Depending on the conditions, this will lead to a single bubble, a train of bubbles, or even a column formation.

We simulate the bottom layer of air as a set of hot air parcels trapped on the ground, modeled as 2D particles. The ground heating due to the sun is modeled by creating new hot air parcels at random. One may use a texture indicating the kind of soil, thus controlling how much energy the ground releases at each point. The rising is due to the difference in air density ρ relative to the upper air layer, which occurs because of the difference in temperature. The buoyancy force per unit mass is $g(T - T^*)/T^*$, where T is the parcel temperature and T^* is the background temperature. However, the buoyancy force is opposed by friction, and the temperature stratification near the ground makes it difficult to define a 'background temperature'. We assume that the rising force is proportional to the heat gained $E = (T - T^*)$ provided by the sun, with an ascendancy coefficient to control the rising ability: the rising force is $f_r(i) = c_{asc}.m(i).E(i)$ for the air parcel i.

We also compute the attraction force created between the parcels by the vacuum effect of the displaced (rising) air. We assume a $1/d^2$ decrease law for this attraction: $f_a(P) = \sum_i \frac{P(i) - P}{\|P(i) - P\|^3}.f_r(i)$. A $1/d$ law would tend to favor a single hot spot attracting all hot air parcels. We also consider a viscosity coefficient to control the stability of the air flux along the surface. From these terms we compute the 2D air transport toward the hot spots. Parcels closer than a given distance are merged. When the rising force exceeds a threshold, which will occur at the hot spots, we consider that a bubble is born, to be given to the model managing the bubble transportation in air. The corresponding mass is subtracted from the remaining parcel of ground air.

The fact that the surrounding air is displaced towards a hot spot supposes that fresh air comes from above, which will decrease the chance for this same location to heat further, thus stabilizing the air transport (main hot spots tend to stay at the same place). We expect that this may emulate Benard cell behavior, but more studies should be done with respect to the resulting distribution of hot spots as a function of the value of the ascendancy and viscosity coefficients, and of the attraction law.

---

[1]Moist air is lighter than dry air, due to the molecular masses of H_2O and air (80% N_2, 20% O_2). Air density is also inversely proportional to temperature. We can merge the two parameters in one, the *virtual temperature*. Typically, 3% of vapor is roughly equivalent to 3 degrees of heat. Thus, in this whole section, T is the virtual temperature.

3.2 Cloud evolution

As explained in the introduction, we do not model within the scope on this paper the bubble rising from the ground to the dew point altitude. The bubble becomes visible at the dew point altitude because of condensation, thus marking the boundary forming the floor of the clouds. We assume that the bubble generated at the previous stage appears directly at the dew point altitude, above the initial point of formation. One may add some bias in order to take into account horizontal displacements attributable to wind.

Because of the quantitative changes in the mixing phenomenon and of the dynamics of the motion below and above the dew point altitude (the air is more hot, wet and turbulent inside the cloud), one cannot assume that a same well-defined bubble being born on the ground will rise up to the top of a cloud. The matter is redistributed. We consider a model where the cloud is fed from the earth's surface with bubbles, and where new bubbles are created inside the cloud depending on the local conditions[2].

In our model, the inside of the cloud is composed of static bubbles. The volumetric resolution is thus crudely represented, with sufficient accuracy for air transport to occur. We use *potential temperatures*, i.e. the temperature that an air parcel would have if it was at the sea level, rather than the real temperature, the latter being affected by the pressure decrease with altitude.

The birth of a bubble inside or at the border of a cloud is due to a local temperature gradient (causing a Rayleigh-Taylor instability). Our computational model works as follows. We first look for the hottest neighborhood, assuming that the motion is due to newly arriving matter, and to accumulation of hot matter. We then compute the barycenter of this neighborhood using temperatures as weights, where the new bubble will be born. The new bubble takes the heat of each bubble in the neighborhood, according to a factor decreasing with the distance d, namely $\frac{1}{1+d/D_{\frac{1}{2}}}$, and in a proportion controlled by a global coefficient τ_{conv} (between 0 and 1). $D_{\frac{1}{2}}$ is a coefficient corresponding to the distance contributing at 50%. We chose it to be equal to the bubble radius so that the bubble recomposition is quite local.

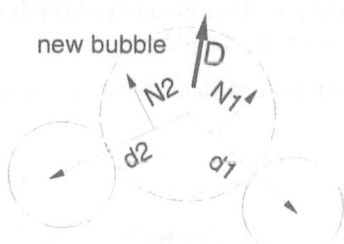

Figure 3: New bubble inside a cloud.

The direction of the bubble displacement depends on the local heat gradient, which is estimated by summing the normals $\vec{N_i}$ (taken in a vertical plane) to each bubble direction $\vec{d_i}$ from which the new bubble is taking heat: $\vec{N_i} = \vec{d_i} \times \vec{horiz}$, $\vec{D} = \frac{1}{nb} \cdot \sum_1^{nb}(\vec{N_i}/\|\vec{N_i}\|)$, see Figure 3. Note that in a homogeneous temperature field,

---

[2]Some heuristico-physical models even consider 3 stages between the floor and the clouds, where the bubbles are rearranged, so that the bubbles reaching the cloud are not the same as the ones that left the floor. These models focus on heat and moisture exchange between successive layers.

the direction is null (no instability), while at the boundary of such a field, the direction follows the boundary normal. Beyond this local potential temperature gradient, there is a vertical gradient of real temperature due to the pressure gradient. This has no effect however, as it is directly counterbalanced by gravity. The density gradient is due to the pressure, which results from hydrostatic equilibrium: $\frac{\partial P}{\partial z} = -\rho.g$. We do need to add the important effect of latent heat released by condensation as long as a wet air parcel rises, as illustrated in Figure 4. This acts as a motor in the cumulus growing. For typical physical values, this is equivalent to adding a unit vertical vector to the computed direction, thus verifying the observation that turrets in natural clouds grow in a direction that is the halfway between the cloud normal and the vertical [14].

Figure 4: The combination of the potential temperature gradient and the latent heat release controls the bubbles motion inside the cloud, and the turrets formation on the border.

Once the bubble has moved a given distance in its chosen direction, one of several things can occur (see Figure 5):

- if the bubble is in a sparse area, we keep it in order to be used in further air transportation. It marks the occupation of this location by cloud matter.

- if the bubble appears on the top of the cloud, we keep it because it is visible. If this hides a neighbor, we can delete the neighbor.

- otherwise we can destroy it and distribute its mass and heat to its new neighbors.

Figure 5: Destiny of the bubble after its move.

In Figure 6 we show the time evolution of the external envelope of bubbles, as visualized by placing a point at the center of each main vortex on a bubble surface. The purpose and use of vortices is described more thoroughly in the next subsection.

Figure 6: Growing 3D cumulus cloud.

3.3 Small scale shape

The surface of the cloud is materialized by structures smaller than the bubbles themselves, i.e. *waves* that become *main vortices* (see D on Figure 2), and subvortices. We assume a recursive structure, as illustrated in Figure 7. A bubble is considered as a sphere, onto which are convected the main vortices, which were initially waves having about 1/10 of the sphere radius [5, 6]. These vortices are also considered to be spherical, and subvortices are themselves advected upon their parent vortex surface in a recursive fashion.

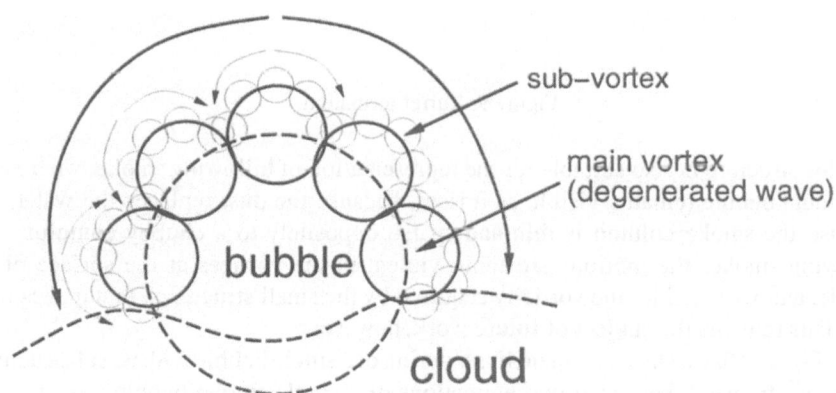

Figure 7: Bubble substructures: main vortices and sub-vortices, each being advected on its parent surface.

In our model, when a bubble reaches and crosses the cloud's top surface, it pushes back this surface, thus 'stealing' the matter (i.e. substructures) from the bubbles residing in the occupied place. These substructures are thus detached from their bubbles and re-attached to the rising one, and advected on its surface as shown in Figure 8. New matter (i.e. waves) appears on the top (in bold in the figure).

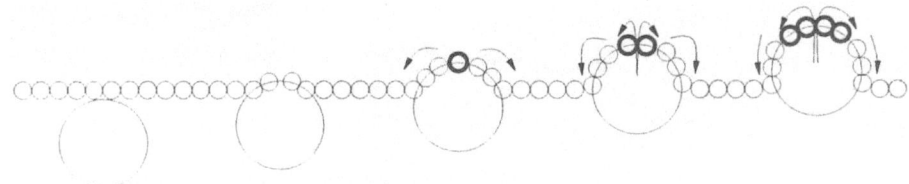

Figure 8: Matter advection.

The matter that appears on the top is advected to the sides where it is then stationary with respect to the background, while the bubble is rising. The rotation around the bubble compensates for the bubble rising, so that the advection acts much like a vertical tank track. If a single bubble rises as a turret, the matter is dropped when it reaches the largest location of the bubble, thus forming a cylindrical column. This is shown in Figure 9.

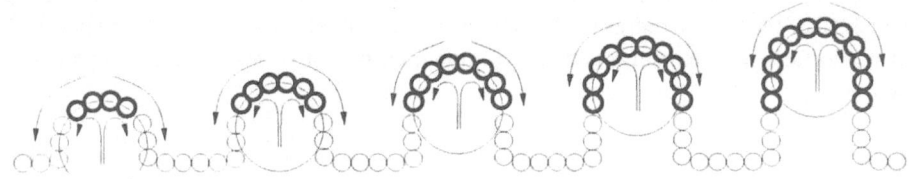

Figure 9: Turret formation.

This structure is also suitable for the representation of billowing smoke, where each individual bubble remains visible as it rises, because the dust replaces the water, and because the smoke column is thin and sparse oppositely to a chubby cumulus. For billowing smoke, the motions are more violent in the vortices at the surface of the bubble, and we consider the vorticity acquired by the small structures, that makes them roll. This remains the subject of future work, however.

In Figure 10, we show an OpenGL rendering of a single bubble with its substructures. These are frames taken from two animations of a single smoke bubble. Shadows on the left image are computed using a shadowmap. The spheres on the right image are textured.

Figure 10: Two bubbles and their substructures rolling on their surfaces.

4 Conclusion

The ongoing work we have presented in this paper proposes to qualitatively simulate the growth and animation of convective clouds. This is achieved by simulating and combining atmospheric structures of various scales. Bubbles are the largest scale structure we use and are responsible for displacements of 3D air parcels in our model. We combine several models to deal with bubbles birth near the ground, bubbles rising up to a cloud, and bubbles moving inside a cloud. Smaller scales are used to add visual complexity for motion and shape on the cloud surface. The smaller-scale substructures are attached to each bubble lying on the cloud periphery, and themselves have substructures. A substructure is advected on the surface of its parent substructure. The largest level of substructure corresponds to waves on a bubble surface that degenerate into main vortices, while finer substructures correspond to the breaking of these vortices into smaller vortices. The general scheme is illustrated in Figure 2.

Our model and implementation are still at an early stage. The various scales have been implemented individually; we have yet to combine them in a single simulation. The following issues also need to be addressed. There are no special provisions for the initial birth and death of a cloud, while the assumption that a cloud is a surface at these instants is not very realistic. The Benard cell structure is not specifically encoded, so there is no guarantee that clouds stay distant from each other. The bubble motion inside the cloud is effected one bubble at a time, while several bubble motion events should be treated simultaneously. Lastly, we have specified the animation of the cloud, but we do not specifically deal with the rendering. The simplest approach to rendering consists of drawing the smaller spherical substructures, possibly with textures. The addition of a global 'skin' upon these structures may also improve the visual aspect of the cloud surface.

Two extensions arise at this point. It would be interesting to deal with larger scale cloud structures, in order to simulate the shape and the evolution of the sky in outdoor scenes. Another issue is that most of the model can also apply to billowing smoke, where the dynamics of advection is more intense, and were substructures play a more important role.

[3]Acknowledgments

Specials thanks are due to Michiel Van de Panne for his fruitful discussions, his help with 3D interfaces, and his patient rereading of the paper.

We gratefully acknowledge the financial support of our research by ITRC (Ontario) and NSERC (Canada).

References

1. Emanuel and K. A. *Atmospheric Convection*. Oxford University Press, 1994.

2. Manuel Noronha Gamito, Pedro Faria Lopes, and Mário Rui Gomes. Two-dimensional simulation of gaseous phenomena using vortex particles. In Dimitri Terzopoulos and Daniel Thalmann, editors, *Computer Animation and Simulation '95*, pages 2–15. Eurographics, Springer-Verlag, September 1995. ISBN 3-211-82738-2.

3. Geoffrey Y. Gardner. Simulation of natural scenes using textured quadric surfaces. In Hank Christiansen, editor, *Computer Graphics (SIGGRAPH '84 Proceedings)*, volume 18, pages 11–20, July 1984.

4. Geoffrey Y. Gardner. Visual simulation of clouds. In B. A. Barsky, editor, *Computer Graphics (SIGGRAPH '85 Proceedings)*, volume 19, pages 297–303, July 1985.

5. W. W. Grabowski and T. L. Clark. Cloud-environment interface instability: Rising thermal calculations in two spatial dimensions. *Journal of the Atmospheric Sciences*, 48:527–546, 1991.

6. W. W. Grabowski and T. L. Clark. Cloud-environment interface instability, part II: Extension to three spatial dimensions. *Journal of the Atmospheric Sciences*, 50:555–573, 1993.

7. W. W. Grabowski and T. L. Clark. Cloud-environment interface instability, part III: Direct influence of environmental shear. *Journal of the Atmospheric Sciences*, 50:3821–3828, 1993.

8. Robert A. Houze Jr. *Cloud Dynamics*. Academic Press.

9. James T. Kajiya and Brian P. Von Herzen. Ray tracing volume densities. In Hank Christiansen, editor, *Computer Graphics (SIGGRAPH '84 Proceedings)*, volume 18, pages 165–174, July 1984.

10. A. Luciani, A. Habibi, A. Vapillon, and Y. Duroc. A physical model of turbulent fluids. In Dimitri Terzopoulos and Daniel Thalmann, editors, *Computer Animation and Simulation '95*, pages 16–29. Eurographics, Springer-Verlag, September 1995. ISBN 3-211-82738-2.

11. Jean Orloff. *personal communications*.

12. Jos Stam and Eugene Fiume. Turbulent wind fields for gaseous phenomena. In James T. Kajiya, editor, *Computer Graphics (SIGGRAPH '93 Proceedings)*, volume 27, pages 369–376, August 1993.

13. Jos Stam and Eugene Fiume. Depicting fire and other gaseous phenomena using diffusion processes. In Robert Cook, editor, *SIGGRAPH 95 Conference Proceedings*, Annual Conference Series, pages 129–136. ACM SIGGRAPH, Addison Wesley, August 1995. held in Los Angeles, California, 06-11 August 1995.

14. Y. Takaya. The motion of uneven structure of convective clouds. *Journal of the Atmospheric Sciences*, 50:574–587, 1993.

15. Wallace, J. M., and P. V. Hobbs. *Atmospheric Science: An Introductory Survey*. Academic Press, 1977.

Visual Model of Plant Development with Respect to Influence of Light

Bedřich Beneš

Department of Computer Science and Engineering,
Czech Technical University,
Karlovo nám. 13, Prague, Czech Republic,
e–mail: benes@sgi.felk.cvut.cz

Abstract. This paper deals with simulation of plant development and focuses on influence of light. Most of the previously published methods dealing with light in these simulations use sky discretization, source of aliasing error which was never mentioned in literature. This paper investigates the problem and proposes a solution to it. The second influence which strongly affects the shape of a plant is the relationship between the amount of light and the activity of buds. We offer here a simplified model to demonstrate this dependency.

1 Introduction

As the technology and methods involved in computer graphics grows more advanced, the provided methods and algorithms become correspondingly more precise and accurate. This tendency can be observed in the area of visual plants simulation, where it presents itself somewhat specifically. Although *ad hoc* methods [14, 16, 19, 27, 28, 29] are still popular and frequently used, biology has begun to exert a beneficial pressure on this area of computer graphics *e.g.,* [9, 15, 18, 20, 21, 23, 25, 26], an impact equally useful in both fields.

As mentioned in [18], the interaction between the plant and the environment is often times neglected. The bulk of previous work mostly considered the plant as a closed system. The former works approximate the fact that the shapes of the plants differ due to their interactions with a surrounding environment by injecting randomness into the model generation phase. Plant–environment interactions has not been entirely excluded from scholarship, and with the tremendously useful aid of computer graphics [1, 2, 12, 13] and this area has found its way into scholarship more and more frequently [3, 4, 6, 7, 18, 24].

This paper is structured as follows. Section 2 reviews previously published methods and findings. The growth model is dependent on the calculation of the light, so the algorithm for the skylight approximation is briefly discussed in Section 3. Section 4 deals with the growth model with modules description and their typical actions. Section 5 focuses on the influence of light and the resulting error caused by a fixed number of lights in scene. Finally, the results of our simulations are presented in concluding Section 6.

2   Previous work

Begin with year in 1984, Aono and Kunii [1] used light, wind, and gravity for bending the branches of trees in certain directions. The phenomenon of self-shadowing of branches however did not fall within the scope of their study.

In 1988, Arvo and Kirk [2] introduced *environment sensitive automata*–ESA in order to investigate the simulation of the climbing plants as well as the spreading grass. This method is based on ray-tracing algorithm. The ESA detect their surrounding environment by casting rays. The information obtained is then used to measure the distance to the obstacle and determine whether or not the ESA will fall into shadow. The second function of this information is also used for varying the size of the blade of grass.

Greene [12, 13] used voxel space automata to simulate roots searching for viable paths on stony ground and to simulate growth of climbing plants. He uses stochastic growth (the random walk). In order to decide a new position of the growing element, multiple random trials are made, position and orientation of a growing element are randomly perturbed, the fitness function is evaluated, and the element is moved to the best place. 3DDA sampling of the trajectory of the sun calculates locally the amount of light. Several rays are cast for every growth element and the coefficient of the sky exposure is evaluated as a relative number of occluded and free rays.

An alternative method of the light direction and the light amount estimation is found in the work of Chiba *et al.* [7]. They introduce a leaf-ball, an approximation of a cluster of leaves with the growing element in the center. The amount of light is estimated by the projection of these balls on the celestial sphere in the center of which the leaf-ball concerned is located. A hidden surface algorithm or 3DDA in voxel space estimates the amount of skylight. If the amount of light remains under a certain threshold, then the branch is treated as withered and is removed. The direction towards the brightest spot is defined by summing the participating vectors associated with each ray reaching the celestial sphere. In 1996, Chiba *et al.* used the same algorithm to calculate both the amount of the light and the direction to the brightest point for leaves [6]. The maximum is used for bending leaves to the direction of the light, while the amount of the light is used for coloring leaves.

The theory of L-systems is well-known in computer graphics. The survey of L-systems is presented in the book [22] while the latest results can be found in [18, 25]. Furthermore, there are two important environmentally sensitive extensions of L-systems published in [18, 24]. The context sensitive parametric L-systems were extended by query modules [24]. The query modules are parametrized components of the rewriting process and they can ask the surrounding environment for some values; *e.g.*, distance from the obstacle. Parameters of the module are set when the rewriting process asks the query module for them. Drawback of this conception is that the whole plant in the string rewriting phase must always be constructed. *Open L-systems* [18], however, do not suffer from this drawback. The rewriting step is preceded by a scanning phase, in which every so called communication module has set parameters without geometrical interpretation of the string. The plant and the environment are treated as processes communicating via the exchange of messages. The communication modules can ask the environment for values (*e.g.,* location or presence of an obstacle, amount of the light, *etc.,*) and they can also inform the environment of certain values (*e.g.,* carbon dioxide).

The author of this paper published his findings of an efficient estimation of the light flux affecting every leaf [3, 4]. Here, the amount of light and the direction of the brightest point are simultaneously calculated for every leaf and bud in the scene by using a sampling of the scene from the light sources. The amount of light is used simply for changing the growth direction of branches and for a simulation of dying leaves owing to lack of light.

3   Approximation of the skylight

Most of the plants develop in outdoor conditions where both the skylight and sunlight play important roles. Although methods for the skylight approximation exist and are in fact applied *e.g.,* [8, 10], in the course of this particular study we will not directly address them. Instead, we suppose the sky to be approximated (discretized) by total number p light sources denoted by S_k, $k = 1, ..., p$. These lights are regularly spaced on a hemisphere with a very large radius (for example, using the algorithm of Max *et al.* [17]). The lights S_k have flux densities denoted by B_k, assigned according to the area of the sky which is approximated by S_k. We should note here that the assumption of the sky approximation fits in well with most of the algorithms for plant–light interaction published [3, 4, 5, 6, 18]. One problem however, relating to this approximation (aliasing caused by finite number of lights), will be discussed in Section 5.1.

4   The growth model

We use a biologically based stochastic model introduced by de Reffye *et al.* [9, 15] (see also [11, pp:1028-1030]).

The plant has a modular structure. The modules used in this paper are outlined in Figure 1. Although it was proven [22] that the class of plants describable in this model can be modeled by L-systems, this model has several advantages to L-systems. First, it is inherently parallel; in contradiction both to a sequential turtle graphics interpretation of the string of modules and to the sequential scanning phase of modules in Open L-systems [18]. Next, this model is intuitive; in contradiction to the textual form of L-system productions. Finally, this model is biologically based, it can be immediately and readily used by biologists; there is no need for an explanation of complex rules as is the case of L-systems. The principal intention of de Reffye's model is the simulation of plant development; on the other hand the simulation of plant development is only one of many possible applications of L-systems (but probably the most important one).

128

4.1 Modular structure

The model of a plant possesses a modular structure [25]. The plant is thought to consist of the modules as outlined in Figure 1. The goal of the simulation is to describe behavior of the modules so that a plant shape will emerge.

The most important module of the plant is a *bud*, which can assume one of two forms: an *apical bud* is always located at the extremity of the main trunk or lateral branch, whereas a *lateral bud* is situated at the leaf's axil (it is also called *axillar bud*). A *leaf* is always adjacent to a lateral bud. A *node* consists of one or more lateral buds and an identical number of leaves. An *internode* is a piece of stem located between two successive nodes. The node is either situated between two internodes, or at the tip of the branch. An *apex* is an apical segment with its apical bud.

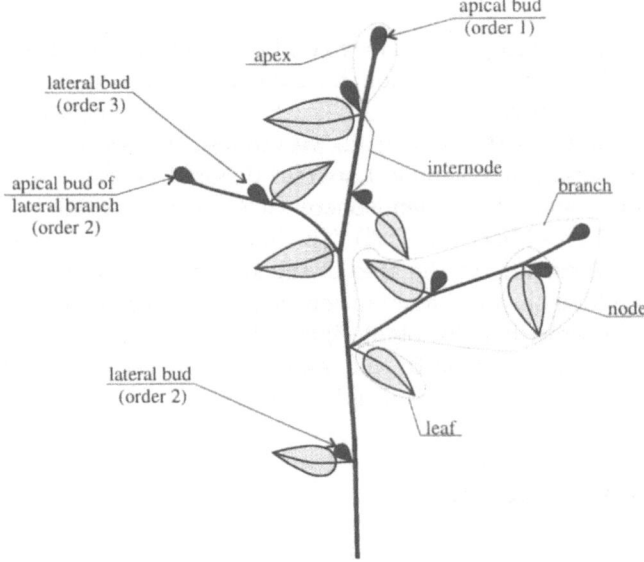

Fig. 1. Diagram identifies the ordering of plant modules. The modules are marked by arrows, whereas the group of modules are encircled in dashed lines.

4.2 Action of modules

The bud is a basic growing element (plant engine [18]) which can perform several actions. Its actions depend on both environmental conditions of the plant (light, water, nutrients, *etc.,*) and internal ones (age, amount of meristem, *etc*). A bud can either *die*, or *bloom and die*, or *become dormant*, or *become an internode*. This final possibility, the process of becoming an internode, is the most important action because it causes growing and branching. This process consists of three steps. At first, one or more lateral leaves appear beside the bud and the same number of new buds appear at their axils. Then the apical bud produces a piece of stem - the new internode. It is obvious, then, that every branch is a result of activity of its apical bud.

The branches as well as the buds are ordered in such a way (see in Figure 1) that the main trunk and its apical bud have ordering number one assigned. Every lateral bud as well as every lateral branch has its ordering number one higher than its bearing branch.

The bud's behavior depends on its ordering number in our simulation. The ordering number is used for indexing the table of attributes. This table is set either by the user or according to an applied architectural model used [9]. The table contains values which describe the lifetime of the bud, the geometry of the internode produced by the bud, the branching angle, *etc.*

The original model [9] is band on discrete time simulation, whereas our is band on continuous time simulation; [3] provides further details.

5 Influence of the light

In general, the plant development depends on many conditions. In order to understand what our model provides for simulating light influence, we will regard the other parameters of the model as fixed, supposing that they do not affect the plant at all. We will work only with light.

Assume, we have n buds denoted by D_i, $i = 1, ..., n$. These buds are represented by spheres of constant radius r - so they are of equal size, thereby easing the task of preparing the calculations. Let $A_D = \pi r^2$ denote the projected area of the bud. If the bud D is completely exposed to the light S_k (see in Section 3), the appropriate light flux contribution from this light to the bud is [8]

$$\Phi_{D,k} = B_k \, A_D.$$

The maximal light flux to the bud from all lights approximating the sky is

$$\Phi_D = \sum_{k=1}^{p} \Phi_{D,k} + \Phi_a, \tag{1}$$

where Φ_a denotes the flux of the ambient light in the crown of the plant. We use a constant amount of ambient light in the crown, in contrast to Reeves and Blau [27] who use exponential scaling of this coefficient. However, constant ambient light does not change the shape of the plant significantly if the directional lights are considered. The value of maximal possible light flux Φ_D is equal for all buds in scene.

Let $A^e_{D_i,k}$ denote the effective projected area of a bud D_i which is affected by light source S_k (we use the algorithm from [3, 4] for this calculation). Next we calculate the effective light flux denoted by $\Phi^e_{D_i,k}$, which takes into account the shadows cast by the other objects in scene from S_k to D_i. This value depends on shadowing the bud and it differs from bud to bud. It is equal to

$$\Phi^e_{D_i,k} = B_k \, A^e_{D_i,k},$$

Analogous to (1) the total effective light flux from all light sources to the bud D_i is

$$\Phi_{D_i}^e = \sum_{k=1}^{p} \Phi_{D_i,k}^e + \Phi_a. \tag{2}$$

Next we denote by ϕ_{D_i} the relative light flux to i−th bud which is from (1) and (2) equal to

$$\phi_{D_i} = \frac{\Phi_{D_i}^e}{\Phi_D}; \quad 0 \le \phi_{D_i} \le 1. \tag{3}$$

This value corresponds to the percentage of the amount of light obtained by the i−th bud from the sky. The relative light flux from the k−th light to the i−th bud is denoted by $\phi_{D_i,k}$ and it is equal to

$$\phi_{D_i,k} = \frac{\Phi_{D_i,k}^e}{\Phi_{D_i,k}}. \tag{4}$$

The relative light fluxes help us to more accurately determine the amount of light needed for the plant lifetime. It is also easier to manipulate with percentage values ϕ_{D_i} instead of the light fluxes $\Phi_{D_i}^e$.

5.1 Phototropism

There are several ways in which light affects the growth of the plant. The most commonly cited effect is *phototropism*. It has mostly the form of *heliotropism*, also called *sun seeking*. Phototropism [22, pp:58-61] is a change in the growth direction of a bud towards towards its light sources (*c.f.*, Figure 2). In order to simulate phototropism we calculate the new growth direction denoted by $\mathbf{d}_i'$ of i-th bud from its original growth direction $\mathbf{d}_i$, direction to the light $\mathbf{v}_k$, and the coefficient of phototropism $0 \le H \le 1$ as follows (see Figure 2)

$$\mathbf{d}_i' = (1 - H)\mathbf{d}_i + H\mathbf{v}_k. \tag{5}$$

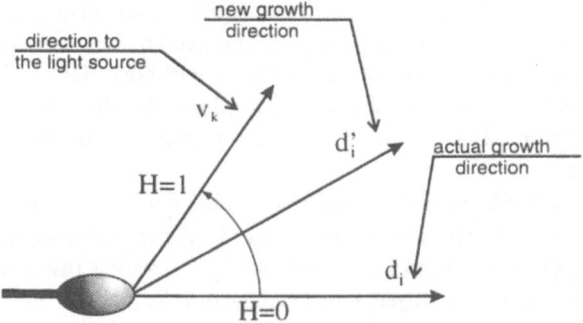

Fig. 2. Calculation of a new growth direction $\mathbf{d}_i'$ of a bud.

Let $\mathbf{v_k}$ denote the direction from which the light flux $\Phi_{D_i,k}$ comes to bud D_i. The direction to the brightest spot on the sky as seen by the bud D_i is *de facto* the direction to the light source contributing with $max\{\phi_{D_i,k}; k = 1, ..., p\}$. However choosing the simple maximum gives rise to an error as shown on Figure 3. Here, the sources have almost the same contribution. The one light source differs by a very small value. Using the maximum value causes a strong and undesirable change in the growth direction as shown in Figure 3(b).

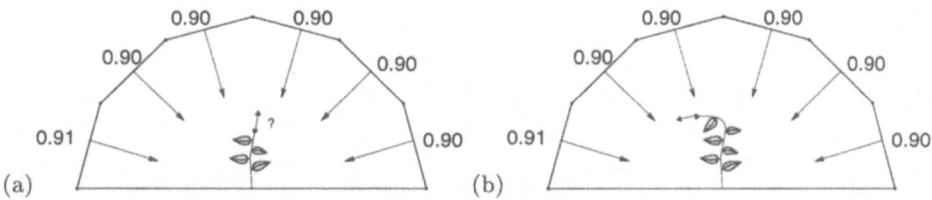

Fig. 3. A small difference in the amount of light causes a sudden change in the growth direction in which the plant is growing if the maximum of the light is simply chosen.

We would like to suggest a solution to this problem. The bud tends to grow in a certain direction, and it changes this direction only if it is really necessary. We denote by α_k the angle between actual growth direction $\mathbf{d}_i$ and direction to the light source S_k. We *scale down* the light flux $\Phi_{D_i,k}^e$, *i.e.*, we multiply it by $\cos(\alpha_k/2)$.

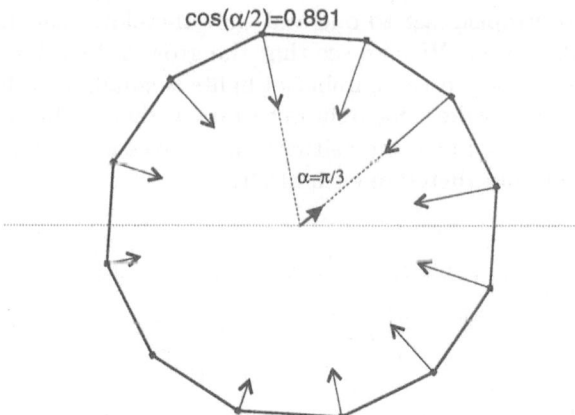

Fig. 4. Influence of the light depends on growth direction of the bud with $\cos(\alpha/2)$, where α denotes the angle between the actual growth direction of the bud and the direction of the light. Note, that the light shining from the back has no effect. For the sake of clarity, all of the directions are displayed; it is however only possible to describe and represent graphically the activity of the bud in upper half of the circle with a given growth direction and with an approximation of the skylight by hemisphere.

After this operation, the effective light flux is calculated for every bud according to (3) and (4). This solution is demonstrated in Figure 4. Meanwhile, we make the assumption that all light sources have equal contributions $\Phi^e_{D_i,k}$. We can then solve the dilemma of choosing specifically one light source by scaling down their contributions according to $\cos(\alpha_k/2)$ *i.e.*, the growth direction remains unchanged.

This author is aware, the number of lights approximating the sky is source of one subtle error. Figure 5 demonstrates behavior of the hyphotetical plant

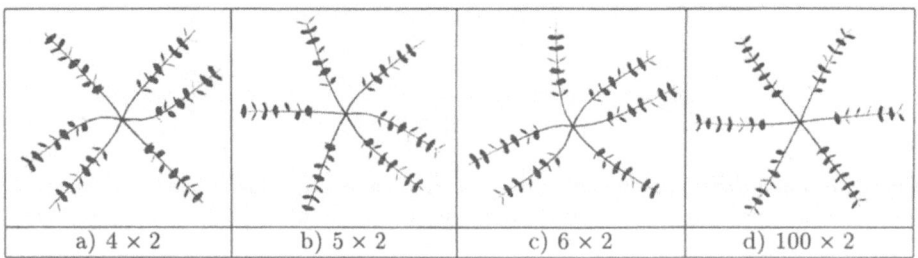

| a) 4×2 | b) 5×2 | c) 6×2 | d) 100×2 |

Fig. 5. Shape of a plant resulting from different number of lights approximating the skylight. The $a \times b$ means a subdivision in a horizontal and b subdivision in a vertical direction. A small number of the lights causes visual errors. Branches in (a)-(c) tend to grow in pairs towards certain light sources.

with only six branches strongly influenced with the light. The branches have coefficient of phototropism set to one and they therefore tend to grow towards the strongest light source. We can see that the growth direction *depends on the approximation of the sky*. If the number of lights is small, as in Figure 5 (a)-(c), several branches grow to the same light in certain distance. This distance depends on the size of the apical buds; they situate themselves at certain distances so as not to inhibit itself and therefore each other.

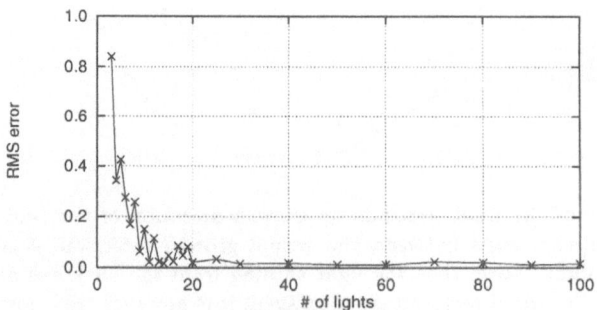

Fig. 6. Presents the error in the plant's shape due to approximation of the skylight.

Quantification of this effect is rather difficult. It cannot be quantified during the plant development, because next stage of the plant depends on the previous one, and therefore the error grows rapidly. We have tested virtual plant with about 200 buds and 3000 leaves. We run one simulation step, *i.e.*, we measured the amount of light, and we have saved the growth direction of the control plant. The control plant was measured with sky approximation by 10^4 light sources. Then the resolution was decreased, and the simulation was run again. The growth direction of the buds was measured once again, the data from which allowed us to generate the following normalized RMS error (see Figure 6).

We meet here a typical computer graphics problem - *aliasing*. Nonetheless, arriving at a solution is a straightforward task. We must increase the precision of the skylight approximation, *i.e.*, the number of lights. The approximation with 20 lights was visually sufficient in most of our simulations and below the level of recognition compared to the approximation with 10^4 lights. The branches are visually chaotical, so this error is registered only if the number of light is too small.

5.2 The others influence of light

The change in the growth direction of buds is one of several influences of light. As the light reaches leaves, they produce photosynthates [18] which are then transported to the adjacent buds. The amount transported has a great influence on the bud's activity. Their insufficiency causes buds to become dormant; on the other hand if there is a lot of photosynthates, the bud gives raise to a lateral bud. In [18], the influence of the light is simulated by two threshold values. If the amount of the photosynthates in the bud is above the first threshold, the bud produces lateral buds. If the amount is between these two thresholds, the bud grows. Insufficiency of the photosynthates, meanwhile, causes the bud to become dormant (inactive). These findings are in keeping with a well observed tendency of the plants for spreading more extensively if the light is enough.

However, this rather complex model can be simplified by remaping the influence of the light to the bud's growth rate. Let t_g and t_b denote time of birth of a bud and time of generation of the lateral bud respectively. The value t_b is set to a constant value T when the lateral bud is born. This constant is unique for the plant and typical for species. The bud D_i produces total length of internode denoted by l in the time $t_b - t_g$. Let t denote actual time and $t_g < t < t_b$. We denote by l_0 the length of an internode which was already produced by the bud in time $t - t_g$. The length denoted by

$$\Delta l = l - l_0$$

would be produced in time $t_b - t$ if the amount of light ϕ_{D_i} (*c.f.*, (3)) reaching the bud is equal to one. According to the relative light flux reaching the bud we *shift* the time of lateral bud production t_b to

$$t_b' = t + (t_b - t)\frac{1}{\phi_{D_i}}. \tag{6}$$

However, the remaining length of the internode Δl which will be produced does not change. So it will be produced in longer time *i.e.,* the bud is inhibited according to the incoming amount of light. According to [18], we should measure the amount of light coming to the adjacent leaf, but a direct measuring of the light reaching the bud enhances the calculation. The error caused by this simplification should be quantified.

We do not require any constant for a simulation of this influence of light. If the amount of light is low, the bud decelerates its growth by lengthening the time of next lateral bud generation.

6   Implementation and results

The program was implemented in *C*, uses *OpenGL* for the amount of light determination, and was run on *Silicon Graphics Indigo*[2] workstation with Extreme graphics board and R4400 on 200MHz MIPS processor. We use previously published algorithm [3, 4] for the light calculation. The shaded pictures were raytraced in POVRay.

Color plates demonstrates the plant growing near the obstacle and therefore spreading more extensively in the direction of incoming light. The branches are bend in the direction of the light as well. Another example shows the plant with branches strongly searching the light. We can see, that strong phototropism helps the branches to finding their way around the obstacles (no collision detection has been solved). Last two color plates show the same plant growing in different light conditions.

For more information visit http://sgi.felk.cvut.cz/~benes/cas97.html.

7   Conclusions

The purposes of this paper were to once again alert to the significance of the relationship between the plant and its environment and to study the light influence to visual plant development. We presented that the discretization of the skylight causes alias which presents itself somewhat specifically - with growing several branches parallel towards the light. Finally, we introduced the simplified model of bud growth with response to incoming light.

8   Acknowledgments

I would like to thank to Radomír Měch and Nelson Max for fruitful discussions and comments.

References

1. M. Aono and T. Kunii. Botanical Tree Image Generation. *IEEE Computer Graphics and Applications*, 4(5):10–34, 1984.
2. J. Arvo and D. Kirk. Modeling Plants with Environment-Sensitive Automata. In *Proceedings of Ausgraph'88*, pages 27–33, 1988.
3. B. Beneš. An Efficient Estimation of Light in Simulation of Plant Development. In *Computer Animation and Simulation'96*, Springer Computer Science, pages 153–165. Springer–Verlag Wien New York, 1996.
4. B. Beneš. Fast Estimation of Light in Simulation of Plant Development. In *Proceedings of WSCG'97*, volume I, pages 1–10. University of West Bohemia Press, Feb. 1997.
5. N. Chiba, K. Ohshida, K. Muroaka, and S. Nobuji. A Growth Model Having the Abilities of Growth-Regulations for Simulating Visual Nature of Botanical Trees. *Computer & Graphics*, 18:469–479, 1994.
6. N. Chiba, K. Ohshida, K. Muroaka, and S. Nobuji. Visual Simulation of Leaf Arrangement and Autumn Colors. *The Journal of Visualization and Computer Animation*, 7:79–93, 1996.
7. N. Chiba, S. Okawa, K. Muroaka, and M. Muira. Visual Simulation of Botanical Trees Based on Virtual Heliotropism and Dormancy Break. *The Journal of Visualization and Computer Animation*, 5:3–15, 1994.
8. M. Cohen and J. Wallace. *Radiosity and Realistic Image Synthesis*. Academic Press Professional, 1993.
9. P. de Reffye, C. Edelin, J. Fraçon, M. Jaeger, and C. Puech. Plants Models Faithful to Botanical Structure and Development. In *Proceedings of SIGGRAPH '88*, volume 22(4) of *Annual Conference Series*, pages 151–158, 1988.
10. Y. Dobashi, K. Kazufimo, H. Yamashita, and N. Tomoyuki. Method for Calculation of Sky Light Luminance Aiming at an Interactive Architectural Design. In *Computer Graphics Forum*, volume 15(3), pages C–109–C–118, 1996.
11. J. Foley, A. van Dam, S. Feiner, and J. Hughes. *Computer Graphics: Principles and Practice*. Addison-Wesley, Reading, 1990.
12. N. Greene. Voxel Space Automata: Modeling with Stochastic Growth Processes in Voxel Space. In *Proceedings of SIGGRAPH '89*, volume 23(4) of *Annual Conference Series 1989*, pages 175–184, 1989.
13. N. Greene. Detailing Tree Skeleton with Voxel Automata. *SIGGRAPH'91, Course Notes on Photorealistic Volume Modeling and Rendering Techniques*, 1991.
14. M. Holton. Strands, Gravity and Botanical Tree Imagery. *Computer Graphics Forum*, 13(I):57–67, 1994.
15. R. Lecoustre, P. de Reffye, M. Jaeger, and P. Dinouard. Controlling the Architectural Geometry of Plant's Growth – Application to the Begonia Genus. In *Computer Animation'92*, pages 199–214, 1992.
16. B. Lintermann and O. Deusen. Interactive Modelling and Animation of Branching Botanical Structures. In *Computer Animation and Simulation'96*, Springer Computer Science, pages 139–151. Springer–Verlag Wien New York, 1996.
17. N. Max and K. Ohsaki. Rendering Trees from Precomputed Z-Buffer Views. In *EG WS on Rendering'95*, Springer Computer Science, pages 74–81. Springer–Verlag Wien New York, 1995.
18. R. Měch and P. Prusinkiewicz. Visual Models of Plants Interacting With Their Environment. In *Proceedings of SIGGRAPH '96*, volume 30(4) of *Annual Conference Series 1996*, pages 397–410, 1996.

19. P. Oppenheimer. Real Time Design and Animation of Fractal Plants and Trees. In *Proceedings of SIGGRAPH '86*, volume 20(4) of *Annual Conference Series 1986*, pages 55–64, 1986.
20. P. Prusinkiewicz. Modeling and Visualization of Biological Structures. In *Proceedings of Graphics Interface '93*, volume I, pages 128–137, 1993.
21. P. Prusinkiewicz. A Look to Visual Modeling of Plants. In *German Conference on Bioinformatics*, Springer Computer Science. Springer–Verlag Wien New York, 1997. to be published.
22. P. Prusinkiewicz and J. Hanan. Visualization of Botanical structures and Processes using parametric L-systems. In *Scientific Visualization and Graphics simulation '90*, volume 22(4), pages 183–201. J.Wiley & Sons, Ltd, 1990.
23. P. Prusinkiewicz, J. Hanan, M. Hammel, and R. Měch. L-systems: from the Theory to Visual Models of Plants. *Machine Graphics and Vision*, 2(4):12–22, 1993.
24. P. Prusinkiewicz, M. James, and R. Měch. Synthetic Topiary. In *Proceedings of SIGGRAPH '94*, volume I of *Annual Conference Series*, pages 351–358, 1993.
25. P. Prusinkiewicz, M. James, R. Měch, and J. Hannan. The Artificial Life of Plants. In *Course Notes of SIGGRAPH '95, Computer Graphics, Annual Conference Series 1995*, volume I, pages 1–38, 1995.
26. P. Prusinkiewicz and A. Lindenmayer. *The Algorithmic Beauty of Plants*. Springer–Verlag, New York, 1990.
27. W. Reeves and R. Blau. Approximate and Probabilistic Algorithms for Shading and Rendering Structured Particle Systems. In *Proceedings of SIGGRAPH '85*, volume 19(3) of *Annual Conference Series*, pages 313–322, 1985.
28. X. Viennot, G. Eyrolles, N. Janey, and D. Arques. Combinatorial Analysis of Ramified Patterns and Computer Imagery Trees. In *Proceedings of SIGGRAPH '89*, volume 23(3) of *Annual Conference Series*, pages 31–40, 1989.
29. J. Weber and J. Penn. Creation and Rendering of Realistic Trees. In *Proceedings of SIGGRAPH '95*, volume 22(4) of *Annual Conference Series*. SIGGRAPH New York, 1995.

Editors' Note: see Appendix, p. 199 for colored figure of this paper

A phenomenological model of coastal scenes based on physical considerations

Jean-Christophe Gonzato and Bertrand Le Saëc

LaBRI *
351 cours de la libération, 33405 Talence (France)
`[gonzato|lesaec]@labri.u-bordeaux.fr`

In this article, we present a dynamic version of wave tracing previously introduce in computer graphics by Ts'o and Barsky. An empirical model of water waves based on Gerstner, Biesel models and the Fournier method is also proposed.

Keywords. Ocean, water waves, plunging breakers, wave tracing

1 Introduction

The complexity of natural phenomena has led many researchers to try to produce realistic pictures. One such natural object interesting to model is ocean surface flow. An important use is to predict the wave form inside a port or to determine the best place for a sea wall. Other researchers try to predict the arrival of tsunamis on the coast. The ocean surface is complex to model near the shore. A lot of phenomena take part in this complexity: reflection, refraction, diffraction of waves, breaking waves, whirlpools.

Wave modeling can be split into two categories: complete physical modelisation such in [KM90] [FM96] [CL95] that solves Navier-Stokes equations on the one hand; and an empirical approach [FR86] [Pea86] [TB87] [IZ95] based on the classical wave model of Gerstner and Biesel et al. [Bie52] [Lac65] [AA85]. The former leads to very accurate, but expensive algorithms and the latter has the opposite characteristics.

Our work is dedicated to the geometric modelization of waves. A complete rendering model is currently in developement, unavoidable stage to animate scenes realistically. As a result, we will not deal with rendering and animation.

In this paper, first, we propose a geometric model of vertical section of the sea that can be viewed as an improved version of the Fournier and Reeves model [FR86]. It can be manipulated easily and advances the Fournier-Reeves limits of modelisation.

Then, we introduce a new algorithm to control the wave refraction based on Descartes law. In comparison to Ts'o-Barsky algorithm [TB87], our model is more precise near the shoreline and can be also used with more general form of floor (baies and islands for instance).

* Laboratoire Bordelais de Recherche en Informatique *(Université Bordeaux I* and *Centre National de la Recherche Scientifique)*. The present work is also supported by the *Conseil Régional d'Aquitaine*.

In this model, waves are described from two views: a side view, taking a vertical section of sea; and a bird's eye view, taking an overhead view of sea. The first one helps us to manage the profile of the waves (general form, breaking, beach arrival). The second one is used to control diffraction, refraction and reflection phenomena.

2 Vertical section of the sea

In this section, we first introduce the main classical wave model developed by Guerstner in 1804. In 1952, Biesel enhance this work to introduce plunging breakers. Then, we present the different previous works made in computer graphics. Finally, our model of waves is introduced.

2.1 Classical wave models

Here, we present the Biesel extension of the Gerstner model. Let us recall the assumptions of this model:

— the atmospheric pressure is constant;
— the ocean is composed of a perfect and homogenous liquid;
— the wind is not blowing anymore;
— there are only plunging waves;
— there are no currents and no friction with the bottom.

The *wavelength* is denoted by λ and the *amplitude A*. We denote by $\gamma = \frac{A}{\lambda}$ the *curvature*, T the period of the wave and h the *depth*. The free surface is the surface of sea with no undulations. The *reference point* is situated in the open sea, the x-axis is directed horizontally to the beach, the y-axis is horizontal and perpendicular to the x-axis, and the z-axis is directed to the top. (Fig. 1)

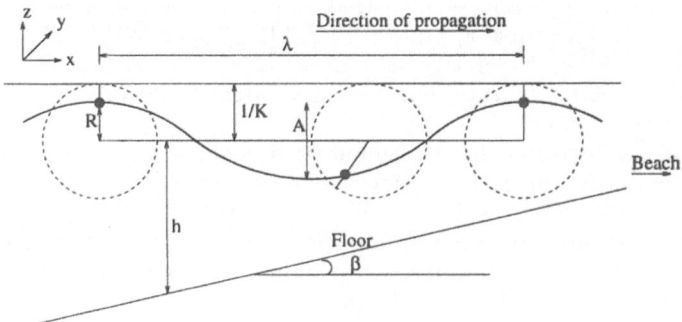

Fig. 1. General definitions.

A first theory was proposed by Gerstner in 1804. It is rigorous for an infinite depth. Each particle of water revolves around a fixed point $M(x_0, z_0)$ describing a circle of radius R. This circle is included in a disc whose radius is $\frac{1}{K}$. K is the wave number, ω is the angular speed.

The (x, z) coordinates of each particle are :

$$\begin{cases} x = x_0 - R_0 e^{Kz_0} \sin(Kx_0 - \omega t) \\ z = z_0 + R_0 e^{Kz_0} \cos(Kx_0 - \omega t) \end{cases} \tag{1}$$

In order to simplify, we set $R = R_0 e^{Kz_0}$. Some data can be determined by physical laws : $\lambda = \frac{2\pi}{K} = \frac{gT^2}{2\pi}$, $A = 2R$, and free surface $z_0 = \frac{\pi A^2}{4\lambda}$. The maximal curvature is obtained when $R = \frac{1}{K}$, so $\gamma_{max} = \frac{A_{max}}{\lambda} = \frac{\frac{2}{K}}{\lambda} = \frac{1}{\pi} = 0,31$.

Guerstner theory is usable with a great depth, but the influence of the bottom on waves is essential near the shore. When waves arrive on the beach, only the period seems to be invariant [Kin65], the wavelength decreases. All variables marked with an ∞ are used at an infinite depth. In the sequel, h is the depth at the current point x.

$$\frac{\lambda}{\lambda_\infty} = \tanh(Kh) \tag{2}$$

The amplitude decreases progressively to 91% of its open sea value and it increases to the breaking point.

$$\left(\frac{A}{A_\infty}\right)^2 = \frac{1}{\tanh(Kh)(1 + \frac{2Kh}{\sinh(2Kh)})} \tag{3}$$

Biesel improves the previous model showing that the circles have to be progressively replaced by ellipses with the major axis oriented along the ground slope when the depth is taken in account. This change entails the formation of breaking waves near the beach.

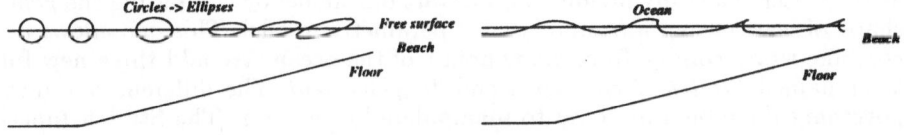

Fig. 2. From Biesel

2.2 Previous work

A first approach uses sinusoidal functions [Pea86]. With this kind of function, we get only one height per point (x, y) of sea. So this point can be stored in a height field, a matrix where are stored the different heights of the sea surface. It is not possible to simulate plunging breakers. The second type of modelization is directly based on Gerstner waves [FR86][IZ95]. Imamiya-Zang propose to use a genetic algorithm to obtain the shape of the waves. Their function simulates a breaking wave, but is limited by a lot of hypotheses. For instance, the slope of the bottom must be constant. The Fournier-Reeves model is the base of our work and will be described in the next part.

Fournier-Reeves model. [FR86] Their waves follow physical laws the most closely. The authors adapt Biesel equations to an approximation easy to compute.

The model is controlled by three factors. A scale factor K_0 determines the influence of the depth on the slope of the ellipses. K_x is an enlargement factor of the ellipse major axis. K_z is a reduction factor of the minor axis. These factors are mainly ranged from 0 to 1. β is the slope of bottom (fig 1).

$$\text{Fournier-Reeves model} \begin{cases} x = x_0 + R\cos(\alpha)S_x \sin(\Phi) + R\sin(\alpha)S_z \cos(\Phi) \\ z = z_0 - R\cos(\alpha)S_z \cos(\Phi) + R\sin(\alpha)S_x \sin(\Phi) \\ S_x = \frac{1}{1-e^{-K_x h}}, S_z = S_x(1 - e^{-K_z h}) \\ \sin(\alpha) = \sin(\beta)e^{-K_0 h} \\ \Phi = -\omega t + \sum_0^{x_0} K(x)\Delta x \\ K(x) = \frac{K_\infty}{\sqrt{\tanh(K_\infty h)}} \end{cases} \tag{4}$$

With this model, the terrain cannot have a negative bottom slope because the waves would break on the reverse wave train propagation (fig. 3 : sixth crest). It is sometimes difficult to control the function on its arrival on the beach, because it predicts that the water goes below the ground, which is impossible. This comes from the fact that the major axis tends to ∞ when h goes to 0. So manipulating each scale factor is unavoidable.

Fig. 3. A limitation of Fournier-Reeves model.

2.3 Our model

We want to create a geometric model with more intuitive parameters, that an average user can easily handle. So, we start our model by computing the general shape of waves using a comprehensive parametric model. This one allows us to combine waves coming from many points of the ocean. We add three new functions named *Stretch*, *Orientation* and *Displacement*. The different parameters governing these ones are easy to manipulate by the user. The Stretch function is used to simulate the acceleration of particles at the crest of the waves. The Orientation and Displacement functions are combined to simulate the influence of gravity. This allows us to simulate plunging breakers.

In the Fournier-Reeves model, which is the base of our model, the major axis of each ellipse tends to ∞ when $h \to 0$. So the coefficients K_0, K_x and K_z are necessary to control the general form of the wave near the coast. This becomes a problem when, in the scene, there are many types of varying depths (gentle and steep slopes).

In the Gerstner model, the circles described by the particles of water are restricted to the disc (equivalent to $R \le \frac{1}{K}$). When $R > \frac{1}{K}$, loops in the wave shape may occur, which does not occur in nature (fig 4.left). An other point is that the major axis of the ellipses becomes greater than the main disc radius. This increase simulates the beginning of plunging waves at medium depth

Fig. 4. Left : A problem with Fournier model ; Right : a limitation with our first model.

but, near the shore, the shape wave goes below the ground and the model is inoperative.

Therefore, we propose to limit the major axis of the ellipses to the disc. Since the main disc tends to 0 when h goes to 0, this modification guaranties a predictable arrival of waves on the beach.The limit shape we obtain is presented in fig 4.right.

At this step of our modelisation, two limitations appear: the amplitude of the wave decreases near the shore, and no starting plunging breakers can occur. But, we do not need to modify the parameters (K_0, K_x and K_z) to adapt the wave shape to the ground definition. We want to manipulate the wave shape by more comprehensive parameters. $K_0 = 0.1$, $K_x = 0.11$ and $K_z = 0.09$ seems to be the best values for our model. They have been choosen empiricaly after many simulations.

Stretch. In order to reproduce the Biesel laws, we propose to add an enlargement factor to our first model. This factor allows us to stretch progressively waves on the crest in the direction of the major axis while making no modification to the trough of the waves. The maximal stretch length St_{max} is chosen by the user. We use also a factor scale named K_s which determines the influence of the depth on the stretch function.

A parabolic function of phase Φ named $Stretch(\Phi, \lambda)$ is used. The trough of the sea is determined by this equation (by searching the minimum of z in the parametric equation of ellips).

$$\Phi_{min} = atan \left(\frac{\sin(\alpha)S_x}{\cos(\alpha)S_z} \right) \tag{5}$$

$$\text{Stretch}(\phi, St_{max}) = \frac{1}{\pi^2}(St_{max}\phi^2 - 2St_{max}\Phi_{min}\phi + St_{max}\Phi_{min}^2). \tag{6}$$

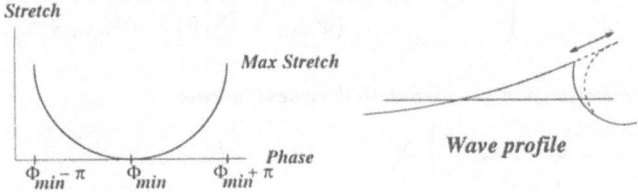

Wave stretch function

Fig. 5. A stretch function

142

Plunging waves adaptation. The stretch function is not sufficient for representing real plunging breakers. In fact, due to gravity, water falls down. So we propose to add an orientation function for crests. Our new function modifies the shape on the crest and progressively adds another stretch that decreases in the direction from the angle of the major ellipse axis to the vertical.

This orientation function (named $Orientation(\Phi)$) is combined with a progressively vertical displacement function (named $Displacement(\Phi, A)$). We limit this displacement to A in order to avoid any touching between the crest and the trough of the sea. Moreover, we use a factor scale named K_d which determines the influence of depth on the displacement function.

At the top of the crest, the particle speed is important, but just below it, this velocity is weak, so we have to reconnect to the original wave form more slowly (part 1 of the function). We decide to cut these functions in three empirical parts :

- $\Phi_{min} - \pi \le \phi < \Phi_{min} - \frac{\pi}{3}$ for the descendant part.
- $\Phi_{min} - \frac{\pi}{3} \le \phi < \Phi_{min} + \frac{7\pi}{8}$ for the trough part,
- $\Phi_{min} + \frac{7\pi}{8} \le \phi < \Phi_{min} - \pi$ for the ascendant part.

$$
Orientation(\phi, \beta) = \begin{cases}
if(\Phi_{min} - \pi \le \phi < \Phi_{min} - \frac{\pi}{3}) \Rightarrow \\
\quad \text{the equation of the line passing through} \\
\qquad (\Phi_{min} - \pi, -\frac{\pi}{4}) \ \& \ (\Phi_{min} - \frac{\pi}{3}, \beta) \\[4pt]
if(\Phi_{min} - \frac{\pi}{3} \le \phi < \Phi_{min} + \frac{7\pi}{8}) \Rightarrow \beta \\[4pt]
if(\Phi_{min} + \frac{7\pi}{8} \le \phi < \Phi_{min} + \pi) \Rightarrow \\
\quad \text{the equation of the line passing through} \\
\qquad (\Phi_{min} + \frac{7\pi}{8}, \beta) \ \& \ (\Phi_{min} + \pi, -\frac{\pi}{4}) \ .
\end{cases}
$$

$$
Displacement(\phi, A) = \begin{cases}
if(\Phi_{min} - \pi \le \phi < \Phi_{min} - \frac{\pi}{3}) \Rightarrow \\
\quad \text{the equation of the line passing through} \\
\qquad (\Phi_{min} - \pi, A) \ \& \ (\Phi_{min} - \frac{\pi}{3}, 0) \\[4pt]
if(\Phi_{min} - \frac{\pi}{3} \le \phi < \Phi_{min} + \frac{7\pi}{8}) \Rightarrow 0 \\[4pt]
if(\Phi_{min} + \frac{7\pi}{8} \le \phi < \Phi_{min} + \pi) \Rightarrow \\
\quad \text{the equation of the line passing through} \\
\qquad (\Phi_{min} + \frac{7\pi}{8}, 0) \ \& \ (\Phi_{min} + \pi, A) \ .
\end{cases}
$$

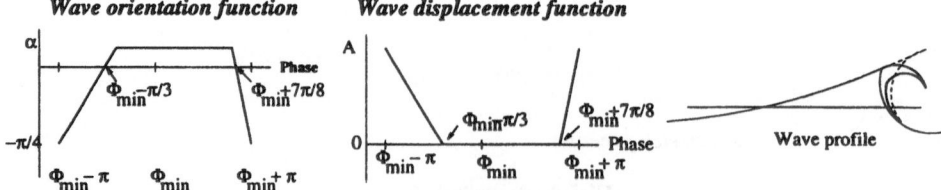

Wave orientation function *Wave displacement function*

Fig. 6. Plunging breaker.

2.4 Negative slopes.

With Fournier-Reeves model, it is not possible to use negative slopes. Indeed, with negative slopes, the waves break on the reverse wave train propagation. So, in order to avoid this problem, we limit the slope of major axis of ellipse to a positive angle.

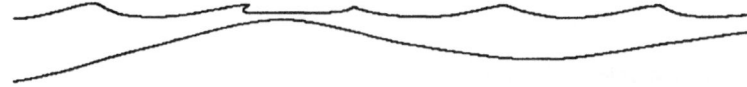

Fig. 7. Wave profile with negative slopes.

2.5 The general form of equations

$$
\begin{cases}
x = x_0 + R\tau'_\beta S_x \sin(\Phi) + R\tau_\beta S_z \cos(\Phi) + Stretch(\Phi, St_{max})\tau'_\beta e^{-K_s h} \\
\quad + Displacement(\Phi, A)\cos(Orientation(\Phi, \beta))e^{-K_d h} \\
z = z_0 - R\tau'_\beta S_z \cos(\Phi) + R\tau_\beta S_x \sin(\Phi) + Stretch(\Phi, St_{max})\tau_\beta e^{-K_s h} \\
\quad + Displacement(\Phi, A)\sin(Orientation(\Phi, \beta))e^{-K_d h}
\end{cases} \quad (7)
$$

with
$\tau_\beta = \sin(\beta)e^{-0.1h}$, $\tau'_\beta = \sqrt{1 - \tau_\beta}$ (β is the slope bottom).
$S_x = \frac{1}{1 - e^{-0.11h}}$ (Increase of major axis)
$S_z = S_x(1 - e^{-0.09h})$ (Descrease of minor axis)
$\Phi = -\omega t + \sum_0^{x_0} K(x)\Delta x$.

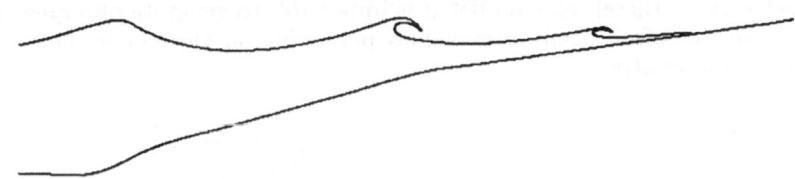

Fig. 8. An example using our model.

3 Wave trains

3.1 Principles

In order to have a complete description of the waves near the shore, we have to position the wave crest lines. The shape of a crest line depends on the form of ocean floor it passes over. Refraction of waves is the principal phenomenon of the depth effect [Kin65][Lac65] . Waves deflect, like light rays throught different media. They tend to align themselves slowly to the contour line and, by extension, to the beach. We can apply the refraction given by Descartes law to wave trains by using wave orthogonals and the velocity C_1 and C_2 of waves before and after the contour line.

$$\frac{\sin(i_1)}{C_1} = \frac{\sin(i_2)}{C_2} \qquad (8)$$

3.2 Previous work

Fournier-Reeves, Peachey. The wave trains built by these models are only formulated using the depth. They only take refraction into consideration in the (x,z) plane. But to model islands and bays, we must include refraction effects in the whole scene i.e. the (x, z) and (x, y) planes.

Ts'o, Imamiya. Wave-refraction calculation was introduced in computer graphics by Ts'o and Barsky [TB87]. Like the ray-tracing algorithm, wave-tracing launches orthogonal wave rays from the open sea along the direction of wave propagation. Descartes's law (eq. 8) is applied to calculate the deflection of the rays. These rays are embedded in uniform grid. The authors approximate the propagation of rays by the well-known Bresenham algorithm. At each point of the grid encountered, the algorithm computes the height of the wave using a 2D model as above. Imamiya follows this work [IZ95].

With this algorithm, it is possible to vizualise the refraction factors in bays and along islands. But two problems remain: the first one comes from the fact that 2 consecutive rays can diverge a lot, and so many details can be missed: it is too inaccurate to deal with bays and islands. Second, with the models derived from the Gerstner-Biesel wave model, it is impossible to generate plunging waves (in this case, we often need three values per point on the height field) : the algorithm is inoperative.

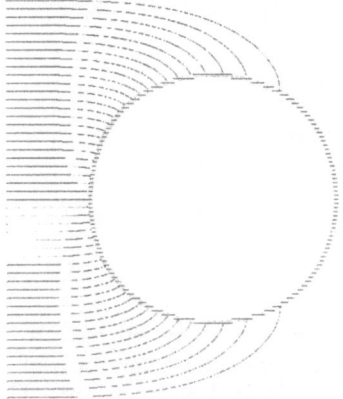 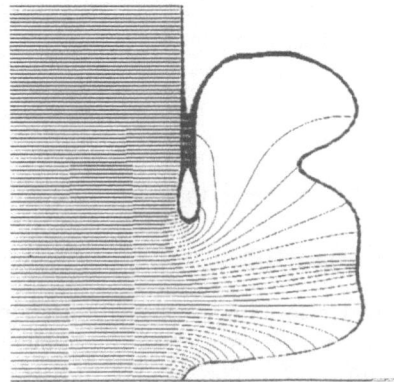

Fig. 9. Ts'o-Barsky wave tracing for an island and a bay

3.3 Our algorithm

Principles The idea of our algorithm is simple: in order to preserve the precision, when two consecutives rays diverge too much, we send a new ray between them.

This could lead to generate an infinite number of rays, each of which can have an infinite length! So, we first have to control the lifetime of rays and their appearences. When these problems are solved, it remains to define clearly the computation of the refraction and how to obtain the tesselation of the sea surface.

At the beginning of the algorithm, we create a list composed of rays that come from the open sea. These rays are separated by a same predefined distance. At each step, they progress incrementally in the scene. We compute their initial depths.

With each ray is associated a flag that can have four values : **DEAD**, **ALIVE**, **FLAT** and **AGROUND**. Their use will be detailed later.

For each ray, during the propagation, the corresponding refraction factor is computed. In order to do that, we need to compute the contour line at the current position.

Contour line calculation. The ground is described by an $m \times n$ matrix named *SEAFLOOR*. To determine the depth at any point of the scene, we use a cubic interpolation. As the bottom is not described by the different contour lines, we have to retrieve them. For each point $M(x, y)$ of the scene, we want to extract three data : the depth, the slope and the contour line. We surround the point M by an equilateral triangle. We approximate the contour line by the line passing through the 2 points on the triangle having a depth value of M.

So we can compute the refraction factor at each step of the wave tracing algorithm using equation 8. The ground is thus decomposed into a scale whole step is the step ray progression. Comparatively, in Ts'o algorithm [TB87], the scene is defined by a set of contour lines given by spline curves. This obliges the author to compute the refraction factor only when an orthogonal wave ray crosses the contour lines (fig. 10). With Ts'o-Barsky method, the distance between two sampling points is not constant. This problem implies a loss of precision.

Ray progression. Each ray progresses along the direction of refraction. We search the contour line passing through the point of calculation. We then compute the new refraction direction and propagate the ray one step. The propagation length is fixed by the user.

When a ray leaves the scene, its flag value is changed to DEAD and no further computation is associated with it. When a ray touches the beach its flag value is set to AGROUND. In this case, the ray follows the seashore. When it is between two other AGROUND rays, its flag become DEAD. This kind of ray is only useful for eventually generating new rays.

Amplitude computation. When two rays diverge, the main amplitude of the wave decreases. When two rays converge, amplitude increases. When two rays are distant by L_∞ on the open sea, for a local distance L, the local amplitude is

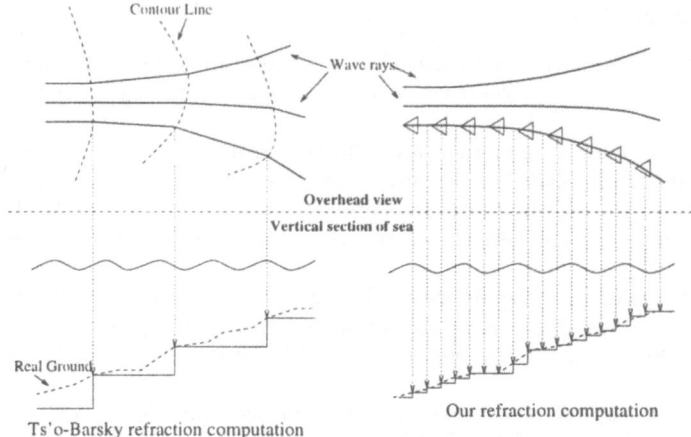

Fig. 10. Computing refraction factors with the Ts'o-Barsky and our model

$$A = A_\infty \sqrt{\frac{L}{L_\infty}} \tag{9}$$

The value of A_∞ is in fact $2 \times R_\infty$ where R_∞ is the value of R we use in our model described in the section 2.3. In the same way, A is equal to $2 \times R$.

Over-sampling. A ray is created when the distance between two rays is greater than a threshold value. The new ray is cast. Its current position is computed by interpolation between its two neighboring rays (case 1 fig. 11.Left). When a ray moves away the coast (case 2 fig. 11.Left), our algorithm creates a new ray between the coast and this ray. Since a ray flagged AGROUND, follows the shoreline, we can easily compute the distance between a ray and the coast. The creation of the ray is made by the insertion of an element in the list of rays.

When a ray is flagged DEAD, the corresponding element in the list is removed.

A ray is FLAT when its amplitude is below a given threshold. When two neighbor rays are FLAT, we do not create new rays when the distance is too large. In fact, when rays are FLAT, there are no undulations on the free surface.

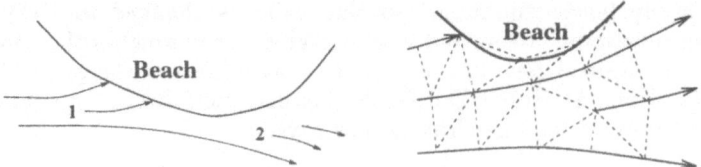

Fig. 11. Left : Two examples of oversampling, Right : Tesselation

Tesselation. After each ray propagation and oversampling, we create two or three facets between each ray position and its last position, depending on the current configuration (fig 11.Right). Facets are created between rays flagged ALIVE, FLAT or AGROUND.

Some crossover may occur between rays. In this case, the two corresponding tesselations are preserved. They will be used for the rendering.

3.4 Results

In figure 9, two different scenes have been introduced. This first one represents a bay and the second an island. In this figure, we apply the Ts'o-Barsky wave tracing.

In figure 12, we apply our dynamic wave tracing on the same scenes. Finally, a bird's eye view of the sea surface is presented in figure 13.

The bay scene is 100 meters long (x axis) and 100 meters large (y axis). We trace one ray per meter (= 100 rays) and sample along rays each 0.4 meter. New rays are created if the distance between two rays is greater than 1.2 meter. Our algorithm creates, in this scene, 209 new rays and 39097 facets to define the scene. it runs on an Onyx Silicon Graphics with R10000 processor and takes 2 seconds to compute the entire scene (Dynamic wave tracing and tesselation).

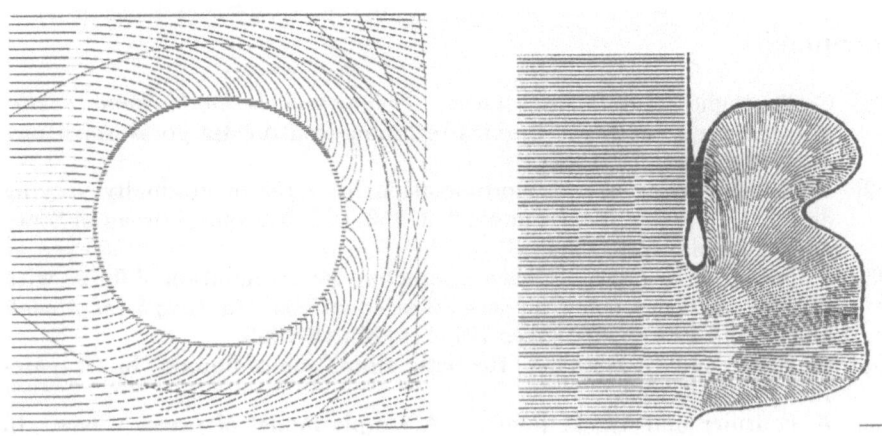

Fig. 12. Dynamic wave tracing for the example of fig. 9

4 Conclusion

In this article, we propose a combination of two algorithms based on physical considerations to modelize ocean scenes. In our model, on the one hand, the manipulation of three intuitive and quasi-independant parameters allows the user a better control on the shape of waves. On the other hand, our *Dynamic Wave Tracing* permits a modelization of more complex scenes than the different previous same type of works.

These tools are integrated in a unique software package (Plates 1-2 see Appendix) and a specific technic of rendering is in the process of elaboration and will be integrated soon.

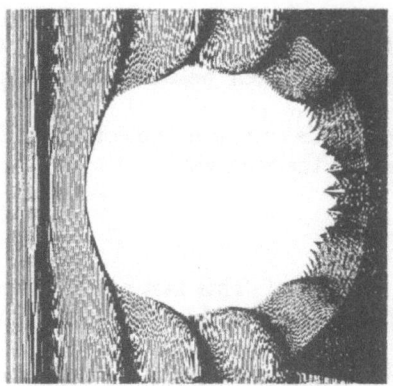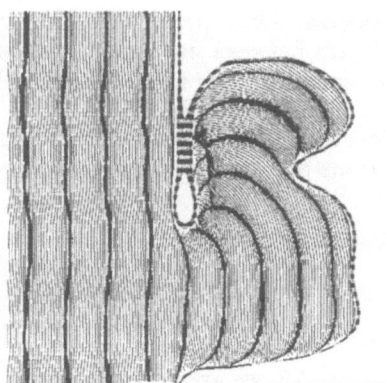

Fig. 13. A bird's eye view of the same scene

In the state of our works, we use Open Inventor for the rendering of our scenes (Plates 3-4 see Appendix).

References

[AA85] C. Aristaghes and P. Aristaghes. *Théories de la houle, houle réelle, propagation de la houle.* Service technique central des ports maritimes et voies navigables, 1985.

[Bie52] F. Biesel. Study of wave propagation in water of gradually varying depth. In *Gravity Waves*, pages 243–253. U.S. National Bureau of Standards Circular 521, 1952.

[CL95] J. Chen and N. Lobo. Toward interactive-rate simulation of fluids with moving obstacles using navier-stokes equations. In *Graphical Models and Image Processing*, pages 107–116, March 1995.

[FM96] N. Foster and D. Metaxas. Realistic animation of liquids. In *Graphics Interface '96*, 1996.

[FR86] A. Fournier and W. T. Reeves. A simple model of ocean waves. In *SIGGRAPH'86*, volume 20, pages 75–84, 1986.

[IZ95] A. Imamiya and D. Zhang. Modelling breaking ocean waves, influence of floor and refraction. In *Pacific Graphics 95*, 1995.

[Kin65] B. Kinsman. *Wind Waves, their generation and propagation on the ocean surface.* Prentice-Hall, Inc., Englewood Cliffs, New Jersey, 1965.

[KM90] M. Kass and G. Miller. Rapid, stable fluid dynamics for computer graphics. In *SIGGRAPH'90*, volume 24, 1990.

[Lac65] H. Lacombes. *Cours d'Océanographie Physique.* Gauthier-Villars, Paris, 1965.

[Pea86] D. R. Peachey. Modeling waves and surf. In *SIGGRAPH'86*, volume 20, pages 65–74, 1986.

[TB87] P. Y. Ts'o and B. A. Barsky. Modeling and rendering waves : Wave-tracing using beta-splines and reflective and refractive texture mapping. In *ACM Transactions on Graphics*, volume 6, pages 191–214, July 1987.

Practical experience in the physical animation and destruction of trees.

Hiromi Ono, Industrial Light and Magic

Abstract

Much attention has been paid to generating realistic trees and plants as part of landscapes and scenery, but little attention has been paid to their realistic motion as part of the scene. This paper describes realistic animation of trees under varying conditions of wind and collisions. The intent is not to present rigorous analysis of trees, but rather to demonstrate how practical results can often be achieved in a production environment with radically simplified "physics". Leaves, branches, and trunks of extremely complex trees have been animated, using a simplified physical model for the tree branches and leaves, and exciting them with a simulated turbulent wind field. Techniques are presented to minimize the computational cost. Techniques for realistic loss of leaves, breaking of branches, and uprooting of trees under high wind conditions are also presented.

Introduction

Real trees in real settings are not just inanimate objects. On all but the quietest, *deadest* day, trees *move* – leaves flutter, branches flex, limbs sway, and even the trunk bends. And when the wind picks up, the motion of a tree becomes dramatic indeed. Under these conditions, a tree that did not move realistically would stand out like a sore thumb.

Trees are among the most complex physical objects commonly modeled. Even a small tree can have thousands of branches and many thousands of leaves. For a large tree, this can number in the hundreds of thousands. Each of these is a mechanical element, with each element interacting with its environment and with its neighbors.

As a result, building a realistic tree is a challenge. Most study of trees in Computer Graphics to date has focused on this challenge [LINDENMAYER85]. Attention has been given to the growth process as a result of interaction with their environment [MECH96]. Only a few examples of trees animated with any detail exist [Rhythm&Hues94] [ILM96], although one commercial product has recently brought this to market [ONYX96].

As there were no tools available to us capable of handling such a large physical simulation, we constructed our own special-purpose system in C++.

In this paper, we demonstrate the simple techniques we used in this system. These techniques were loosely based on selected physical phenomena, but with an eye on visual adequacy, not physical accuracy. The goal is to produce a tree that *seems* real, without needing to control too many factors or consume too many computing resources.

This is in contrast to most papers on the topic of computer graphic trees, which have attempted to establish a flexible formalism and mathematical rigor.

This paper describes our experiences in a production environment. In making practical trees we needed to control the essential behaviors without needing to change too many parameters. We also needed it to run quickly enough to make many adjustments by trial and error, to get results suited to the scene.

In addition, in a production environment, programming time is a critical factor. Even where a more physically or mathematically rigorous approach could be made sufficiently efficient, the time available for programming for a particular scene is very short.

Creating a tree

When creating a tree, rather than use a production system, we used a recursive growth process. This seemed a more natural way to express the idea in software than production systems based on symbol replacement [LINDENMAYER85], although there is little difference in the final result.

The growth process mimics the natural growth processes, much as we later mimic the natural physical motion. In the example we present here, the trees were designed to approximately match original trees from the background plate (that were later painted out).

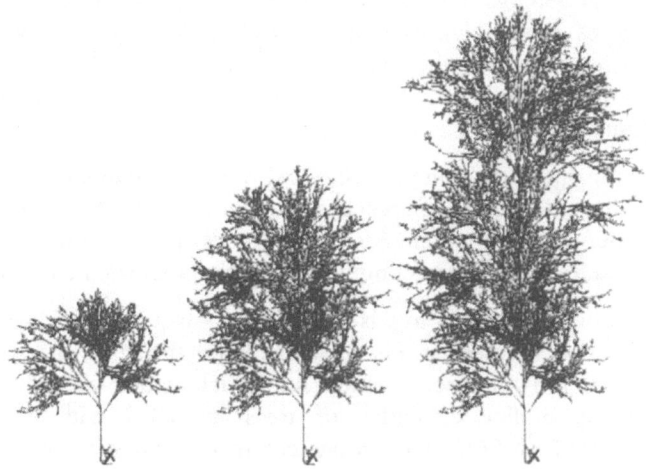

Figure 1: Tree growth (skeleton w/ Leaves)

Trees have many elements. Even a moderate size tree may have >10,000 branch segments, and >5000 leaves. Clearly this is too many to control in detail, so we must specify it algorithmically.

Physical model for animation.

To animate a tree, we use an extremely simplified physical model of a tree's mechanical properties, together with a simplified "physics", where we ignore any factors which we do not expect to be visually significant.

Physical behavior of natural trees.

The starting point for all animation (as with all visual art), is *observation*. The first thing you notice about real trees is that their motion is complex, and hard to predict visually. This complexity is typical of chaotic systems, and the turbulent wind flow is a predominant source of the complexity.

Trees respond to the wind by bending. With sufficient wind, even the largest tree will be seen to bend even at the trunk. Every part of a tree has a different stiffness, a different resonant period, and a different drag. In interacting with the wind, each part of the tree has a different response.

In addition, trees have internal friction, which damps out the motion. In addition to friction, the drag of leaves through the air as the branches move exerts a damping effect on the motion of the tree.

Simplifying assumptions.

To model the physical processes driving tree animation, we first make a number of simplifying assumptions. These assumptions allow a simpler model. As complex as trees are, we don't need to be physically accurate, but we do need to be perceptually realistic.

Most of these assumptions are not essential; they could be relaxed if needed without incurring a major cost. But taken as a whole, they result in a significantly simpler model.

- Branches have a uniform modulus of elasticity; stiffness varies with length and diameter in a uniform way.

- Leaves are of uniform size.

- The density of the tree is uniform.

- Branches move by bending, and not due to torsion.

- Forces are transmitted through sideways bending forces, and not through tension.

- Gravitational forces are roughly balanced by spring forces, and the effect of gravity on the dynamic motion is not visually significant.

- No collisions occur between branches or leaves.

- While the wind affects the tree, the tree does not modify the wind flow.

- Whenever the mechanics become complex, ignore the complexity.

152

- Linear acceleration is an adequate approximation of the motion, without considerations of angular velocity or momentum. This is perhaps our most important simplification.

Many of these assumptions are clearly untrue. For example, torsion is definitely a real factor, as can readily be seen when looking at the broken ends of limbs that have broken off.

However, much apparently twisting motion will be seen even without torsion. Branches extend out to the sides from their parents, so flexing of the child branches in a direction perpendicular to the parent's axis will produce motion around the parent's axis. The difference will only be visible if you are close enough to the join to see that the join does not rotate.

Thus, for most purposes, we can completely eliminate torsion calculations and state from the tree, and eliminate the need to calculate and propagate moments up the tree.

We go further, however. Rather than calculate moment of inertia, angular velocity and angular acceleration, we work entirely with translations orthogonal to the branch's orientation at rest. The assumption we made is that the translations and the rotations are tightly correlated, and that there is therefore little to be gained, visually, from performing the extra calculations.

These simplifications were not arrived at by starting from a formal dynamic description, and discarding parts which were expensive. We approached this from the other direction; only adding that which was needed to achieve results. The simplifications may seem less ad hoc when viewed from this perspective; the simplifications are the things we decided we didn't need to put in, not things that needed to be removed for efficiency.

The Model

Each branch segment is modeled as a flexible spring and mass. A typical branch will have several segments, each one thinner than the one below. Since the stiffness of a branch is proportional to the square of the diameter, branches become more flexible near their ends.

The diameter of branches is derived from the position in the tree. We derive this using the following recurrence relation [See Equation 1]

$$A_i = a + g\sum A_{i+1} \tag{1}$$

Where:

A_i is the cross-sectional area of the ith branch

a is the cross-sectional area of the smallest branches

g is a growth factor, relating the areas of successive generations

Intuitively, Equation 1 says that each branch has to be large enough to support all of its children. All of the children's fibers connect to the parent. The parameter g accommodates any mismatch between the generations, such as splitting. It can be regarded as a 'fudge factor' covering any discrepancy between the simple model and reality.

No doubt, a biometric survey would reveal a great deal more subtlety, but this suffices to express the tree diameters in just a couple of parameters. We viewed this as an important feature of a practical system, as our experience is that the more parameters a dynamic model has, the more time you spend looking for the right values.

We define stiffness S as the ratio of applied force Fs to the displacement d (see Equation 2). The displacement used is the displacement of the outer end of the branch

$$S = \frac{F_s}{d}$$

(2)

segment from its rest position (relative to the base).

We compute the stiffness from the modulus of elasticity for the wood of the tree. This takes into account the dimensions of the branch – thicker branches are stiffer, and

$$S = \frac{r^2}{l^2} M$$

(3)

longer ones bend more.

Where M is the modulus (defined in relative units).

In order to compute the motion, we need to compute the total wind forces plus the spring forces.

$$\Gamma_{w_i} = \sum F_{wi+1}$$

(4)

We compute the wind forces on a particular branch B as a recurrence relation. Each child pulls on its parent in some direction. In calculating the forces, we only consider the current wind force of the children. In reality, the force is a combination of bending forces transmitted laterally through the children, and tension. The branches bend, but don't stretch (wood is extremely strong in tension), so the bent branches would continue to apply forces even after the wind is removed. We simply ignore this, and aggregate all the forces as the current wind force.

A further simplification is applied in damping – we do nothing! However, there is a degree of implicit damping in the method of numerical integration we use (simply adding the acceleration * time to get velocity, and adding the velocity * time to get position, and renormalizing the length). This proved to be sufficient for our purposes, somewhat to our surprise.

These are then combined with the spring force (2) to give the acceleration as follows:

$$a_i = \frac{\left(F_{wi} + F_{s_i}\right)_i}{m} \tag{5}$$

where m is a computed value we term *effective mass*. This is perhaps closer to being a moment of inertia, but as we work with translations rather than rotations, the term "moment of inertia" would seem to be a little misleading. For each branch segment, we simply sum the effective mass for the children, and add it to the effective mass around the base of the branch segment.

$$m_{e_i} = dm + \sum m_{e_{i+1}} \tag{6}$$

Where d is the distance to the center of the segment, and m is the mass of the branch segment and m_{e_i} is the effective mass of the ith segment.

The effective mass merges the effects of the various masses in a single unified calculation. This avoids the need to calculate moments for each node, and deal with torsion. The calculation is cached, which allows us to calculate it in linear time.

Then the problem becomes one of integrating the acceleration twice to get displacement, and adding that displacement to the current offset for the branch. This displacement is then used to compute the spring force in the next round. We do the integration in nearly the simplest way possible.

The result is a displaced branch position, relative to the parent's position. What is calculated is a linear displacement; we then normalize the length back to the original length. This effectively gives us rotation around the base of the branch segment. Thus, the linear motion stands in for the angular motion as well.

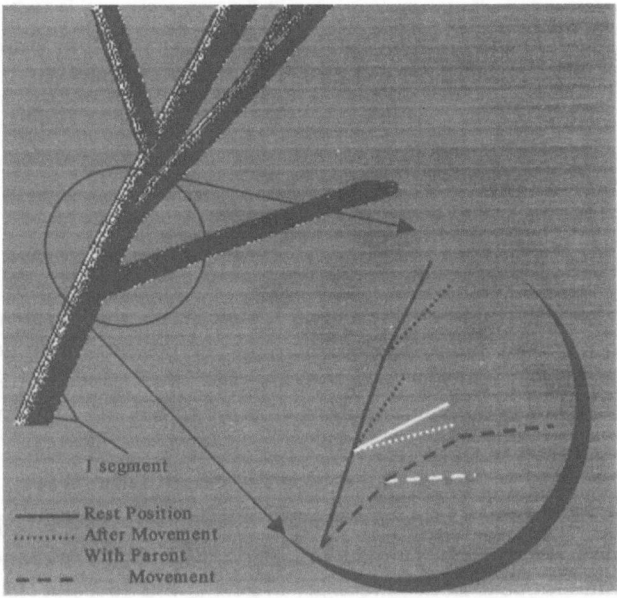

Figure 2: Branch Segmentation and Motion

The leaves are rotated randomly, rather than via any oscillatory or turbulent model. This makes sense at high motion rates compared to frame rates, as will be true in all but gentle winds. Under gentle wind conditions, in close shots this could be expected to be inadequate. In our work, we did not have gentle wind conditions, so we did not explore this.

The motion of leaves is certainly an important part of the visual gestalt of a tree, when seen from close enough to discern individual leaves or clumps of leaves.

Response to external shocks.

In addition to motion due to wind, trees respond to external shocks such as from animals, or from collisions (or other motion) of cut or broken trees or limbs. The technique we have presented so far is not suited to this, as it presumes that forces propagate toward the trunk of the tree.

However, such motions are made simpler by one overriding fact: the motions and forces involved stem from a single (or small number) of simple accelerations or forces.

This fact allows us to employ a much simpler technique. Rather than use detailed simulation of the physical forces and processes, we can treat each branch as a resonant system, excited by whatever forces or accelerations we wish to impose.

Thus, for shocks, we can simply compute a damped sinusoid. For more complex stimuli, we can convolve this response with the stimulus over some interval.

Of course, this is just the behavior you would expect from a full dynamic model. However, in [Rhythm&Hues94] we have actually used this to *dispense with* the dynamic model entirely, with good results.

This approach worked very well for trees such as pines, but we can expect that trees with large leaves might need to have the leaves animated separately based on the velocity of the branch through the air.

Turbulent wind field

We excite our trees using fractal turbulence built using the Perlin noise function [PERLIN]. The frequency range of this function must extend from much longer than the tree to much smaller than the tree. In addition to the turbulence, an (optionally) animated non-turbulent component is added, and the turbulent field is moved past the tree at the same rate.

In our simulations, we moved a fixed turbulent field past the tree. The turbulent field did not change except for translation. This is unrealistic, but proved adequate for animating a single tree or small number of trees, because a given feature is on scene for too short a time for us to notice that a given gust or lull does not change with time.

The drag force that the wind applies depends on its velocity, and the presented cross-sectional area. As a simplification, we leave out the trigonometry, and just use the total cross-sectional area.

Breaking apart the tree.

When winds are high enough, trees break apart. This process begins with leaves, weakened limbs, and eventually can result in the uprooting of the tree, or if the trunk is weakened by decay, or in extreme cases such as tornadoes, twisting off at the base.

This can be simulated nicely by comparing the total force against a threshold (which needs to vary with the size of the limb). This threshold can be varied over some probability distribution to spread out the probability of the threshold being exceeded and make it easier to control.

Once the branch or leaf has been broken off, its behavior changes. It is no longer subject to the bending forces that broke it off, and it goes into flight, subject only to aerodynamic and gravitational forces.

At this point, the branches and leaves essentially become particles in a particle system, caught up in the turbulent wind field. There is no more spring force, and the wind force now is free to act on the object as a whole.

For branches at this point, rotation becomes important, and the physical turning forces (and perhaps gravity) may be needed for good animation. This is especially likely to be true for larger branches. However, leaves can continue to be rotated randomly.

The trajectory of the tree trunk appearing in the color plates was hand-animated to meet the dramatic needs of the scene.

Performance issues

There are several performance issues that need to be addressed to avoid becoming very slow. Most important is to keep the renderer happy, by generating output that is as simple for it to work with as possible. In our case, that meant combining branch segments into larger patches wherever possible. This cuts down on the number of objects that must be rendered.

However, even though the rendering is more expensive than the animation, the animation performance is important. Motion checks done on the skeleton data are important feedback in tuning the animation.

The algorithm as presented here requires exponential time in the number of branches, as we must recurse down each branch to sum the forces and moments of inertia. For sufficiently large models, this could cause the animation to become more expensive than the rendering! This is alleviated through the use of per-branch caches for force, the position of the head of a branch, and the moment of inertia. Thus these values are only calculated once per frame, and the exponential behavior is avoided.

Once this was done, the time was dominated by the rendering time, so we did not do any rigorous performance measurements of the animation.

Our implementation does not support multiple processors. However, in our approach the tree can be partitioned beyond a certain point, and the task of computing the children's forces can be handed to separate threads. When the threads finish, the results would then be summed normally.

Conclusions

The most important conclusion to be drawn from this work is that, unlike in engineering, visually satisfying results do *not* depend on physical accuracy. This system's physics is only a rough approximation of real-world physics. It seems the eye responds more to the overall patterns and rhythms of motion than to physical accuracy.

We believe the success of the effort was due to the resulting fractal complexity of the motion, and the observable "physics-like" properties of coordinated, resonant, damped motion, distributed evenly throughout the trees. There might even be simpler ways to achieve these results involving no simulation.

There is no doubt that had tools with sufficient performance been available to us, a more accurate model could have been constructed with less work. However, we don't consider the accuracy of the model to be the most important factor in film production work; performance and ease of control are more important to successfully creating the illusion of realism.

We feel that the overall *animation* quality would stand up to closer scrutiny as a foreground element. However, there are several areas where additional work would need to be done for adequate *image* quality.

- No collision calculations are being done. If the tree were sufficiently close, this would be disturbing for the larger, closer parts.

- More sophisticated and detailed generation of the tree itself might be required. There are no detailed growth features included, such as broken branches, knotholes, bark damage, etc.

- The joins between the branches would need more detail if you're close enough to see them clearly.

- The leaf motion might need to include rotation to show a "fluttering" motion, especially for lower wind speeds!

Future Work

Leaves and branches were not subjected to torsion. This would add realism to close-ups. (We had no close-ups).

Collision handling could be improved, and an integrated user interface for controlling the parameters and seeing the results would be most helpful.

Acknowledgements

I'd like to express my thanks to Bob Kerns for helping with the preparation of this paper and serving as a sounding board as I developed these ideas.

Thanks to Industrial Light and Magic, especially Henry LaBonta and Stephan Fragmeyer, for giving me the chance to do this work even in a production environment. And to Jim Harrington wrote the library that showed me how to code tree generation in Dynamation.

And to the Twister crew, who helped to create these scenes.

References

[ILM96] 1996 Industrial Light and Magic. Movie "Twister", directed by Jan De Bont, Produced by Amblin Entertainment. Distributed by Warner Bros.

[LINDENMAYER85] A. Lindenmayer. Mathematical models for cellular interaction in development, Parts I and II. *Journal of Theoretical Biology*, 18:280-315, 1968

[MECH96] Radomir Mech and Przemyslaw Prusinkiewicz, "Visual Models of Plants Interacting With Their Environment", *Computer Graphics Proceedings*, 1996.

[ONYX96] TREE ELAS Storm, Onyx Computing, Inc., 10 Avon Street, Cambridge, MA 02138, U.S.A

159

[PERLIN85] Perlin, Ken. "An Image Synthesizer." *Computer Graphics* 19(3) (1985): 287-296.

[Rhythm&Hues94] 1994 Rhythm & Hues, Inc. Commercial for Coca Cola featuring polar bear cubs toting a Christmas Tree.

Color plates: Three frames from the movie "Twister" [ILM96] showing blowing leaves and a collision with the ground. By the last frame, few leaves remain. All the trees along the roadway are digital; the trees in the background plate they replace were hand-painted out.

Editors' Note: see Appendix, p. 201 ff. for colored figures of this paper

5

Collision processing

REACT: REal-time Adaptive Collision Testing
An *Interactive Vision* approach

Carol A. O'Sullivan   Ronan G. Reilly

University College Dublin
Trinity College Dublin
email: cosulliv@cslan.ucd.ie, Ronan.Reilly@ucd.ie

Abstract. As the demand for high levels of interaction in computer systems increases, so too does the need for real-time, interactive animation. Detecting collisions between geometrically modelled objects remains a major bottleneck in areas such as Virtual Reality (VR). In order to maintain a constant frame-rate, a trade-off between speed and accuracy is necessary. This is possible if, at each frame, potential collisions are graded by their importance to the viewer's perception. An appropriate Level Of Detail (LOD) at which to test each object may then be chosen, based on the importance of the collision in which it is involved. We adopt some ideas from an emerging area of research, Interactive Vision, and propose a scheme which uses an eye-tracking device to locate the position of the user's gaze. This, along with other perceptual criteria, may be used to choose an appropriate LOD for each colliding object at each frame, allowing the application to degrade detection accuracy where it is least likely to affect the user's perception of the collision.

1 Introduction

The demand for highly interactive computer systems is increasing rapidly, as people wish to communicate with computers in a more natural fashion. This need for interaction adds to the pressure on developers of systems to produce realistic, real-time animations. However, this high degree of interaction with the user may also be exploited, in order to adaptively improve the realism of real-time animations. In order to maintain a user's immersion in the animation, a high and constant frame rate is necessary. Realistic rendering, motion synthesis, and collision handling all place an impossibly high computational load on graphics workstations. In a scene with many moving objects, maintaining the target frame rate, while rendering each frame to the highest level of image realism, and controlling motion and interaction of objects to full accuracy is virtually impossible with single-processor work-stations.

In some applications, such as scientific simulation, fully accurate physically-based collision response is necessary. In these cases, solutions must be considered such as degrading the image realism to maintain physically-based response, or increasing the number of processors and developing parallel algorithms for tasks such as rendering and collision detection. However, in a growing number of applications, what is important is that the viewer perceive events, such as collision response, to be accurate. Testing all potentially colliding objects at full resolution is not always necessary to achieve this goal. In fact, in some cases this testing may be fully redundant, for example, if the viewer is not actually looking at the objects when they collide. The application should adapt at each frame to the perceptual capabilities of the viewer while maintaining a high and constant frame rate (e.g. 10-20 frames per second). In order to achieve this type of adaptation, some form of eye tracking will be an important component of the system.

In Section 2 of this paper, an overview of the proposed approach is given. Section 3 outlines the heuristics to be used, and Section 4 discusses collision testing issues. Section 5 offers conclusions and plans for future work.

2 Overview of approach

An approach is proposed that will maximise the realism of the collision response achieved in a target frame time (e.g. 50 milliseconds), by choosing an LOD representation for each object based on an evaluation of the perceptual importance of the collision in which that object is possibly involved. We propose to build on previous work [O'Sullivan 1996] by taking the full scene and motion complexity into account when grading collisions. Factors which affect the viewer's perception of potential collisions are also allowed for in this approach, as is the current attention focus of the viewer, by tracking their fixation location.

2.1 Previous Work

One solution to the problems of bottlenecks in real-time animation and rendering has been to throw more processing power at the problem. In [Van Reeth et al 1993], networks of transputers are used to implement parallel rendering algorithms. They claim that animation systems can be linearly expanded in performance by adding new processors. However, [Casciola and Morigi 1995] found that, although advantages are gained in the computation phase by parallel processing, display can be a bottleneck. This can sometimes degrade performance to such an extent as to make parallelization a waste of time.

Another possible solution would be to incorporate some intelligence into the system, to enable it to use processing resources more efficiently. The main research into Artificial Intelligence (AI) techniques for collision detection comes from the robotics community, where either neural nets have been trained to predict and/or avoid collisions, or heuristics were developed to do this. (See [Chande et al 1993], [Hiraga et al 1993], [Payeur et al 1994], [Tseng and Wu 1995], [Yuan 1995]).

Adaptive techniques have been proposed, where accuracy of processing is traded against speed. In [Funkhouser and Sequin 1993], a heuristic approach is used to determine the importance of objects, and to choose a suitable level of detail (LOD) to render each object at. A cost heuristic is based on polygon and pixel capacity, and the benefit is a weighted average of factors such as object size, accuracy and importance. The optimization is a version of the knapsack problem, and is incrementally and approximately solved at each frame.

[Hubbard 1995] also proposes the use of LODs, this time for collision detection. An object is approximated by various levels of sphere-trees, the lowest being a single sphere, which is subsequently refined in higher levels to provide successively tighter approximations to the object's surface. When two objects are deemed to be close to colliding, the application tests for collisions between these LODs, starting at the lowest level, and continuing to test at higher and higher resolutions until the time allotted for collision testing has expired. At this point, the testing process is terminated, and collision response is handled. What is not catered for in this approach is the fact that some collisions are less 'important' than others. No grading of potential collisions takes place. It is, however, recommended that the broad phase should be able to *"selectively ignore objects that the application temporarily designated less important" (page 229)*.

By adopting a heuristic-based approach similar to that in [Funkhouser and Sequin 1993], and combining it with an adaptive refinement approach to narrow-phase collision testing, as in [Hubbard 1995], it is possible to grade potential collisions based on their importance, and then to choose a suitable LOD for each object involved in a potential collision, or to trivially ignore or accept 'unimportant' collisions. This will allow for degradation of accuracy where it least affects the perception of the user, allowing the system to put more processing effort into more 'noticeable' collisions.

2.2 Interactive Vision

The objective of all real-time animation applications is to achieve as constant a frame rate as possible, while maintaining high visual realism. In many applications, such as VR, the accuracy of the collision detection is only important insofar as it allows believable collision response.

As an alternative to the orthodoxy they call 'Pure Vision', [Churchland et al 1995] present the idea of 'Interactive Vision'. Pure Vision theorists claim that the human visual system creates a detailed replica of the visual world, works in a strictly hierarchical fashion, and operates independently of other senses. Interactive Vision researchers draw on experimental results that suggest that other sensory systems do play a significant role in what is seen; that the brain is only approximately hierarchical; and most particularly, that the brain does not maintain a fully developed model of the world, but rather assumes the world is constant, and uses it as a type of 'external memory'. They introduce the idea of 'Visual Semiworlds', and claim:

"What we see at any given moment is a partially elaborated representation of the visual scene; only immediately relevant information is explicitly represented. ... Although unattended objects may be represented in some minimal fashion (sufficient to guide attentional shifts and eye movements, for example) they are not literally seen in the sense of 'visually experienced'." (Page 25).

We use the ideas from this area of research to identify and use some factors which influence a viewer's perception of a collision to some degree, i.e:

a) Eye movements and direction of gaze
b) Number of moving/colliding objects in scene
c) Speed at which objects are travelling
d) Size of objects
e) Visibility of intersection points
f) Input from other sensory organs, e.g. sound, touch.
g) Semantics, i.e. meaning of objects

A heuristic approach to grading collisions is proposed, similar to that described in [Funkhouser and Sequin 1993], with the benefit heuristic being a weighted combination of the above factors, and the cost heuristic being the time needed to process intersections between multi-level LOD representations. This may be expressed as a version of the Knapsack problem, and approximately optimised at each frame. LODs may in this way be chosen for each potentially colliding object to maximise benefit for a fixed cost (i.e. the target frame rate). It is not necessary to find a global minimum, as local minima are usually very good for this type of problem. As we do not have the problem of smooth progession between successive LODs at each frame which occurs with adaptive rendering techniques, the number of LODs available per object may be kept reasonably low, so that the time to find a minimum will be acceptable. However, it may be the case that the overhead of solving for a minimum may be excessive, in which case a simpler, sub-optimal solution must be considered.

2.3 Eye tracking

When viewing a still picture (or reading text), the eye picks up information in a series of fixations lasting on average about 220 msecs and interspersed with rapid jumps called saccades lasting around 20-40 msecs. During saccade, it appears that no useful information is acquired by the eye. The issue is more complicated when the eye is viewing one or more moving objects. In this case, it is the time that the eye concentrates on a particular moving object that is important, rather than the actual fixation time. The 'danger' time, from our perspective, is when the eye is distracted from one moving object and moves to view a different part of the screen. If this happens within a frame, after the eye-position has been determined and before rendering occurs, it is possible that the viewer will perceive a collision response anomaly. How likely this is to occur, and how significant its effect would be, is one of the main questions which arises. This can only be answered after fully implementing and testing the proposed system. However, certain speculations and assumptions may be made at this stage.

Let us consider an animation consisting of 1000 frames, produced at a rate of 20 per second, (i.e. 50 milliseconds per frame). We need to predict the average time the eye spends concentrating on one moving object in the animation. It seems reasonable to assume this time to be at least equal to the average fixation time while viewing a still image i.e. 220 milliseconds. We know that saccades last between 20 and 40 milliseconds. Therefore, each fixation-saccade cycle can then be estimated to last 250 milliseconds, i.e. 5 frames. In an animation consisting of 1000 frames, the 'danger time' will then occur 200 times.

On the basis of these tentative calculations, we may predict that there is a 20% likelihood at each frame that the eye will fixate in a new position. The chances that this fixation will occur where it is not expected, i.e. after position has been recorded and before rendering, are less again, while the probability that a collision is occurring at the new point of fixation exactly at that time is significantly smaller. These speculations indicate that the probability of a viewer perceiving a significant collision response anomaly is very low.

Since the turn of the century researchers have been developing systems for determining the exact location of a person's eye during picture viewing or reading. Eye tracking technology has currently reached a level where reasonably non-intrusive instruments can be used to measure fixation location with a useful level of accuracy (e.g., one degree of visual arc). There is, however, a tradeoff between accurate registration of fixation location and intrusiveness of the instrumentation required. For resolutions finer than one degree one usually needs to employ head restraints and bite bars to reduce head and body movement.

In the application being considered in this paper, a high-resolution eye tracker (AMTech ET3; horizontal resolution 2 minutes; vertical 10 minutes) will be used (see Figure 1). This may be more resolution than is required in a final system, but is nonetheless a good place to start. A high degree of accuracy in measuring eye position will be quite important while we explore the sensitivity of viewers to degradations in collision handling accuracy. The frequency at which the eye-tracking processor is polled to received the fixation location is also crucial. Ideally, this should occur once at the beginning of each frame, e.g. every 50 milliseconds. The extent to which this affects overall efficiency must be assessed and compared to the benefit gained in collision detection performance.

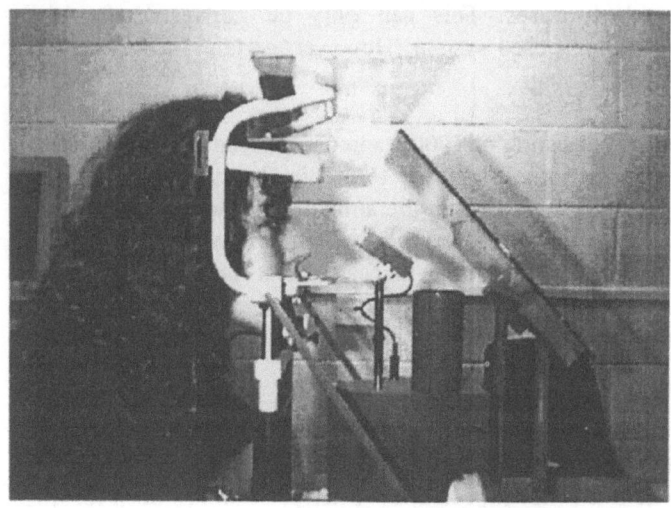

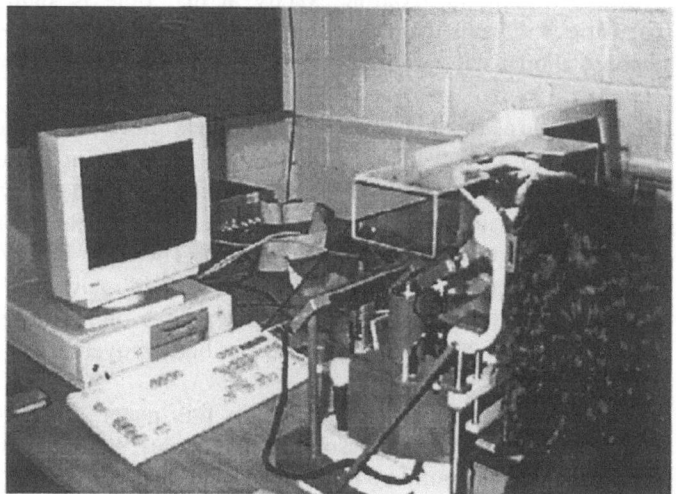

Fig. 1. The Eye-tracking hardware

3 Heuristic approach

We propose adopting an approach similar to that described in [Funkhouser and Sequin 1993], and define a collision tuple (O1, L1, O2, L2) as being a collision of object 1 at LOD 1 and object 2 at LOD 2. We can define two heuristics for these collision tuples:

Cost(O1, L1, O2, L2) which estimates the time it takes to test for collisions between the objects at those levels of detail, and

Benefit(O1,L1,O2,L2), which estimates the benefit to the overall perceived realism of the animation of that collision at those LODs.

If we define C to be the set of all collision tuples occuring in a frame, and T to be the target frame time, then we can choose a level of detail for each colliding object in that frame by:

$$\text{Maximising: } \sum_C \textbf{\textit{Benefit}}(O1,L1,O2,L2)$$

$$\text{subject to: } \sum_C \textbf{\textit{Cost}}(O1,L1,O2,L2) \leq T$$

The cost heuristic is an estimate of the time required to test both objects at those LODs for intersection. This depends on the intersection testing algorithm used, but is usually directly proportional to the number of vertices, and should be a conservative estimate. A collision testing algorithm is needed for which the processing time can be accurately estimated in advance , i.e. no worst or best time. The benefit heuristic should be based on Interactive Vision ideas, and should be a weighted sum of the factors listed above. An attempt to quantify the effect of these factors follows:

3.1 Eye movements and direction of gaze

In [McConkie 1990], an experiment is described, where viewers were asked to gaze at an image on a screen. As they allowed their eyes to roam over the display, foveating it to absorb all its detail, their eye movements were tracked. Major display changes were made during saccades which went completely unnoticed. Objects were added or removed, or their colours altered, while the viewer retained the impression that they were viewing a completely unchanging picture.

As yet, research on human visual collision detection has not involved eye movement recording. A key question is the degree to which motion discontinuities are detected at different regions of the retina, partially with what range of motion parameters are acceptable as indicating normal response from collisions, and partially with the degree to which motion discontinuities at different retinal regions grab attention. Observations have shown that collisions occuring on the periphery of subject's foveal region are perceptible at a very low resolution. Objects could be repulsed at quite a significant distance, but still be perceived by the subjects as having collided.

[Funkhouser and Sequin 1993] do not track eye movements in their adaptive display algorithm, but simply reduce the benefit of each object by an amount proportional to its distance from the middle of the screen. If an eye-tracker is used, it may detect if the viewer's eye is moving, the (x,y) location of the point of focus if the eye has rested, and the distance of the eye from the point of focus. As the above experiment has shown, as the eye is moving, major changes will go unnoticed, so the benefit of each collision may be calculated as being equal. Otherwise, the midpoint between the centres of two potentially colliding objects is calculated, and the benefit of this collision will be reduced by an amount proportional to the distance of this midpoint from the point of focus.

3.2 Number of moving/colliding objects

In [Verghese and Pelli 1992], an experiment called "find the dead fly" was devised in which subjects were first presented with a large number of moving spots, and one stationary one, and secondly with a large number of stationary spots, and one moving one. They found that increasing the number of moving objects in the former case reduced the ability of the observer to detect the stationary one by an inverse proportion, whereas in the latter case, the ability to pick out the moving object was independent of the number of stationary ones. Hence, although the time available to process each collision (and hence accuracy of response) is reduced depending on the number of colliding objects, the attention of the viewer to individual collisions is also reduced, leading to an overall decreased ability to notice response anomalies.

3.3 Speed at which objects are moving

Objects which approach each other and bounce off at high speed will appear blurred, as the viewer's eye and brain cannot process the motion in time. Hence, the benefit of a collision can be reduced by an amount proportional to the sum of the perceived relative speed of both objects involved in it.

3.4 Size of objects

The size on screen of colliding objects, measured by pixel coverage, also contributes to how noticeable a collision is. Hence, the benefit of a collision can be increased by an amount proportional to the sum of the screen sizes of the objects involved in it.

3.5 Visibility of intersection points

Further observations have shown that even if a subject is looking directly at colliding objects, if the potential points of collision are obscured, they cannot tell if the colliding objects have actually touched or not. This is particularly true for objects which approach each other along paths almost coinciding with the users direction of gaze. This is the case for quite significant gaps of repulsion. However, if the collision points are on the visible silhouette of both objects, and the objects are approaching each other along paths almost perpendicular to the users direction of gaze, the subject's perception of the collision is extremely acute. This indicates that the benefit of a collision should be reduced by an amount proportional to the angle that the vector between the centres of the objects makes with the view-plane. It also implies the need for very accurate collision tests on the visible silhouettes of objects, less accurate tests on visible interior faces, and very approximate tests on occluded back faces.

3.6 Input from other sensory organs, e.g. sound, touch

[Churchland et al 1995] describe subjective motion experiments which show that adding auditory stimuli affects the way in which subjects 'see' events. First they showed a blinking dot and a shaded square, and subjects perceived no motion. Then they added a tone to the left ear whenever the dot blinked on, and to the right ear when it blinked off. This led to subjects perceiving the dot as moving in and out behind the shaded square.

Undergraduate students in our laboratory have incorporated sound and colour changes (e.g. colliding objects flashing bright red and beeping) into a very basic collision response handling system for their animation projects. This increases the realism of collisions, convincing the viewer that a collision has occurred, even when the collision detection is not completely accurate. This need not, however, be taken into account as part of the benefit heuristic, but simply noted as a useful device to increase the realism of a collision

3.7 Semantics

[Churchland et al 1995] introduce the concept that animals and humans have a 'relevant to my lifestyle' model of the world, as opposed to a 'world with all its perceptual possibilities'. They claim that the purpose of visual perception is to: *"facilitate the organisms thriving at the four Fs: feeding, fighting, fleeing and reproduction" (Page 25)*. Hence, it could be claimed that people only 'see' things in detail which are relevant to the task that they are currently involved in.

Some objects in the animation may have a more important "meaning" to the user than others. For example, in an interactive football game, the ball will be the most important object, and collisions between it, the players, and the goal-posts will be much more attended than say collisions between the players themselves. These 'importance ratings' can be set by the application, and the benefit of each collision should be increased by an amount proportional to the sum of the importance of both colliding objects.

4 Collision testing

Hybrid collision detection is a term used by [Kitamura et al 1994] to refer to collision detection methods which first perform approximate tests to identify interfering objects in the entire workspace and then perform more accurate tests to identify the object parts causing interference. [Hubbard 1995] and [Cohen et al 1995] both propose hybrid algorithms for collision detection. Hubbard calls the two phases of the algorithm the "broad phase", where approximate intersections are detected, and the "narrow phase", where exact collision detection is performed. [Palmer and Grimsdale 1995] proposes an algorithm with three stages, the first stage using bounding volumes, the second stage using sphere-trees to approximate an object's geometry, and the third stage performing very accurate polygon intersection tests. As in previous work [O'Sullivan 1996] a Hybrid Algorithm is proposed, which first runs a Broad Phase, testing for approximate collisions between all pairs of objects, grades them by importance, and then triggers a Narrow Phase, performing more accurate tests only on pairs of objects between which approximate collisions have been detected.

The strategy of projecting higher dimensional objects onto a lower dimension, and testing for intersections between these projections has been used by [Cohen et al 1995] , [Shinya and Forgue 1995], [Thalmann and Volino 1996] and [O'Sullivan 1996] among others. This approach is advantageous for the following reasons:

- Dimension reduction: the dimension in which manipulations are performed is reduced by 1, making it simpler to implement
- Robustness: because of the limited use of topological information, i.e. not many different special cases.

The down-side of using dimension-reduction techniques is loss of information, especially if used in the narrow phase. However, the purpose of this research is not to develop a highly accurate collision detection routine, which always produces the actual points of collision. If two objects are so close to each other as to look to the viewer as if they were colliding, this can usually be taken to be a collision. A dimension-reduction approach is proposed for both phases of the collision detection algorithm: A Broad Phase which culminates in the "grading" of the approximate collisions detected, and the selection of LODs for each object involved in these collisions, and a narrow phase which tests for intersection between these objects at the chosen LODs. The narrow phase should be such that it is possible to accurately predict the time needed to perform testing.

Trading speed for accuracy will give rise to anomalies which will be of one of the following types: 1) Missed collisions, i.e. collisions which occur and go undetected, or 2) non-existent collisions, i.e. collisions which have not occurred but are nevertheless detected. Either one or the other anomaly must be accepted - but which one? Which is most noticeable, or most disturbing for the user?

The choice of accepted anomaly determines the type of LOD representation to be used for objects. If anomalies of type 1 are to be avoided, i.e. no collisions should go undetected, a superset of all collisions must be detected. In this case, each LOD representation of an object should totally enclose the object. Hence LOD generation should start with the lowest LOD being a loose boundary of the object, which is refined to produce closer and closer approximations to the boundary of the object. The higher the level of detail, the less likely that non-existent collisions will be detected. Sphere-trees [Hubbard 1995] provide this type of conservative approximation, as do Oriented Bounding Box (OBB) trees, described by [Gottschalk et al 1996].

If, however, collisions which have not occurred should never be mistakenly detected, i.e. type 2 anomalies should be avoided, only a subset of all collisions can be detected. Therefore, LOD generation should start with the most accurate representation of the object, and lose detail gradually, preserving local features, but losing more of the global nature of the object. The higher the level of detail, the lower the chance of missing a collision.

5 Conclusions and Future work

An approach has been described in this paper, which proposes an adaptive collision detection algorithm that allows degradation of detection accuracy where it least affects the perception of the viewer. In this way, maximum realism should be attained within a target frame time. The proposed approach could be applied not only to the collision detection problem, but to any kind of multiresolution problem in real-time animation systems.

The major issues involved in the proposed approach have been discussed, and some informal investigations into its feasibility have been described. We now intend to rigorously test all the perceptual criteria proposed, in order to assess their impact. The eye tracker described in section 2 will be central to these investigations. This is necessary to enable us to quantify each of the factors discussed in section 3, in order to schedule the accuracy of the collision test for each object pair. Once these factors have been quantified, implementation and testing may occur, and the benefit of the proposed approach may be measured. At the moment, the proposed technique is valid for only one viewer. Whether the ideas proposed can be adapted to cater for multiple viewers is another area worthy of further investigation.

Hardware constraints must also be considered. The equipment described in section 2 is quite intrusive. The viewer's head is kept immobile with the use of supports and bite bars (not unlike some mediaeval instruments of torture). However, we are not suggesting that this be adopted as the method of eye-tracking in interactive animation systems such as VR. What we do wish to establish is that eye-movement tracking can be used to improve the perception of computer-generated animations. The high resolution offered by the intrusive equipment will be invaluable in assessing this. Once the principle has been established, more non-intrusive methods can be considered, as can issues relating to the compatibility of eye-trackers and other viewing systems such as Head Mounted Displays (HMD).

References:

[Casciola and Morigi 1995] G. Casciola, S. Morigi. "Graphics in parallel computation for rendering 3D modelled scenes." *In Parallel Computing* Vol.21 Pages 1365-82, Aug.1995.

[Chande et al 1993] P.K.Chande, M.Shrivastava, G.N.Sharma. "Neural Assisted Robot Arm Collision Avoidance." in *SICE 93 Proc. of the 32nd SICE Ann. Conf. Inter. Sess.* Kanusawa, Japan. Pages 1547-1550, Aug. 1993.

[Churchland et al 1995] P.S.Churchland, V.S.Ramachandran, T.j.Sejnowski. "A Critique of Pure Vision" in eds.C.Koch, J.L.Davis *Large-Scale Neuronal Theories of the Brain,* MIT press, 1995.

[Cohen et al 1995] J.D.Cohen, M.C.Lin, D. Manocha, M.K.Ponamgi, "I-COLLIDE: An Interactive and Exact Collision Detection System for Large-Scale Environments" in *Proc. 1995 Symp. Interactive 3D graphics,* Monterey, Calif. pages 189-196, 1995.

[Funkhouser and Sequin 1993] T.A.Funkhouser, C.H.Sequin. "Adaptive Display Algorithm for Interactive Frame Rates During Visualization of Complex Virtual Environments." in *ACM SIGGRAPH 93,* Annaheim, Calif. published as Computer Graphics, Annual Conference Series, 1993. Pages 247-254. Aug. 1993.

[Gottschalk et al 1996] S.Gottschalk, M.C.Lin, D.Manocha. "OBB-Tree: A Hierarchical Structure for Rapid Interference Detection." To appear in *Proc. of ACM Siggraph '96.* 1996.

[Hiraga et al 1993] I.Hiraga, T,Furuhashi, Y. Uchikawa, S.Nakayama. "Knowledge Acquisition for Collision Avoidance Using Fuzzy Neural Networks". in *IJCNN 93 Proc. of the 1993 Int. Joint Conf. on Neural Networks,* Nayoya, Japan. Vol.1. Pages 673-6. Oct. 1993.

[Hubbard 1995] Philip M.Hubbard. "Collision Detection for Interactive graphics applications." In *IEEE Transactions on Visualization and Computer Graphics,* Vol. 1, No. 3 pages 218-230

[McConkie 1990] G.W.McConkie "Where vision and congnition meet". *Paper presented at the HFSP Workshop on Object and Scene Perception,* Leuven, Belgium. 1990.

[Kitamura et al 1994] Y.Kitamura, H.Takemura, N.Ahuja, F.Kishino. "Efficient Collision Detection Among Objects in Arbitrary Motion Using Multiple Shape Representations". in *Proc.12th IAPR Int. Conf. on Pattern Recognition,* Jerusalem. Vol.1. Pages 390-6. Dec.1994.

[O'Sullivan 1996] C.A.O'Sullivan. "Real-time Collision Detection for Computer Graphics." *M.Sc dissertation.* Dublin City University. Oct.1996.

[Palmer and Grimsdale 1995] I.J.Palmer, R.L.Grimsdale. "Collision Detection for Animation using Sphere-Trees." in *Computer Graphics Forum.* Vol.14. Pages 105-16. June 1995.

[Payeur et al 1994] P.Payeur. H.Le-Huy, C.Gosselin. "Robot Path Planning Using Neural Networks and Fuzzy Logic." in *IECON 94 Int. Conf. on Ind. Electronics, Control and Inst.* Bologna. Vol.2. Pages 800-5. Sept. 1994.

[Shinya and Forgue 1995] M.Shinya, M.Forgue. "Laying out objects with geometric and physical constraints." in *Visual Computer*. Vol.11, pages 188-201, 1995

[Thalmann and Volino 1996] N.M.Thalmann and P.Volino. "Sculpting, Clothing and Hairdressing our Virtual Humans" in eds N.M.Thalmann, D.Thalmann *Interactive Computer Animation* Prentice Hall, 1996.

[Tseng and Wu 1995] C.Tseng, C.Wu. "Collision Detection for Multiple Robot Manipulators by using Orthogonal Neural Networks." in *Journal of Robotic Systems*, Vol.12 Pages 479-90.1995.

[Van-Reeth et al 1993] F.Van Reeth, E. Flerackers, W. Lamotte. "Animating architectural scenes utilizing parallel processing." in *Visualization and Intelligent Design in Engineering and Architecture*, Southampton. Pages 149-64, Apr. 1996.

[Verghese and Pelli 1992] Verghese,P. and Pelli,D.G. "The information capacity of visual attention", in Vision Research, Vol 32, Pages 983-95, 1992.

[Yuan 1995] J.Yuan. "A Neural Network Measuring the Intersection of m-dimensional Convex Polyhedra." in *Automatica*. Vol.31. Pages 517-29. April 1995.

Collision and self-collision handling in cloth model dedicated to design garments

Xavier PROVOT

Institut National de Recherche en Informatique et Automatique (INRIA)

B.P. 105, 78153 Le Chesnay Cedex, France

Xavier.Provot@inria.fr

Abstract

This article presents a method for collision handling applied to the semi-rigid mass-spring cloth model formerly described in [Pro95].

This method deals with the four main difficulties encountered in collision handling. The first is collision detection. The second is optimization of collision detection, which is otherwise excessively time consuming. The third is collision response. The fourth is conservation of collision consistency. The latter is discussed in detail, and related to cases of interfering multiple collisions. An original method for computation of collision response in this case of multiple collisions is presented, providing a robust conservation of collision consistency.

Results obtained with this approach, in the case of building real garments on a mannequin, are presented and validate our cloth model and collision handling method.

Introduction

Collision handling was first considered in the case of colliding *rigid* objects [MW88, Bar90]. However, cloth animation required the study of the more general case of collisions between deformable surfaces. Cloth models, like our semi-rigid mass-spring model [Pro95], describe the inherent mechanical behavior of the matter of woven fabrics, when submitted to forces of various nature. However, they do not include forces designed to avoid collisions as in [TPBF87] or in [LMTT91]. More generally, it does not tackle the problem of *contact*.

The phenomenon of contact is of a completely different nature from internal mechanical behavior, and it is natural to handle it with a different method. In [CYMTT92], a new method inspired from "inverse dynamics" methods is proposed for collision response computation. This method applies the macroscopic Coulombian laws of friction to the case of a cloth model. This is much more adapted than using an artificial repulsing force. It is also later used in [LKC96].

But in order to handle collision response, the colliding elements of the meshes of the colliding objects must be detected. The main problem of this collision detection is that it requires a very important computation time.

There are different ways to carry out this collision detection, so as to reduce computation time. Some methods can just locate *at each iteration* the regions where meshes interpenetrate, and then modify these regions so that interpenetration is avoided, as in [VMT94]. The advantage is that really fast algorithms can be implemented in this case. The drawback is that if objects have a very high velocity and if the time-step is too large, some objects may cross each other completely while no collision will have been detected.

Another way is to detect whether collisions occur or not *during each time-step interval*, as in [LMTT91, LKC96]. This is more time-consuming but more accurate. Optimizations are however possible, and some are presented in this article.

Finally, another problem of collision handling is that methods always consider *individual* collisions between two elements of the meshes implied. They do not handle all simultaneous collisions as a whole. As explained in this article, this leads to collision inconsistency, *i.e.* collision detection and response computation as described above does not succeed in avoiding all interpenetration. This is not only due to numerical inaccuracies (as explained in [VMT95]), but also to the fact that multiple collisions may interfere with each other, and the individual treatment of these collisions is not sufficient to solve them, as will be detailed later.

However, Volino *et al* [VMT95, VCMT95] propose an interesting and efficient method for solving this collision consistency problem. This present article presents an alternative method, which circumscribes zones where these multiple interfering collisions occur, and handle them in a specific way to solve completely the collision response problem.

This paper will be structured as follows: we will first present our collision detection method, then the optimizations of this detection, we will explain how we tackle the simple collision response problem, and finally the multiple collision response problem, in order to keep collision consistency.

1   Collision detection

The general case of collision handling is the one involving a cloth object and another moving object of the scene. A particular case is the case of self-collisions, *i.e.* collisions of the deformable cloth object with itself. Regarding both detection and response, both cases are basically handled in the same way, the only difference lies in the optimization of self-collision detection described in 2.2. Therefore, in this section we will not make any difference between self-collision and collision between two different objects. Also, we will only deal in this paper with objects represented by a set of triangles.

Let t_0 be an instant when there is no interpenetration between the cloth and the object. Consider a time interval $[t_0, t_0 + \Delta t]$. Knowing the positions and velocities of each node of our model at time t_0, it is possible to compute its position at time $t_0 + \Delta t$. Collision detection then consists in finding out if one or more collisions occurred during this interval.

These collisions can be of two types:

- either a node of one of the mesh went through a triangle of the other mesh ("point-triangle" collision);

- or the edge of a triangle of one of the mesh went through another edge of the other mesh ("edge-edge" collision).

Note that the numerical integration used in our model is the explicit Euler method (see [Pro95] for more details). The approximation of this integration is that, during the interval $[t_0, t_0 + \Delta t]$, each node moves at a *constant* velocity. This feature is very important for our collision detection method.

1.1 "Point-triangle" collision

Let $P(t)$ be the moving point, and $A(t)$, $B(t)$, $C(t)$ the vertices of the moving triangle. Let also $\overrightarrow{V}$, $\overrightarrow{V}_A$, $\overrightarrow{V}_B$, $\overrightarrow{V}_C$ be their respective constant velocities during $[t_0, t_0 + \Delta t]$. We have of course: $A(t) = A(t_0) + t\overrightarrow{V}_A$, $B(t) = B(t_0) + t\overrightarrow{V}_B$, $C(t) = C(t_0) + t\overrightarrow{V}_C$.

If there is collision, then the point $P(t)$ will belong to the triangle $ABC(t)$. This can be written using the following relation:

$$\exists\, t \in [t_0, t_0 + \Delta t] \text{ such that}$$
$$\exists u, v \in [0, 1],\ u + v \leq 1,\ \overrightarrow{AP}(t) = u\overrightarrow{AB}(t) + v\overrightarrow{AC}(t) \tag{1}$$

Unfortunately, this vectorial equation yields a *non linear* system of equations. In order to solve this system, another condition expressing that point P belongs to ABC can be used. Indeed, since the vectorial product $\overrightarrow{N}(t) = \overrightarrow{AB}(t) \wedge \overrightarrow{AC}(t)$ is perpendicular to the plane of triangle ABC, the following relation will be satisfied at the time of collision:

$$\overrightarrow{AP}(t) \cdot \overrightarrow{N}(t) = 0$$

This new relation is necessary, though *not sufficient*: it only means that A, B, C and P are coplanar. It is nevertheless useful since it allows the determination of collision time t in a straightforward way. $\overrightarrow{N}(t)$ is a t^2 term, $\overrightarrow{AP}(t)$ is a t term, and their dot product yields therefore a third degree equation that can be solved easily. Three values of t can yet be obtained, among which only those belonging to the interval $[t_0, t_0 + \Delta t]$ can correspond to a collision.

In order to check whether these values of t really correspond to a collision, and not only to coplanarities, they are injected back in equation 1 — which then becomes a *linear* system —.

If several values of (t, u, v) are solutions to the system, the only collision that we must consider is the one that occurred the soonest, *i.e.* the one corresponding to the smallest value of t.

1.2 "Edge-edge" collision

What is concerned here is the detection of a collision, during interval $[t_0, t_0 + \Delta t]$, between an edge of the cloth and an edge of the moving object.

Let $AB(t)$ be the first edge and $CD(t)$ be the other one. This time, there will be collision if and only if:

$$\exists\, t \in [t_0, t_0 + \Delta t] \text{ so that} \\ \exists u, v \in [0, 1],\ u\overrightarrow{AB}(t) = v\overrightarrow{CD}(t) \tag{2}$$

Like before, this leads us to a non linear system. Another relation can nevertheless be used once more in order to find out the value of t without solving the general system above. At the time of collision indeed, the four point A, B, C, D will also lie in a same plane, which can be written:

$$(\overrightarrow{AB}(t) \wedge \overrightarrow{CD}(t)) \cdot \overrightarrow{AC}(t) = 0 \tag{3}$$

This relation yields once again a third degree equation, and allows to compute u and v after having injected t in equation 2. It can thus be detected whether a collision occurred or not.

2 Collision detection optimization

2.1 Bounding boxes hierarchy

Collision handling, and especially collision detection, is the most time-consuming part in cloth animation. Indeed, the collision detection between a cloth model with N mass points and an object of the scene with M nodes has a $\mathcal{O}(MN)$ complexity. The self-collision detection has a $\mathcal{O}(N^2)$ complexity. As soon as we must deal with significantly discretized meshes, this complexity becomes very limitative, and there is a need to reduce it.

We implemented a first simple optimization which consists in dividing the piece of fabric recursively in zones imbricating with each other. The criterion for this recursive partitioning of the triangles of the cloth object is their position in the 2D texture space. At each iteration, a bounding box of these zones can be computed. Then, the collision detection algorithm can be significantly improved by parsing the bounding box tree while eliminating rapidly collisions tests between elements that belong to two zones whose bounding boxes do not intersect. In order to be accurate, the bounding box of each zone does not only bound the position of the zone at iteration $t_0 + \Delta t$, but both its positions at t_0 and $t_0 + \Delta t$.

2.2 Surface curvature and self-collision detection

In the case of self-collision detection, another optimization, inspired from [VMT94], has been implemented.

This optimization is based on the following property: when a given zone (provided it is connex[1]) has a sufficiently "low curvature", it cannot self-intersect, and all the zones it includes do not intersect with each other.

Figure 1: Cone including normals to triangles of a zone of the cloth surface.

The "curvature" of a zone will be in our case evaluated by the set of normals of the triangle belonging to the zone (figure 1). We compute a cone which includes these normals, and the angle α at its vertex is sufficient to build a test that discriminates zones that cannot self-intersect and zones that may: if $\alpha < \pi$, the zone *cannot* self-intersect.

Cones are computed using the hierarchical tree described in previous section (the tree is therefore *not reconstructed* at each time step).

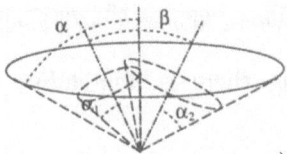

Figure 2: Cone (angle α) enclosing its two "descendant" cones in the hierarchical tree (angles α_1 and α_2).

At the bottom of the tree, each leaf node has a single normal, and therefore $\alpha = 0$, the axis vector of the cone is the normal of the triangle. Then for each tree node for which the cones of its two descendants are known, the cone is computed using the two angles of the descendant cones, α_1 and α_2, and the angle β between the two axes of the descendant cones. The axis vector is computed as the mean vector of the two axis vectors of the descendant cones. The new angle α is then computed as: $\alpha = \beta/2 + \max(\alpha_1, \alpha_2)$ (figure 2).

This is of course only valid if the two descendant zones of each node are *adjacent*. The hierarchical tree described in section 4.4 verifies this property in most cases. Cases of non-adjacency would only occur if the 2D contour of the cloth object were severely non-convex. It never happened in our simulations, even when modeling clothes using real clothes patterns (see section 4.4).

With this technique, it is possible to avoid unnecessary self-collision tests in whole branches of the tree provided they correspond to a zone with

---

[1] As mentioned in [VMT94], this condition is theoretically not sufficient. It always has been sufficient in practice in the cases we needed to model.

a sufficiently low curvature. At the beginning of an animation for instance, if the piece of cloth is almost flat, no self-collision tests are computed at all.

3 Collision response

3.1 Contact and friction

When two objects collide, there is a time at which they are in *contact*[2]. General macroscopic laws of *friction* describe the forces that are applied to each of the objects when they are in contact. These Coulombian laws can be written as follows.

Consider a mass point P in contact with a motionless rigid surface, at a point H of this surface. Let $\overrightarrow{N}$ be a unit normal of the surface at point H. Let $\overrightarrow{F}$ be the force applied to P in order to keep the contact. Let $\overrightarrow{F}_N = (\overrightarrow{F} \cdot \overrightarrow{N})\overrightarrow{N}$ be the component of $\overrightarrow{F}$ perpendicular to the surface and $\overrightarrow{F}_T = \overrightarrow{F} - \overrightarrow{F}_N$ its tangential component.

The laws of friction are:

- if $\|\overrightarrow{F}_T\| \geq k_f \|\overrightarrow{F}_N\|$, there is sliding contact, with friction, *i.e.* the point moves parallel to the surface, under the action of a force $\overrightarrow{F}_s = \overrightarrow{F}_T - k_f \|\overrightarrow{F}_N\| \overrightarrow{u}_T$, where $\overrightarrow{u}_T = \overrightarrow{F}_T / \|\overrightarrow{F}_T\|$;

- if $\|\overrightarrow{F}_T\| < k_f \|\overrightarrow{F}_N\|$, there is *non-sliding* contact, the point remains motionless, $\overrightarrow{F}_s = 0$.

k_f is called the *friction coefficient* $(k_f \in \mathbf{R}^+)$. Note that if $k_f = 0$, there is sliding with *no friction*, and if $k_f = \infty$, there is necessarily no sliding at all. This coefficient is characteristic of the fabric's friction behavior. It has to be specified with its other characteristics (stiffness, elongation rate, it etc.).

In our model, these macroscopic laws of contact are adapted to the situation of collisions. They can indeed not be applied as such in a straightforward way, since the situation of contact occurs during an *infinitely small* time interval. This situation is at the limit of validity of Coulombian friction laws.

Consider a "point-triangle" collision where the triangle is motionless. The force generated by the impact of the point on the triangle (and *vice-versa*) is an unknown. Only the velocity $\overrightarrow{v}$ of the point *before the shock* is known. If $\overrightarrow{v}'$ is its velocity *after the shock*, then the acceleration of the point during $[t_0, t_0 + \Delta t]$ could approximated to $(\overrightarrow{v}' - \overrightarrow{v})/\Delta t$, and the force applied to this point by the triangle to $\overrightarrow{F}_c = \mu(\overrightarrow{v}' - \overrightarrow{v})/\Delta t$. But the thing is that $\overrightarrow{v}'$ is precisely what we have to determine, and is therefore also an unknown.

In order to solve this problem, we need to make an approximation so that the force generated by the impact can be evaluated. This approximation consists in considering that the forces implied are proportional to velocities, since it is obvious that the greater the impact velocity, the greater the force generated.

---

[2]We will consider in this section that the collision is *perfectly inelastic*, *i.e.* that there is no "bouncing" effect.

Whatever the coefficient of proportionality, the laws of friction described above can then be exactly rewritten by replacing $\vec{F}$ with $\vec{v}$ and $\vec{F}_s$ by $\vec{v}'$.

These relations therefore give us the velocity of the point *right after collision* against the triangle. Since the velocity of the point should be constant during $[t_0, t_0 + \Delta t]$, the algorithm simply replaces the velocity $\vec{v}$ of the point during the interval by $\vec{v}'$ and computes the corresponding trajectory from $P(t_0)$ to $P(t_0 + \Delta t)$. This is actually equivalent to considering that the collision precisely takes place at t_0, whatever the collision time $t \in [t_0, t_0 + \Delta t]$ that had been computed in the collision detection process.

3.2 Impact and dissipation

Another phenomenon during a collision is *impact* (in opposition to contact) and the collateral "bouncing" effect. During an "elastic" collision, there is no dissipation of energy at all. During an "inelastic" collision, there is such a dissipation, and a "perfectly inelastic" collision is a collision where the entire energy is dissipated.

This can be expressed with simple empirical relations. With the same notations as before, the velocity of the point P colliding the motionless triangle becomes after the shock: $\vec{v}' = \vec{v}_T - k_d \vec{v}_N$, where k_d is the dissipation coefficient ($0 \leq k_d \leq 1$). This coefficient is also part of the mechanical characteristics of the fabric.

3.3 Total response

In the general case, the velocity $\vec{v} = \vec{v}_T + \vec{v}_N$ of a point P before its collision with a motionless object therefore becomes after the collision:

$$\begin{cases} \text{If } \|\vec{v}_T\| \geq k_f \|\vec{v}_N\|, & \vec{v}' = \vec{v}_T - k_f \|\vec{v}_N\| \dfrac{\vec{v}_T}{\|\vec{v}_T\|} - k_d \vec{v}_N \\ \text{If } \|\vec{v}_T\| < k_f \|\vec{v}_N\|, & \vec{v}' = -k_d \vec{v}_N \end{cases} \tag{4}$$

In the case of moving objects, these relations are only applied to velocities once computed *in a reference frame moving at the velocity of the center of mass* of the object. In the case of self-collisions, the velocities are computed in a reference frame moving at the velocity of the center of mass of all elements involved in the collision (the point and the triangle, or the two edges).

In order to decompose the initial velocity of each mass point between its normal and tangential components, the normal used is the normal of the triangle at time t_0 in the case of a "point-triangle" collision. In the case of an "edge-edge" collision, the normal chosen is the result of the vectorial product of the two edges.

4 Consistency of multiple collisions

4.1 Multiple collisions

The collision handling algorithm presented so far is in fact insufficient for avoiding every case of self-penetration during a cloth animation. This collision algorithm indeed tackles only the problem of collisions between a *couple* of two elements, point and triangle, or edge and edge. These collisions are handled independently from each other, whereas in fact more than two of these elements may interfere with each other during a collision, over a time-step $[t_0, t_0 + \Delta t]$. Each computation of a collision modifies the positions of the points it involves, and it *also* modifies therefore the position of *all* the triangles and edges linked to these points, not only the ones directly involved in the collision. But nothing guarantees that these modifications did not create any other unpredicted collisions ... If this is the case, we will say that there are *multiple collisions*.

An interesting method for maintaining collision consistency can be found in [VMT95]. Our alternative method is based on the determination of the zones where these multiple collisions appear, and on handling their collisions specifically, with a new hypothesis of collision.

4.2 Determination of a "zone of impact"

The collision handling algorithm basically involves the position of the cloth model at time t_0 and its position at $t_0 + \Delta t$. Once collisions are handled, the computation of collision response has altered the position of the cloth at time $t_0 + \Delta t$.

In order to find out whether this computation has created new collision situations, a first thing to do can be to carry out one more collision detection. If the result of this detection is that there is no new collision, the algorithm can switch to the next time-step. If on the contrary new cases of collision appeared, it could also be possible to carry out another collision response computation, and then iterate. However, this iterative method is not guaranteed to converge.

The first phase of our method will be therefore to circumscribe all the points of the mesh that are involved in multiple interfering collisions. The iterative method described above will be used, with the aim to memorize at each iteration the set of points that are "linked", either because they take part in a *same* "point-triangle" or "edge-edge" collision, or because they take part in *two* different collisions that involve one or more points in common.

At each iteration, these sets of points, that we will name *zones of impact*, are likely to grow when new collision situations appear (see figure 3). During this growing process, if two zones of impact happen to include one or more points in common, *they are merged* so that they form a single larger zone of impact. The iterative method stops when all zones of impact stop to grow and remain stable: they are circumscribed.

This time, this method converges, since zones where multiple collisions occur are generally *local*. Moreover, even if it is not the case, zones of impact can

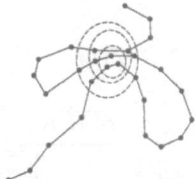

Figure 3: Iterative circumscription of zone of impact (cross-section view).

only grow to the point that they all have merged and have eventually included the whole cloth mesh. This ensures that there will never be an infinite loop.

4.3   Hypothesis of perfectly inelastic impact and non-sliding contact

The mere determination of zones of impact does not solve the handling of multiple collisions. The idea is to handle this zone of impact in a specific way so that no interpenetration occurs within the zone.

Note first that collisions occur between the time t_0 and the time $t_0 + \Delta t$, and it is guaranteed that there is no interpenetration yet at time t_0. Also, zones of impact are made of different elements of the mesh that interfere through multiple collisions: in a certain way, their movement is made difficult by these collision interferences, since they are all in contact with each other.

The idea is then to consider that all these imbricated elements will not be able to move but "as a whole", that is to say while remaining fixed with respect to each other, so that no collision occurrence may appear within the zone. This hypothesis of displacement is actually equivalent to suppose that within the zone, collision response consists in a *perfectly inelastic impact* and *non-sliding contact*. This is justified by the fact that, movement being made difficult by collision interferences, there is no possibility of any bouncing or gliding inside the zone.

Zones of impact eventually act as *rigid objects* during time-step $[t_0, t_0 + \Delta t]$. Their displacement is characterized by a *group velocity* $\vec{V}_G$ and a *group angular velocity* $\vec{\Omega}_G$.

$\vec{V}_G$ is computed as the mean velocity[3] of the n points of the zone of impact $\mathcal{Z}_c$:

$$\vec{V}_G = \frac{1}{n} \sum_{M \in \mathcal{Z}_c} \vec{V}_M$$

$\vec{\Omega}_G$ is computed for instance by reference to the geometric center G of

---

[3]For simplicity, points are all supposed to have the same mass; if it is not the case, then group velocities should be computed by reference to the center of mass.

$\mathcal{Z}_c$:

$$
\begin{cases}
\overrightarrow{OG} = \dfrac{1}{n} \displaystyle\sum_{M \in \mathcal{Z}_c} \overrightarrow{OM} \\[3mm]
\overrightarrow{\Omega}_G = \dfrac{1}{n} \displaystyle\sum_{M \in \mathcal{Z}_c} \dfrac{\overrightarrow{GM} \wedge (\overrightarrow{V}_M - \overrightarrow{V}_G)}{\|\overrightarrow{GM}\|^2}
\end{cases}
$$

The collision response for all M in $\mathcal{Z}_c$ is therefore given by its new velocity:

$$
\forall M \in \mathcal{Z}_c, \overrightarrow{V}'_M = \overrightarrow{V}_G + \overrightarrow{\Omega}_G \wedge \overrightarrow{GM}
$$

4.4 Iteration

The hypothesis described above guarantees that no interpenetration will occur within each zone of impact during $[t_0, t_0 + \Delta t]$. However, to be accurate, nothing guarantees that the computation of their displacement do not create new collision occurrences at their *boundaries*. In order to be completely sure that this will not happen, the iterative circumscription of zones of impact must be coupled with the specific computation of collision response within these zones. The algorithm can be therefore divided in three phases.

1. The initial phase consists in detecting "point-triangle" and "edge-edge" collisions and computing their response without taking into account zones of impact.

2. The second phase consists first in carrying out another collision detection and memorizing zones of impact if new collisions appeared. Then, a specific collision response of detected zones of impact is computed.

3. The third phase consists in iterating the second phase, making zones of impact grow or merge if necessary, until no new collision is detected.

This time again, this iterative method converges since zones of impact are most of the time local. If it were not the case (for instance if the cloth were all rumpled and rolled in a ball), all zones of impact would merge and eventually include the whole cloth, convergence would be however guaranteed.

Note that this iterative method takes place at each time-step. Once zones of contact have been successfully circumscribed and collision response has been fully solved, any memory of these zones of contact is erased, and they have to be computed again at the next time-step. It may then happen that the cloth object evolves in a way that new forces tend to separate some parts of the cloth that were in a same zone of contact. These parts therefore no longer collide with each other. They will hereafter not be included in a same zone of contact, unless they collide again.

In practice, even in the severe collision case of the falling ribbon shown in section 4.4, the crumpled zones unfold smoothly once it is mechanically and dynamically possible for them to do so.

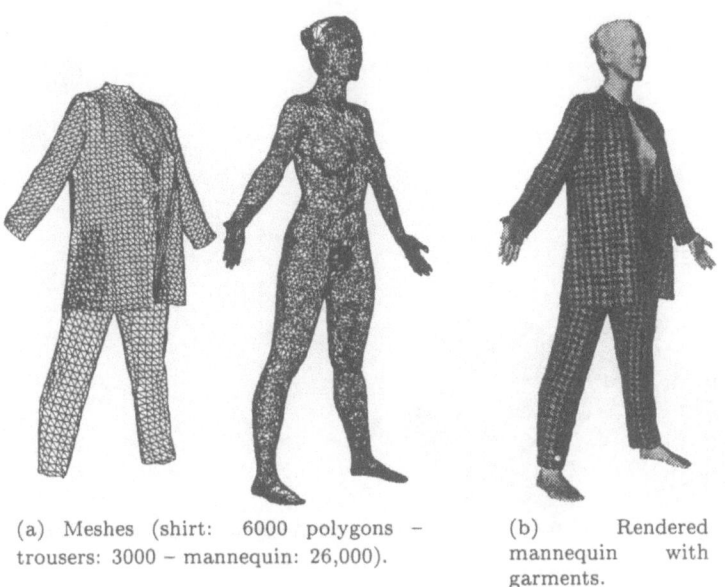

(a) Meshes (shirt: 6000 polygons – trousers: 3000 – mannequin: 26,000).

(b)   Rendered mannequin   with garments.

Figure 4: Garment construction.

Results and conclusion

Our model has been used to simulate cases of cloth objects in various situations. The most achieved example is certainly the realization of garments to dress a virtual 3D mannequin. These garments are semi-automatically built using *real garment patterns* given by *Lectra Systèmes*, a specialized industry working in the field of computer-aided garment design. These patterns are then fit on a mannequin obtained from the scanning of a *real person*[4].

All collisions and self-collisions occurring during this garment construction have been successfully detected and handled, and no interpenetration of the clothes and the mannequin took place. The computation required for the building of clothes such as the shirt or the trousers shown in figure 4 took between one hour and a half to two hours for each, on a SGI Indigo 2. This is still an important computation time, but it is right away lower than the time required by a cloth modelist to build the real garment on a mannequin. Recent optimizations of the algorithm, not implemented at the time of the results presented above, allowed to decrease this computation time by 50 %. They were also tested in the critical case of a long ribbon colliding with a table and rumpling severely. The computation took one hour for six seconds of animation on a Dec Alpha 500/500.

---

[4]The automatic cutting of patterns and fitting on the 3D mannequin will be described in detail in my Ph.D. report [Pro97].

188

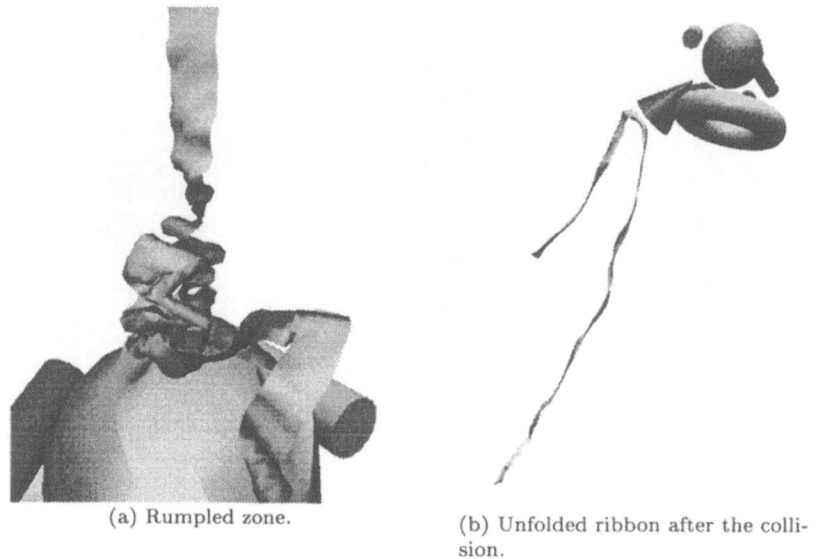

(a) Rumpled zone.

(b) Unfolded ribbon after the collision.

Figure 5: Falling ribbon (4000 polygons).

Acknowledgements

I would like to thank Georges Stamon and André Gagalowicz for their help during all our work, and Jean Marc Surville, from *Lectra Systèmes* (Bordeaux, France), who provided the garment patterns, and gave me many explanations and much advice. I also wish to thank the whole team of the *Projet Syntim* at INRIA, where this work has been carried out.

References

[Bar90]   David Baraff. Curved surfaces and coherence for non-penetrating rigid body simulation. *Computer Graphics (SIGGRAPH'90 proceedings)*, 24(4):19–28, août 1990.

[CYMTT92]   Michel Carignan, Ying Yang, Nadia Magnenat-Thalmann, and Daniel Thalmann. Dressing animated synthetic actors with complex deformable clothes. In Edwin E. Catmull, editor, *Computer Graphics (SIGGRAPH'92 proceedings)*, volume 26, pages 99–104, juillet 1992.

[LKC96]   J. D. Liu, M. T. Ko, and R. C. Chang. Collision avoidance in cloth animation. *The Visual Computer*, 12(5):234–243, 1996. ISSN 0178-2789.

[LMTT91]   Benoit Lafleur, Nadia Magnenat-Thalmann, and Daniel Thalmann. Cloth animation with self-collision detection. In *Proc. of Conference on Modeling in Computer Graphics*. Springer, 1991.

[MW88]   Matthew Moore and Jane Wilhelms. Collision detection and response for computer animation. *Computer Graphics (SIGGRAPH'88 proceedings)*, 22(4):289–298, août 1988.

[Pro95]   X. Provot. Deformation constraints in a mass-spring model to describe rigid cloth behavior. In *Graphics Interface '95*, Québec, Canada, 17-19 mai 1995.

[Pro97]   Xavier Provot. *Animation Réaliste de Vêtements*. PhD thesis, Université de Paris 5, printemps 1997. (to appear).

[TPBF87]   Demetri Terzopoulos, John Platt, Alan Barr, and Kurt Fleischer. Elastically deformable models. In *Computer Graphics (SIGGRAPH'87 proceedings)*, volume 21, pages 205–214, juillet 87.

[VCMT95]   Pascal Volino, Martin Courchesne, and Nadia Magnenat-Thalmann. Versatile and efficient techniques for simulating cloth and other deformable objects. In Edwin E. Catmull, editor, *Computer Graphics (SIGGRAPH'95 proceedings)*, volume 29, pages 137–144, août 1995.

[VMT94]   Pascal Volino and Nadia Magnenat-Thalmann. Efficient self-collision detection on smoothly discretized surface animations using geometrical shape regularity. In *Computer Graphics Forum (EuroGraphics Proc.)*, volume 13, pages 155–166, 1994.

[VMT95]   Pascal Volino and Nadia Magnenat-Thalmann. Collision and self-collision detection: efficient and robust solutions for highly deformable surfaces. In *6th Eurographics Workshop on Animation and Simulation*, pages 55–65, Maastricht, septembre 1995.

Appendix:

Colour Illustrations

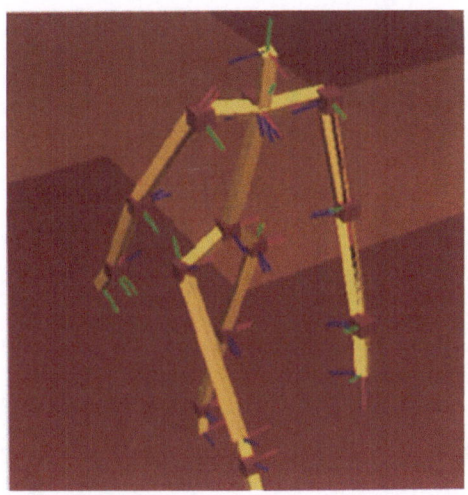

Fit between skeleton (yellow) and data (black) (Bodenheimer et al., Fig. 10)

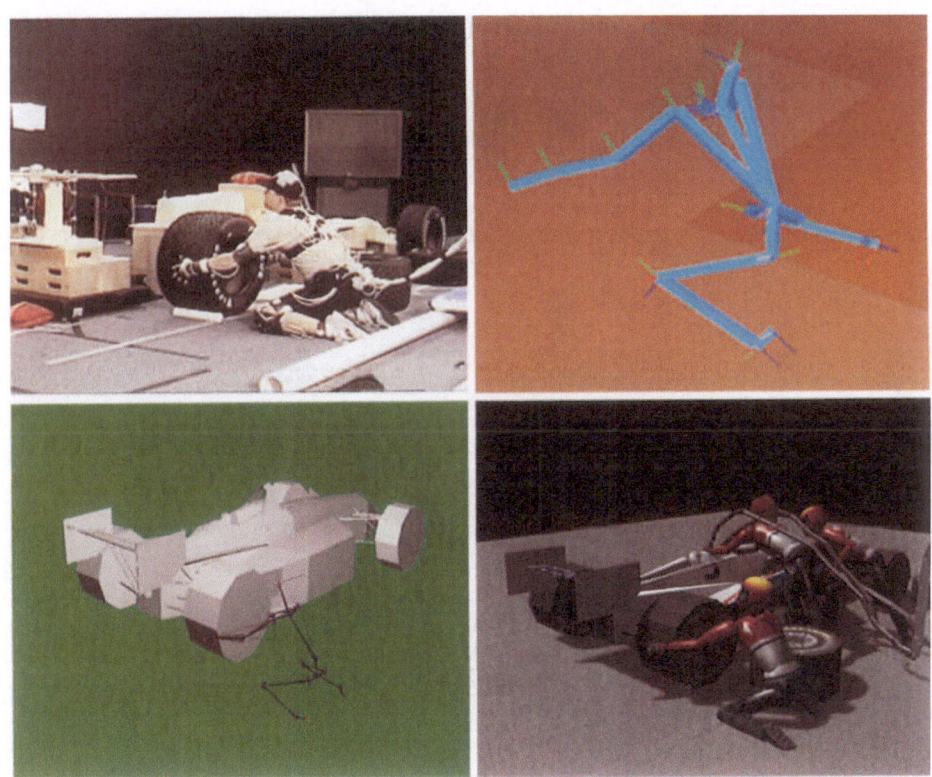

Various phases of the motion capture process (Bodenheimer et al., Fig. 11)

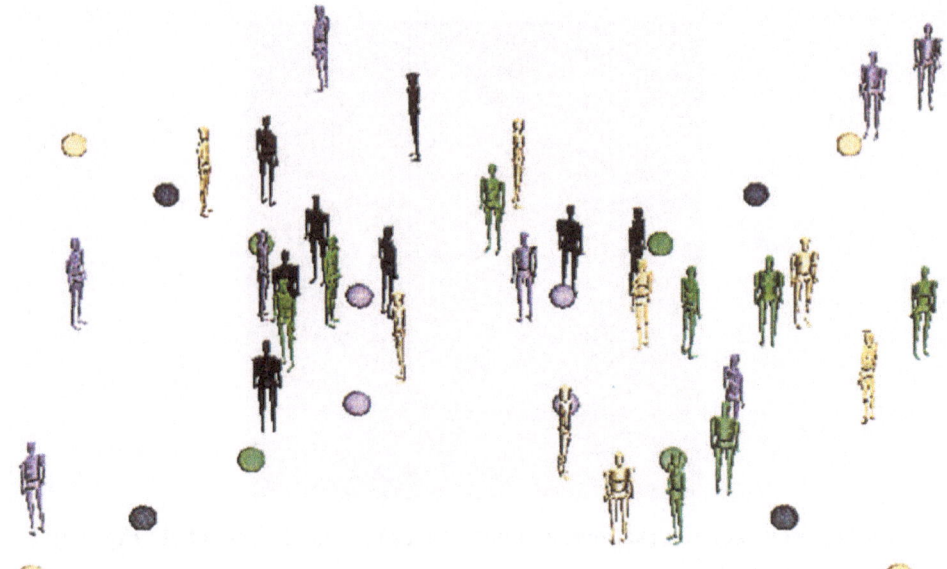

Initial population in sociogram (Musse and Thalmann, Fig. 3)

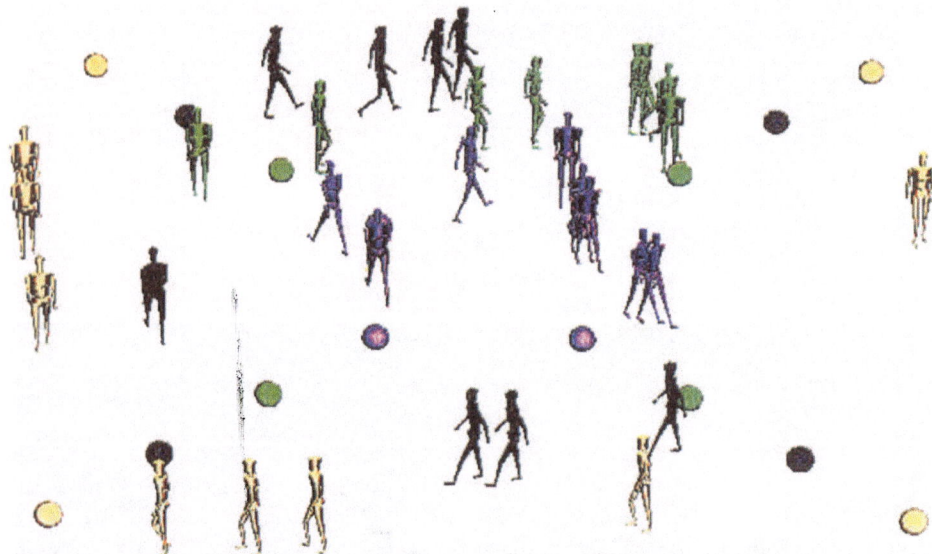

Formed groups in sociogram (Musse and Thalmann, Fig. 4)

Initial population visiting a museum (Musse and Thalmann, Fig. 5)

Formed groups in the museum (Musse and Thalmann, Fig. 6)

Simulation integrated in DIVE (Musse and Thalmann, Fig. 7)

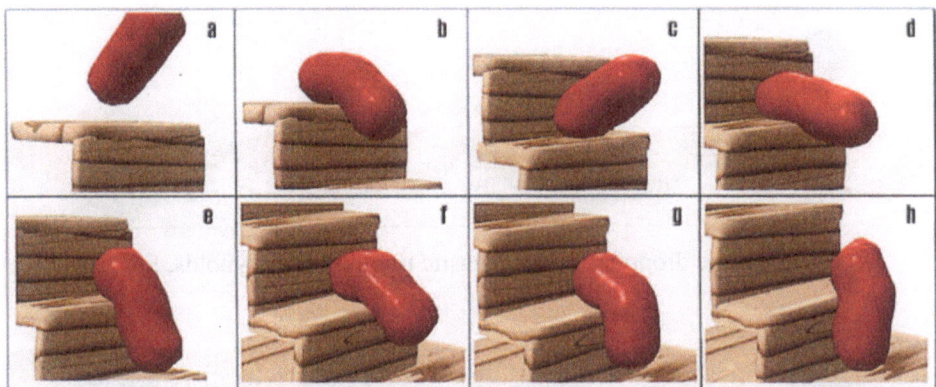

Flexible cylinder falling down steps (Reynolds, Fig. 8)

Localised stresses experienced on striking the top step (Reynolds, Fig. 9)

198

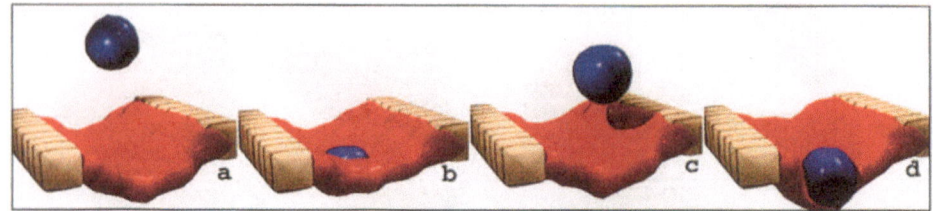

A heavy sphere dropping onto an elastic trampoline (Reynolds, Fig. 10)

Object undergoing elastic deformation (Reynolds, Fig. 11)

Object undergoing plastic deformation (Reynolds, Fig. 12)

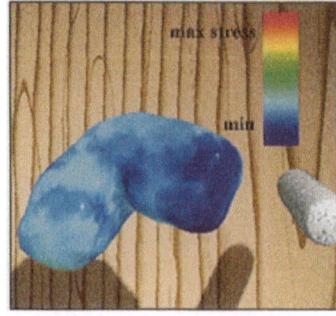

An alternative snapshot of the internal stress after plastic deformation (Reynolds, Fig. 13)

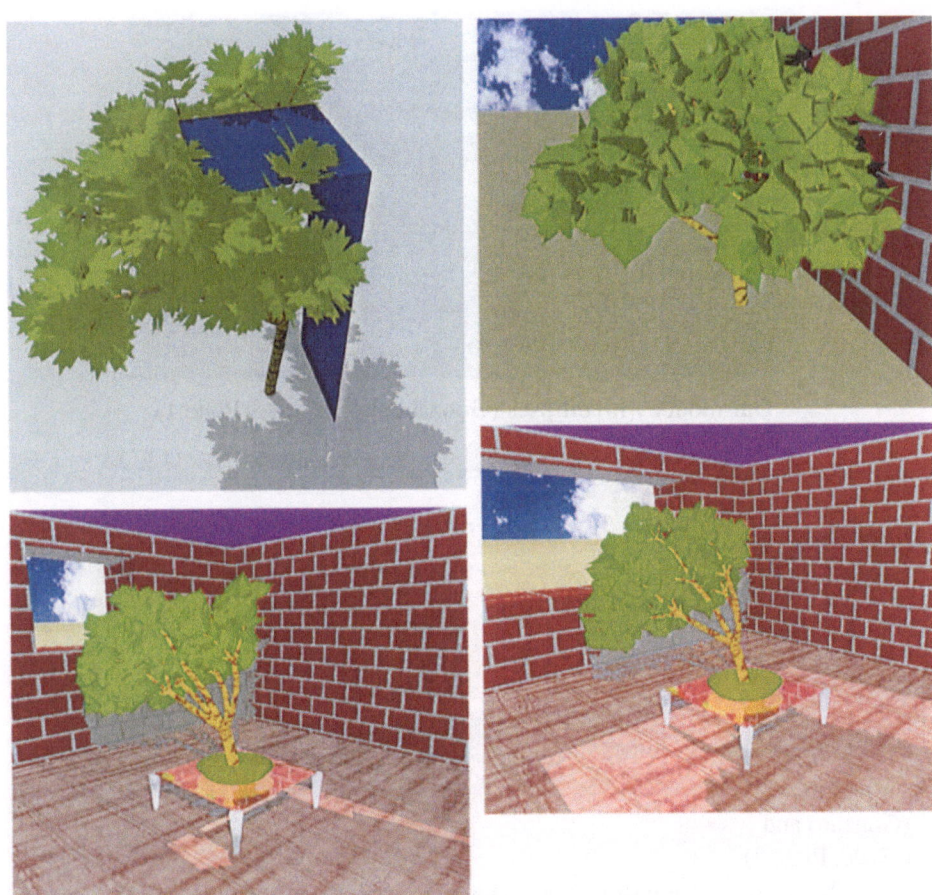

1 The plant with branches strongly searching the light. **2** The plant growing near the obstacle is spreading extensively in direction of incoming light. The branches are also bent in direction of the light. **3–4** The same plant growing in different light conditions (Beneš, Fig. 1)

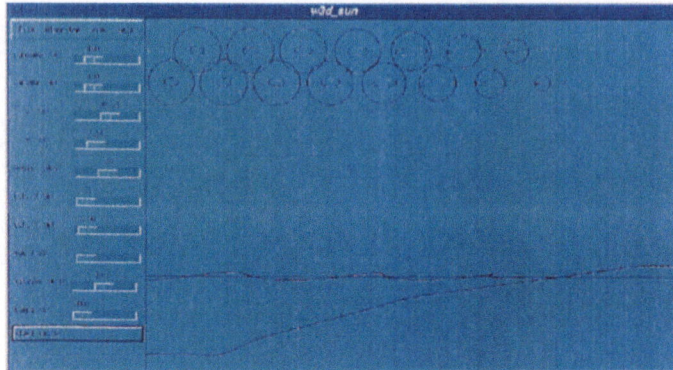

Our model with ellipses (Gonzato and Le Saëc, Plate 1)

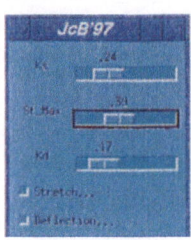

Our parameters
(Gonzato and
Le Saëc, Plate 2)

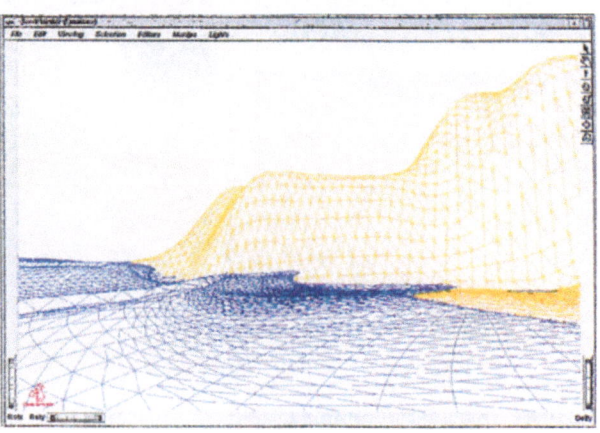

A wireframe Open Inventor view (Gonzato and Le Saëc, Plate 3)

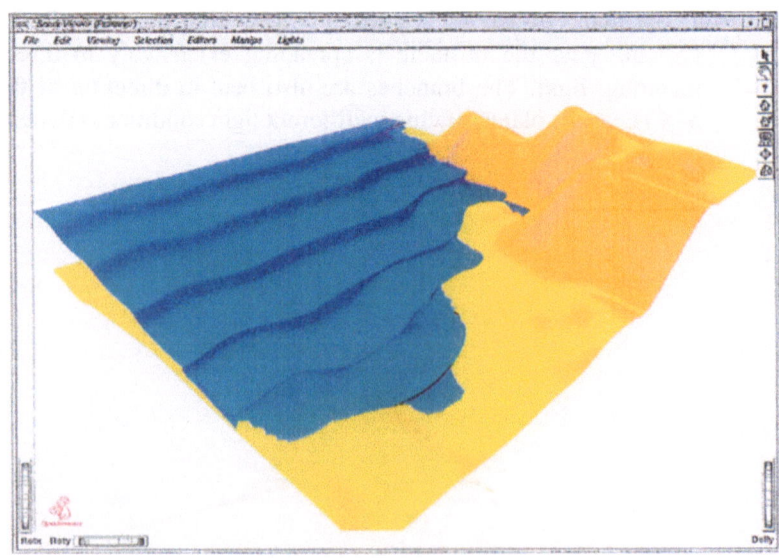

(Gonzato and Le Saëc, Plate 4)

Leaves blowing (and other debris); branches still intact (Ono, Plate 1)

Trees bending wildly; one tree uprooted (Ono, Plate 2)

Broken tree, denuded of leaves, collides with ground and skids across the frame (Ono, Plate 3)

SpringerEurographics

Julie Dorsey, Philipp Slusallek (eds.)
Rendering Techniques '97

Proceedings of the Eurographics Workshop in St. Etienne, France, June 16–18, 1997

1997. 172 partly coloured figures. IX, 342 pages.

Soft cover DM 118,–, öS 826,–

ISBN 3-211-83001-4

The papers in this volume present new research results in the areas of finite-element and Monte-Carlo illumination algorithms, image-based rendering, ray tracing, clustering techniques, texture generation and sampling, and efficient hardware rendering. While some contributions report results from more efficient or elegant algorithms, others pursue new and experimental approaches to find better solutions to the open problems in rendering.

Wilfrid Lefer, Michel Grave (eds.)
Visualization in Scientific Computing '97

Proceedings of the Eurographics Workshop in Boulogne-sur-Mer, France, April 28–30, 1997

1997. 92 partly coloured figures. Approx. 180 pages.

Soft cover DM 85,–, öS 595,–

ISBN 3-211-83049-9

Visualization is now recognized as a powerful approach to get insight in large datasets produced by scientifc experimentations and simulations. The contributions to this book cover technical aspects as well as concrete applications of visualization in various domains such as finance, physics, astronomy and medicine, providing researchers and engineers with valuable information for setting up new powerful environments.

 SpringerWienNewYork

Sachsenplatz 4-6, P.O.Box 89, A-1201 Wien, Fax +43-1-330 24 26, e-mail: order@springer.at, Internet: http://www.springer.at
New York, NY 10010, 175 Fifth Avenue • Heidelberger Platz 3, D-14197 Berlin Tokyo 113, 3-13 • Hongo 3-chome, Bunkyo-ku

SpringerEurographics

Francois Bodart, Jean Vanderdonckt (eds.)
Design, Specification and Verification of Interactive Systems '96

Proceedings of the Eurographics Workshop in Namur, Belgium, June 5–7, 1996
1996. 114 figures. XI, 383 pages.
Soft cover DM 118,–, öS 826,–
ISBN 3-211-82900-8

Making systems easier to use implies an ever increasing complexity in managing communication between users and applications. Indeed an increasing part of the application code is devoted to the user interface portion. In order to manage this complexity, it is important to have tools, notations, and methodologies which support the designer's work during the refinement process from specification to implementation. Selected revised papers from the Eurographics workshop in Namur review the state of the art in this area, comparing the different existing approaches to this field in order to identify the principle requirements and the most suitable notations, and indicate the meaningful results which can be obtained from them.

Xavier Pueyo, Peter Schröder (eds.)
Rendering Techniques '96

Proceedings of the Eurographics Workshop in Porto, Portugal, June 17–19, 1996
1996. 197 partly coloured figures. IX, 294 pages.
Soft cover DM 118,–, öS 826,–
ISBN 3-211-82883-4

Ronan Boulic, Gerard Hégron (eds.)
Computer Animation and Simulation '96

Proceedings of the Eurographics Workshop in Poitiers, France, August 31–September 1, 1996
1996. 152 partly coloured figures. X, 225 pages.
Soft cover DM 89,–, öS 625,–
ISBN 3-211-82885-0

 SpringerWienNewYork

Sachsenplatz 4-6, P.O.Box 89, A-1201 Wien, Fax +43-1-330 24 26, e-mail: order@springer.at, Internet: http://www.springer.at
New York, NY 10010, 175 Fifth Avenue • Heidelberger Platz 3, D-14197 Berlin Tokyo 113, 3-13 • Hongo 3-chome, Bunkyo-ku

SpringerEurographics

Martin Göbel, Jacques David, Pavel Slavik, Jarke J. van Wijk (eds.)
Virtual Environments and Scientific Visualization '96
Proceedings of the Eurographics Workshops in Monte Carlo, Monaco, February 19–20, 1996,
and in Prague, Czech Republic, April 23–25, 1996
1996. 169 partly coloured figures. VIII, 324 pages.
Soft cover DM 118,–, öS 826,–
ISBN 3-211-82886-9

Bodo Urban (ed.)
Multimedia '96
Proceedings of the Eurographics Workshop in Rostock, Federal Republic of Germany,
May 28–30, 1996
1996. 71 figures. VII, 178 pages.
Soft cover DM 85,–, öS 595,–
ISBN 3-211-82876-1

Remco C. Veltkamp, Edwin H. Blake (eds.)
Programming Paradigms in Graphics '95
Proceedings of the Eurographics Workshop in Maastricht, The Netherlands, September 2–3, 1995
1995. 41 partly coloured figures. VIII, 172 pages.
Soft cover DM 94,–, öS 655,–
ISBN 3-211-82788-9

Philippe Palanque, Rémi Bastide (eds.)
Design, Specification and Verification of Interactive Systems '95
Proceedings of the Eurographics Workshop in Toulouse, France, June 7–9, 1995
1995. 153 figures. X, 370 pages.
Soft cover DM 118,–, öS 826,–
ISBN 3-211-82739-0

 SpringerWienNewYork

Sachsenplatz 4-6, P.O.Box 89, A-1201 Wien, Fax +43-1-330 24 26, e-mail: order@springer.at, Internet: http://www.springer.at
New York, NY 10010, 175 Fifth Avenue • Heidelberger Platz 3, D-14197 Berlin Tokyo 113, 3-13 • Hongo 3-chome, Bunkyo-ku

SpringerEurographics

Martin Göbel (ed.)
Virtual Environments '95
Selected papers of the Eurographics Workshops in Barcelona, Spain, 1993,
and Monte Carlo, Monaco, 1995
1995. 134 partly coloured figures. VII, 307 pages.
Soft cover DM 119,–, öS 832,–
ISBN 3-211-82737-4

Demetri Terzopoulos, Daniel Thalmann (eds.)
Computer Animation and Simulation '95
Proceedings of the Eurographics Workshop in Maastricht, The Netherlands, September 2–3, 1995
1995. 156 partly coloured figures. VIII, 235 pages.
Soft cover DM 98,–, öS 688,–
ISBN 3-211-82738-2

Riccardo Scateni, Jarke J. van Wijk, Pietro Zanarini (eds.)
Visualization in Scientific Computing '95
Proceedings of the Eurographics Workshop in Chia, Italy, May 3–5, 1995
1995. 110 partly coloured figures. VII, 161 pages.
Soft cover DM 94,–, öS 655,–
ISBN 3-211-82729-3

Patrick M. Hanrahan, Werner Purgathofer (eds.)
Rendering Techniques '95
Proceedings of the Eurographics Workshop in Dublin, Ireland, June 12–14, 1995
1995. 198 partly coloured figures. XI, 372 pages.
Soft cover DM 118,–, öS 826,–
ISBN 3-211-82733-1

Martin Göbel, Heinrich Müller, Bodo Urban (eds.)
Visualization in Scientific Computing
1995. 150 figures. VIII, 238 pages.
Soft cover DM 118,–, öS 826,–
ISBN 3-211-82633-5

 SpringerWienNewYork

Sachsenplatz 4-6, P.O.Box 89, A-1201 Wien, Fax +43-1-330 24 26, e-mail: order@springer.at, Internet: http://www.springer.at
New York, NY 10010, 175 Fifth Avenue • Heidelberger Platz 3, D-14197 Berlin Tokyo 113, 3-13 • Hongo 3-chome, Bunkyo-ku

Springer-Verlag
and the Environment